Effective Management for Marketing

The Marketing Series is one of the most comprehensive collections of books in marketing and sales available from the UK today.

Published by Butterworth-Heinemann on behalf of the Chartered Institute of Marketing, the series is divided into three distinct groups: *Student* (fulfilling the needs of those taking the Institute's certificate and diploma qualifications); *Professional Development* (for those on formal or self-study vocational training programmes); and *Practitioner* (presented in a more informal, motivating and highly practical manner for the busy marketer).

Formed in 1911, the Chartered Institute of Marketing is now the largest professional marketing management body in Europe with over 24,000 members and 28,000 students located worldwide. Its primary objectives are focused on the development of awareness and understanding of marketing throughout UK industry and commerce and in the raising of standards of professionalism in the education, training and practice of this key business discipline.

GW00507134

The CIM Student Workbook Series: Marketing

Business Communication
Misiura

Effective Management for Marketing
Hatton and Worsam

International Marketing Strategy
Fifield and Lewis

Management Information for Sales and Marketing
Hines

Marketing Communications Strategy
Yeshin

Marketing Fundamentals
Lancaster and Withey

Marketing Operations
Worsam

Promotional Practice
Ace

Sales and Marketing Environment
Oldroyd

Strategic Marketing Management
Gilligan and Fifield

Understanding Customers
Lea-Greenwood

Effective Management for Marketing

Angela Hatton and Mike Worsam

Published on behalf of
the Chartered Institute of Marketing

BUTTERWORTH
HEINEMANN

Butterworth-Heinemann Ltd
Linacre House, Jordan Hill, Oxford OX2 8DP

℞ A member of the Reed Elsevier plc group

OXFORD   LONDON   BOSTON
MUNICH   NEW DELHI   SINGAPORE   SYDNEY
TOKYO   TORONTO   WELLINGTON

First published 1995

British Library Cataloguing in Publication Data
Worsam, Mike
  Effective Management for Marketing. –
  (Marketing Series: Student)
  I. Title II. Hatton, Angela III. Series
  658.8

ISBN 0 7506 1993 7

Composition by Genesis Typesetting, Laser Quay, Rochester, Kent
Printed in Great Britain by Scotprint, Musselburgh, Scotland

Contents

Preface

This workbook covers the essential requirements of managers in today's workplace, whether that be commercial or not-for-profit, for business or socially oriented. Management is concerned with achieving results through people, and that principle holds true whatever the organization, whatever the driving force.

Effective Management for Marketing is seen by the Chartered Institute of Marketing (CIM) as vital to the needs of today's marketers. First examined in December 1994, it was introduced as part of the CIM's major syllabus review and recognizes that it is no longer enough for managers to be taught about functional specialisms – they must also be given help in developing the knowledge and skills essential to a competent manager.

Much of the content and activities within these pages will be equally valued by those on business or management programmes or in any way actively involved in the process of management. Whether you have years of management experience – or only a few weeks – we are confident that the ideas and activities in this workbook will help you to review your own skills and effectively manage your own personal development.

Faced with the rapid changes and growing demands of business in the 1990s, few now question that a career in management represents a commitment to life-long learning. Successfully passing your examination in this subject is only one basis for assessing your development. As a manager you will need to be constantly monitoring and developing your own skills, and also the skills of others. This workbook provides the needed understanding, in easily digestible form.

Written by Angela Hatton (CIM Senior Examiner for EMFM and Co-ordinator of the CIM's Certificate Examinations) and Mike Worsam (LCCIEB Chief Examiner for Marketing) this workbook is presented in a style which you will find easy to work with, and which covers the material you need to tackle the examination confidently.

As with the other CIM/Butterworth-Heinemann workbooks, you will find the material laid out with easy to follow instructions, activities and review questions. It is fun to work with. There are many activities to stimulate your learning. Each unit is targeted on an area of key concern. A full specimen examination paper, with outline answers to all questions is provided.

The best learning happens when you enjoy what you are doing. This workbook has been written especially to help ensure enjoyment. It has been fun writing it, we hope you will have fun working with it.

Good luck in your career, good luck in your examinations.

Angela Hatton
Mike Worsam

A quick word from the Chief Examiner

I am delighted to recommend to you the new series of CIM workbooks. All of these have been written by either the Senior Examiner or Examiners responsible for marking and setting the papers.

Preparing for the CIM Exams is hard work. These workbooks are designed to make that work as interesting and illuminating as possible, as well as providing you with the knowledge you need to pass. I wish you success.

Trevor Watkins
CIM Chief Examiner,
Deputy Vice Chancellor,
South Bank University

How to use your CIM workbook

The authors have been careful to structure your book with the exams in mind. Each unit, therefore, covers an essential part of the syllabus. You need to work through the complete workbook systematically to ensure that you have covered everything you need to know.

This workbook is divided into eleven units each containing the following standard elements:

Objectives tell you what part of the syllabus you will be covering and what you will be expected to know having read the unit.

Study guides tell you how long the unit is and how long its activities take to do.

Questions are designed to give you practice – they will be similar to those you get in the exam.

Answers give you a suggested format for answering exam questions. *Remember* there is no such thing as a model answer – you should use these examples only as guidelines.

Activities give you the chance to put what you have learnt into practice.

Exam hints are tips from the senior examiner or examiner which are designed to help you avoid common mistakes made by previous candidates.

Definitions are used for words you must know to pass the exam.

Extending activity sections are designed to help you use your time most effectively. It is not possible for the workbook to cover *everything* you need to know to pass. What you read here needs to be supplemented by your classes, practical experience at work and day-to-day reading.

Summaries cover what you should have picked up from reading the unit.

The nature of management

In this introductory unit you will:

- Examine the role of the manager.
- Review the changing nature of the management task.
- Consider the characteristics and skills needed by a manager.

By the end of this unit you will:

- Appreciate the nature and purpose of the organization.
- Understand the dynamics which have resulted in changing management philosophies.
- Understand the role of the manager.
- Be aware of recent changes in the nature of the management function.
- Be able to produce list of criteria for a manager's job.

Covering the introductory part of the CIM syllabus this first unit of the *Effective Management for Marketing* workbook will introduce you to the broad subject area of management and examine its significance and value to the marketing manager. You will find the material straightforward, but of central importance as it provides the essential rationale for the subject area. As you will see under Exam Hints later in this unit you will need to be prepared for an examination question which tests your understanding of the management process and the functions of the manager.

We would expect it to take you about 3 hours to work through this first unit and suggest you allow a further 2 hours to undertake the suggested activities. Besides your notebook and writing equipment you will need the following to complete this unit:

- Copies of recent job advertisements for marketing posts.
- Sight of the annual reports of two or three companies, including possibly your own and one of a non-profit organization.

This first unit will also help you to familiarize yourself with the approach and style of our workbooks. It has been developed to ensure that you acquire not only the knowledge necessary for examination success, but also the skills to apply that knowledge, both in the examination and as a practising marketer. You will find clearly signposted boxed panels to guide you as you assess and extend your knowledge. These will be used throughout the workbook so that you can manage your own learning, in terms of both pace and depth. Opportunities are given so that you can practise what you learn.

Organize your study materials from the beginning of your course:

- Use file dividers to keep broad topic areas indexed.
- Look out for relevant articles and current examples, you will find these useful to illustrate examination answers.
- File relevant materials and articles with the applicable notes.
- Incorporate past questions, summary and revision notes as you complete each section of your studies.

In these ways your files will be complete and ready for easy revision for the examination.

Practice is essential. We shall constantly remind you of the importance of putting what you learn into practice at your work, and in your social life.

You will find a full specimen examination paper at the end of this workbook. We strongly suggest that you *immediately* clip that section together with paper clips or – better – staples!

When you have worked through to the point of active revision you should schedule a period for a full mock examination, and take the specimen paper 'cold'. You will find that we give suggested answers, so you will be able to grade your work.

Explanations and definitions

At the beginning of every unit you will find a list of the key technical terms used within it. Some will be explanations, some definitions, some both. Remember that you are expected to use technical terms correctly at work – but especially in your examinations.

1 *Continuing professional development (CPD)* A system adopted by Professional Institutes to encourage Members and Fellows to continue their studies after qualification. Usually a voluntary scheme at first it often becomes a requirement for continuing professional recognition. The CIM introduced CPD in June 1993, with the first register of those who qualified published in August 1994. CIM Members and Fellows who meet the CPD study requirements are entitled to use the designation 'Registered Marketer' in addition to their grade of membership (MCIM or FCIM).

2 *Corporate culture* The prevailing attitude which influences the way in which the organization behaves to its employees, customers and other stakeholders. Corporate culture can usually be traced to the attitude of the senior management. It influences how and what decisions are made and the general approach of the organization to its environment. It has a powerful impact on management style and, therefore, on the morale of all employees.

3 *Effective and efficient* These terms are usually used together because being 'effective' means doing the right things. 'Efficient' means doing them right, and to time. If an organization is not both effective and efficient it may do the right things badly (effective but not efficient) or the wrong things superbly (efficient but not effective).

4 *Stakeholders* Anyone who has a direct or indirect interest in the organization, e.g. employees and shareholders in a private-sector company, the rate payers and local community for a local authority. Other interested groups might include suppliers, the media, merchant and clearing banks, distributors and agents.

5 *Sum of the organization*

What is an organization?	– It can be described in terms of its structure, its procedures and its systems.

PLUS

What it does?	– It can be described in terms of processes.

PLUS

How does it do it?	– It can be described in terms of its style or culture.

6 *Synergy* Definition: 'combined effects that exceed the sum of individual effects' (*Concise Oxford Dictionary*).

Explanation: where a single page can be torn by a baby, only a very few can tear a telephone book in half. Synergy is often expressed as 2 + 2 = 5. Good management is constantly seeking synergy because the gearing effect is usually considerably more than in the 2 + 2 = 5 example.

7 *Total quality management (TQM)* A concept which has evolved from the quality control activities of the production line to encompass all the activities of the organization. It is based on the concept of ensuring that 'quality' systems are developed for every aspect of the organization's activities. If the systems are appropriate and well designed they will deliver good-quality outputs.

The job of marketing

Have you ever stopped to think about the *real* job of the marketing professional?

- How would you describe what he or she does?
- What is their role in the business?

Use this space to jot down your thoughts about the nature of the marketer's work.

Probably your first thoughts were of the operational responsibilities we associate with marketing. Areas such as marketing research and promotion, and the tasks of price setting or influencing new product development. Whilst these activities do catalogue the areas of interest and functional expertise of the marketer, they fail to define adequately the essence of the role that the marketer actually performs.

All the *specialisms* of business – finance, marketing, production, distribution and so on – are critical to an organization's performance, but none exists in isolation. All are functions of management. They are all activities which are planned and controlled by 'the management', even though those managers may also be accountants, engineers or marketers.

Think about the CIM's definition of marketing: 'The *management process* which identifies, anticipates and satisfies customer requirements profitably'.

As is clearly highlighted, the professional marketer is first and foremost a manager. A manager who happens to have specialized in a particular aspect of business – the customer/ organization interface, but essentially still a manager. The tasks of the marketing manager (and every manager of marketing) must therefore be the tasks undertaken by a manager, although performed within the context of the marketing activity. Clearly, before someone can become a successful marketer they must be an effective manager.

The need to continually develop expertise in personal management skills is, not surprisingly, emphasized by the CIM. It is a theme which is of crucial importance outside your studies for this examination. Evidence of your management competencies will be called for throughout other Advanced Certificate and Diploma studies and once you are qualified it will be an area highlighted in the Institute's CPD requirements.

Throughout this workbook we will be examining with you the knowledge and skills necessary to becoming a competent manager and considering the role of the manager working within the marketing function.

The nature of management

Management can be thought of as the coordinating force which runs between and across all aspects of the organization, binding it into an identifiable entity. It is management who are responsible for providing drive, sense of purpose and direction to the organization so that it can develop, grow and change.

To understand the role of the manager it is first necessary to understand the rationale for the organization of which he or she is an agent. Organizations, whether in the private or non-profit sectors exist for a purpose. This purpose is their goal or mission – their reason for being. All those employed within the organization are valuable to it in the context of the contribution which they make to the achievement of that mission. The organization's purpose is normally related to providing some benefit to its stakeholders, all of whom have different needs.

Whilst this mission explains what the organization wants to achieve and therefore its motivation for operating, a business can only exist and continue to exist if it is able to satisfy the needs and wants of its customers. The firm will only make its profit if it finds a buyer for its products. Potential customers will only be attracted to a product if they perceive it will satisfy some need or want which they have.

Mission statements

Do not mistake the general concept of a mission or goal with the more specific mission statement of the organization. Whilst the mission statement may encompass the rationale for the organization, it can also cover other aspects of strategic positioning and culture. If you are unfamiliar with mission statements take time to find out about those of your company and perhaps your competitors. Make a point of identifying the mission statement of your college, or a charity you support. How do these compare with those of organizations in the private sector? You will find that mission statements are often incorporated in annual reports which you will find in good reference libraries. Alternatively, ask your friends about the organizations they work for, and borrow an annual report or mission statement from them.

(**See** Debriefing at the end of this unit.)

Mutually profitable exchange

Business depends upon exchange, and not just that between producer and consumer. Workers exchange their labour for salaries, landlords their space for rent, investors their capital for interest and, finally, manufacturers their goods for a price*. Exchange is fundamental, but will only occur if it is 'mutually profitable'. In other words, both parties must benefit. Managers are concerned to maintain these internal as well as external exchanges, balancing the needs of the stakeholders with those of the customers. Good labour relations, the confidence of bankers, shareholders and landlords are all necessary if the organization is to operate smoothly.

The exchange process is not limited to the private sector. Voters exchange their support, in the form of votes, for promised reform and political policies, taxpayers exchange their earnings for a range of public sector services, the charitable exchange their donations or support for the 'feel-good' factors and status associated with giving. Most activities between the individual and organizations can be viewed in terms of mutually profitable exchange.

Simple economic analysis also provides us with a useful insight into the role of the manager. Again we must first consider the nature of the organization.

---

* The essence of marketing can be clearly seen in this simple economic principle of exchange. To be successful, i.e. achieve its mission, the organization must first satisfy its customers – it needs to be customer oriented.

Think about a company you know, any company will do, Sainsbury's or ICI, McDonald's or the dry cleaners down the road. Use these questions to prompt your thoughts about the nature of business:

- Would you say this company exists?
- If so, in what sense?
- Does it have an identity?
- What does such a business comprise?

(**See** Debriefing at the end of this unit.)

Clearly, organizations do have identities. They even have a pattern of life, from launch through maturity to eventual decline, but it is an existence different from the life of the individual. The organization is a collection of resources – known by economists as the factors of production:

- Land.
- Labour.
- Capital.
- Enterprise.

These scarce resources are combined to create the want-satisfying goods and services which can be offered to the individuals/households who own the factors of production. Business takes the factors of production and transforms them, adds value to them and converts them into products which satisfy the needs of individual consumers – goods they are prepared to accept in exchange for part of their incomes (Figure 1.1).

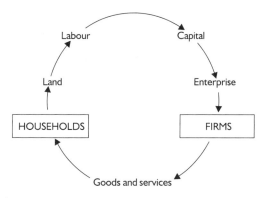

Figure 1.1 Exchange cycle

It is only when the factors of land, labour and capital are brought together that this transformation to want-satisfying goods and services can occur. It is the factor of production called 'enterprise' which acts as the essential catalyst in this process and it is within enterprise that we can see the essential role of management – as guardian and organizer of the scarce resources of the organization in pursuit of its mission.

The role of the manager

The custodian of scarce resources. The central activity of any manager can be seen as the safe-keeper, administrator and user of resources. Because all resources are scarce they have a value and a cost. Successful organizations are those whose managers use their resources effectively and efficiently – getting the most output from any given input.

Resources must be employed in a way which best contributes to the achievement of customer satisfaction and so, in turn, to the organization's mission. The co-ordinating role of the manager ensures that all divisions, departments and sections of an organization are pulling together – using the resources available to strive cooperatively towards a common goal. Managers strive for synergy – adding value and getting more output from the inputs used.

Obviously, there is little point in having ever higher levels of efficiency if you are producing goods which no one wants. One of the functional roles of marketing is to provide the organization with information about what customers' needs are so that the organization does not waste resources by producing goods simply to add to stockpiles.

ACTIVITY 1.4

The manager and resources
Think about your own role as a manager or choose someone you know who has a management function. What sort of tasks do they undertake which demonstrate their responsibility for resources? Use this space to list the relevant activities.

(**See** Debriefing at the end of this unit.)

Taking risks

Resources are the organization's raw materials and managers are charged with their custody, but this role is in no way static. The manager should not be mistaken for a sort of resources' security guard. Management is a process, value can only be added and the organization's mission achieved if and when the factors of production are employed productively.

This resource consumption introduces another aspect of management's role which is also implicit within the economist's view of enterprise – the dimension of risk. The process of transformation into want-satisfying goods involves managers in making decisions – and decision making entails risk. The intention is to add value to the resources. The danger is that in production value is *lost* – perhaps through waste or because the goods are not bought by customers.

Because managers are responsible for the process of transformation, they are the decision makers and risk takers for the organization. All their creative, analytical and decision-making skills are required to achieve successful 'value added' for the organization.

Profit is the economic reward for this entrepreneurial risk-taking, and managers' higher salaries often incorporate a profit element to reward the risk-taking dimension of their role.

Managing people

The manager may be a coordinator of work and activities, but that work is undertaken by people. The business is a complex of systems and of people which must be brought together by the managers. People are the most important core resource of any organization. No matter in which department or what specialist background the manager is employed, he or she has the same central responsibility - the management of people. This responsibility for staff is so critical that it has become the concern which dominates management theory and management thinking.

The core management skills of motivation, delegation, leadership and team building all feature equally prominently in the syllabus of this CIM subject. Working with people is demanding and a far from an exact science. People, unlike machines, can and do behave unpredictably. Their performance cannot be forecast with certainty and is influenced by their environment, attitude, experiences and feelings.

The successful manager must have an empathy with others in the organization and be sensitive to their needs and problems. Here marketing managers can have great strength from the knowledge and skills they acquire through their understanding of customer behaviour. It is essentially because the people dimension is so unpredictable that management has to be considered an art, to be practised and developed, rather than a science with rules and formulae to be simply applied.

Self-check 1.1

Take time to answer the following questions to help you assess your understanding of the material covered so far.

1 Briefly describe the job of a marketing practitioner.
2 What is the function of an organization?
3 What is essential before any form of exchange can successfully take place?
4 What is the difference between efficiency and effectiveness?

(**See** Debriefing at the end of this unit.)

The changing role of managers

The job of the manager, whilst remaining fundamentally the same, is becoming more difficult and more demanding (Figure 1.2). The causes for this change include:

- Competition is increasing, both externally for customers and often internally for resources.
- The wider environment in which the organization operates is changing – constantly and rapidly.

Figure 1.2   The changing role of managers

To keep up-to-date, managers have to review their own activities and philosophies regularly. The relatively recent and widespread adoption of the marketing concept by organizations across all sectors of activity is evidence of how the changing organizational environment forces significant changes in the philosophy of managers.

Changing philosophies of management

Changes in the balance of demand and supply have gradually turned the sellers' markets of the 1960s into the increasingly competitive buyers' markets of the 1990s. This change can be observed in sector after sector, with the need for a shift to a customer-oriented philosophy most recently evident in public sector organizations. Health and education are typical. Their operating environments have been transformed by the competitive dimension introduced by deregulation. Over the years changes in the market and the balance of demand and supply have forced managers to change the emphasis and the priorities of their activities in order to continue to achieve the organization's mission.

   In a seller's market profits could be increased by having more goods to sell. In such circumstances emphasis would be on efficiency and getting more goods produced – almost any goods will do. This creates an organization- or production-oriented culture which is only challenged by a change in the balance of power between buyers and sellers.

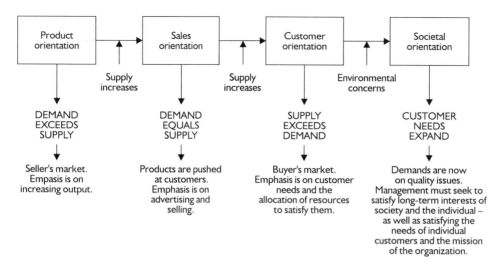

Figure 1.3 Changing management philosophies

It is in circumstances of competition, when customers have a choice, that managers are forced to put them first. Ensuring that the goods which are produced are 'right' for the customer becomes the critical success factor. Then customer orientation replaces the earlier production- or sales-based philosophies. But, adopting the marketing concept is undertaken for only one reason – in a competitive environment customer orientation increases the likelihood that the organization will achieve its objectives. Any future changes in the way managers think about their business will also be stimulated by the same motive – if in doing so they believe they can be more successful.

Certainly change and new challenges are constant. Managers cannot afford to simply sit back. Even organizations confident that they are successfully satisfying both the objectives of their stakeholders and customers must be alert to changes. The increased emphasis on environmental concerns led Kotler to expand the simple marketing concept to the more demanding societal one, charging managers not simply with ensuring that organizations achieve mutually profitable exchange, but also of protecting both the individual's and society's long-term interests in the process.

Customers and stakeholders are becoming better educated and more understanding of business, whilst generally their expectations are being raised. Business itself is more complex, with global markets and competitors and a rapid international interchange of ideas, ideals and innovations. Managers are constantly challenged by new approaches developed to help organizations achieve both efficiency and effectiveness in their operations.

Quality initiatives, introducing the concepts associated with TQM, mean that attention is focused on every aspect of the management process and the organization's activities. TQM has brought with it new ideas and issues as well as harnessing other concepts with which most marketers will already be familiar. The importance of internal customers, the benefits of relationship marketing and the demands of achieving just-in-time standards of delivery and customer response are all quality issues that today's managers are having to address.

Like the marketing orientation, TQM should be recognized as an approach which if adopted will help the organization achieve its mission and objectives. These developments are intrinsically attractive only in so much as they offer managers a means to achieve their ends. Clearly, the challenges and responsibilities facing the manager are becoming ever more demanding, and to be successful the manager must be flexible and willing to change his or her outlook and philosophy of business.

Better tools for the manager

Whilst the job of managers is getting tougher, the tools of management are improving. Information technology (IT), in particular, provides information and techniques which can be used to calculate risk, simulate outcomes and aid decision making (Figure 1.4). Tools of analysis and control are faster and more detailed and managers at all levels and in locations thousands of miles apart can access data and information simultaneously.

The result of the dramatic pace of change in IT has had equally dramatic effects on the work of the manager. Information is yet another resource to be managed. Like people and

Figure 1.4 Better tools for the manager

technology it can, if used well, generate significant competitive advantages. Managers have to be better trained and constantly updated if they are to use the many new tools available to them, and so the need for management training has been an issue increasingly in the forefront of public debate since the early 1980s.

Perhaps the biggest change is in the number and type of management jobs. In the past, large organizations had to employ armies of junior and middle managers to handle information about the resources and to administer their use. Easier access to information has meant senior managers can dispense with the services of many of these management 'foot soldiers'. So a thinning out of middle management has been taking place in organizations across the globe.

Spurred on by the cost-saving necessities forced upon them by the world-wide recession, firms have 'de-layered' their organizations, stripping out hundreds and sometimes thousands of employees – many in the management category. Improved IT can be identified as a major cause of unemployment. Its impact in the 1990s is most strongly felt by white-collar workers, in much the same way that improved production technology impacted on the blue-collar workers of earlier generations. This process of 'de-layering' – flattening the organizational pyramid – has a number of implications:

- Senior managers are in much closer contact with both operational level employees and customers, easing communication problems with both groups. Typically, companies have reported dispensing with up to eight layers of staff between the boardroom and the shop floor.
- With less staff up and down, communication is encouraged across the organization. Old 'functional chimneys' which were barriers to communication are giving way to lateral communication. Today's managers have to be able to communicate across functional specialisms, so they need to learn to work together, often in flexible cross-functional teams.
- There are fewer opportunities for managers to learn 'on the job', so management skills must be developed more formally.
- Individual managers have to take on greater areas of responsibility. Where not managed at a personal level, this increased workload can lead to increasing stress levels, and the potential for deteriorating management working practices.
- With fewer managers, operational staff have to become personally responsible for their own activities and performance. More of the workforce are knowledge rather than manual workers. Improved training and education enable them to work with less supervision.

The manager of today and tomorrow has to get used to working in reshaped organizations, faced with the constant requirement to respond to change caused by the continuing change in the environment.

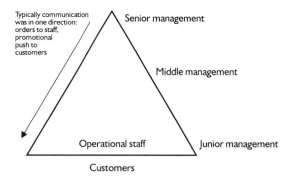

Figure 1.5 Traditional hierarchical organization structure

The traditional organizational structure is formal, highly structured and based on almost military lines of seniority and control, with the organization established to support the senior management team (Figure 1.5). Organizations today tend to be not only flatter, but also of a different conceptual shape. They can be seen as inverted with management's role that of supporting an organization designed to meet customer needs. The customer is at the top, not the bottom, of the system. The task of management is to improve the interface between the organization and its customers. Communication flows are now likely to be multidirectional, both up and down and across the organization (Figure 1.6).

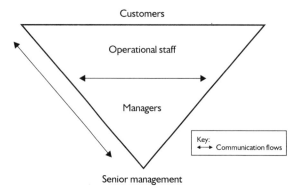

Figure 1.6 A flatter inverted organization structure developed to serve customers

Take your organization, or one with which you are familiar, and find out how it is organized now and if/how its structure has changed over the last few years. Talk to some of those managers involved in the organization and see how the new structure has changed their roles. Remember you can use non-profit-sector entities too. Try your college tutor, church or community service if you do not have access to a business.

- Organization now

- Organization before

- Advantages of the change

- Disadvantages of the change

Management or leadership?

Changes in structure and culture have brought with them further review and analysis of the proper role of the manager, particularly the role of senior managers. It is easy to get caught up in what, at one level, are semantic differences. The term 'management' implies control; it can be seen as inward looking and order giving. Such a traditional style of business was labelled by Douglas McGregor as a 'theory X organization'.

Theory X organizations are authoritarian and work centred. They are based on the belief that people basically do not like work, are lazy and need constant supervision and control. Management have the right to command and the power to enforce obedience.

McGregor also identified theory Y organizations. The assumptions of theory Y are:

- Expending effort at work is as normal as play or rest.
- People will exercise self-direction and self-control in the service of objectives to which they are committed.
- Commitment to objectives is a function of the rewards associated with their achievement.
- Average human beings learn, under proper conditions, not only to accept but to seek responsibility.
- Imagination, ingenuity and creativity are widely, not narrowly, distributed in the population.
- The intellectual potentialities of the average human being are only partly utilized.

Theory Y assumes that people want to work, will take responsibility for their contribution, and need managers to facilitate their activity not to control it. Consensus, discussion and joint responsibility for decisions would be the hallmarks of such an organization. Here the need for leadership rather than management can be seen.* Motivation and a clear common purpose are essential to an effective theory Y organization.

Theory Z was developed by William Ouchi by taking the best from American and Japanese management practices in the 1970s. Its key features are:

- Long-term employment should be guaranteed.
- Decision making should be consensual.
- Individuals should be given responsibility.
- Evaluation and promotion should be at a slower rate.
- Control should be implicit within explicit, formalized measures.
- Career paths should be moderately specialized.
- Concern for employees should be holistic, and extended to include the families.

* We shall return to leadership when we examine team building later in the workbook.

You need to take a view on management style and its effectiveness in different market conditions.

- Can a theory Z organization survive in conditions of recession? The Japanese held on longer than many Western firms, but as their world markets slowed and profits fell they had to lay off staff. Does this negate the theory?
- Can a theory Y manager survive in a theory X organization? Is the need for self-protection such that the extra bar has to be added to the Y?
- What happens to a theory Y section when a theory X manager is appointed to it?

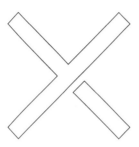

Many of today's business personalities are quoted as inspirational leaders – dynamic, with charisma and the ability to communicate a sense of both purpose and culture, e.g. Anita Roddick of Body Shop, and Richard Branson of Virgin. Interestingly, these and others like them are entrepreneurs, not only managers in the traditional sense. The business is or was solely theirs and they have retained both ownership and control. The acid test may well be how successfully the organizations would (will?) survive without their founders at the helm.

What does it take to be a manager?

Whether you view management as leaders or administrators, the knowledge and skills which are the building blocks of a competent manager need to be analysed and appreciated by every current and aspiring manager:

- They represent the basis on which you can evaluate your own managerial performance and the yardsticks by which personal development goals can be set.
- CIM Advanced Certificate and Diploma examiners will be looking for evidence that you have developed appropriate management skills, from communication to time management, analysis through to decision making.
- You are likely to be involved in interviewing and selecting other people as managers and will need to establish criteria to help you.

The manager's job

Look at the advertisements for marketing management jobs which you have collected and the one below for a management post. Using knowledge of similar types of post, your own experience and what you have learned about the manager's role, draw up a list of all the skills and characteristics you would look for in a candidate for this post.

(**See** Debriefing at the end of this unit.)

EXAM HINTS

Of the Effective Management for Marketing syllabus, 10 per cent is concerned with the nature of management. This unit provides a comprehensive introduction to the topic, but you must extend and build upon it from as wide a range of sources as possible. Classic management textbooks are readily available – you will find that, while there is general agreement on central issues, different authors offer a range of approaches.

Management, as we have seen, is more of an art than a science, and you should not be surprised that there is no one best way of being a manager. Providing that you know your style and the effect it has on others you can be a very effective manager. Theories X, Y and Z are less important than clarity of purpose, because there is need for all three types, depending on the organization and circumstances.

Wide ranging everyday reading will give you considerable insight. A day never goes by without a management example appearing in the quality press. Supplement the press with specialist media, such as *Management Today*, and the marketing press and you will be strongly placed to answer examination questions from a personal understanding that has foundation.

The Chartered Institute of Marketing is increasingly placing more emphasis on the marketer's role in management. This is evidenced by the inclusion of this specialist subject within the Advanced Certificate.

You can expect the role of the manager and the nature of the management to feature in some part of most examination papers – not necessarily as a stand-alone question. Management is, after all, the central issue to marketing success.

The 'nice' organization

There is increased interest from both academics and organizations in the virtue of being a 'nice' company. Evidence that 'niceness' can bring long-term benefits is shown by organizations such as Marks and Spencer, which has long been known for its enlightened staff policies. Body Shop is now investing profits in environmental projects in addition to its long-standing policy of promoting environmentally friendly products and packaging. Dixons has adopted a strategy designed to make the company 'nicer' when pile-them-high sell-them-cheap retailing seemed to no longer satisfy the customers.

Read through the two profiles, extracted from an article in *Management Today*, and compare the approach of two very different companies.

Unipart puts people first

Unipart, the former components division of British Leyland, based in Cowley, Oxford, shows that a leopard can change its spots. It used to have the fractious industrial relations and poor relationships with suppliers characteristic of the motor industry. But recently the company has been enjoying something of a transformation.

Following a MBO in 1987, chief executive John Neill looked at the Japanese manufacturing miracle and decided that, if Britain was to compete, its industry was going to have to work on the basis of co-operation and not the confrontational approach which had dogged Britain's car makers for so long. 'It's no good having these annual all-or-nothing battles with unions. You have to build relationships and work together.'

Many of Neill's ideas originated in Japan, which ironically is now rethinking some of its employment practices, including the jobs for life pledge. All Unipart staff now wear the same uniforms, eradicating 'us and them' demarcations between bosses and workers. Multi-skilling has been introduced so that people are trained, become used to doing a variety of jobs and understand other people's problems.

The unions were de-recognised in October 1991. 'Within 12 months, productivity in our distribution department had gone up by 39%,' says Neill. 'It wasn't that people were working harder, they just felt liberated.'

Unipart began investing heavily in staff training, something that had previously been targeted at management. The company ran a series of two-day training seminars for all staff entitled, Putting People First, and a monthly award programme was launched, to recognise outstanding service to customers.

Quality Circles were encouraged under a 'My Contribution Counts' campaign. Neill says that 1,000 staff have taken part and developed ideas, saving £4 million a year.

A campaign to improve supplier quality and reliability, called 'Ten to Zero' measured supplier performance. Aims are not just quality and reliability but trust and co-operation.

It seems to have worked. Last year profits were up to £20 million (1987 profits: £12 million; sales: £428 million) and, Neill, says: 'Unipart is a much happier ship.'

A mixed bag at Cadbury

Cadbury, Britain's best-known chocolate-maker, has a history of almost sickening niceness. Founded in 1824 by a Quaker, John Cadbury, the company was the archetypal paternal employer. Staff used to be given a restorative cup of cocoa on arrival every morning. And when the company moved to a new factory near Birmingham in 1879, Cadbury built itself an entire village including homes, schools and hospitals for workers, as well as playing fields and leisure facilities in the factory grounds.

Cadbury was proud of its industrial relations record and in 1918 works councils were set up to monitor working conditions, education and training and the social life of the factory and its workers.

Now part of Cadbury Schweppes plc and a company over which the profit-hungry City analysts pore daily, Cadbury is trying to shrug off some of the more anachronistic ideological baggage. 'The trick is try to retain the best of the old without throwing the baby out with the bath water,' says Neil Makin, Cadbury's personnel director.

Such changes have not always been well received. Last year Cadbury announced 450 redundancies. Nearly a year later the unions, chiefly the Transport and General Workers' Union and the Amalgamated Engineering and Electricians' Union, are still in dispute with Cadbury over the redundancies and the length of the working week (the unions want a reduction from 39 to 37 hours per week). They are operating an overtime ban, the first in years. 'We wanted to be properly consulted about it, which we had been before,' says union convenor John Tiler.

But the Quaker roots still show through. Pensioners have an annual get-together – at Bournville – which is so well attended it has to be staged over three nights. And old-timers still get a bag of goodies each which the company confesses 'costs more to send out than the value of the contents'. Cadbury pensioners are entitled to use the canteen as long as it is before 1.30pm.

Such nannying is now deemed unnecessary. 'People make more of a distinction between their working life and their home life,' says Makin.

- List the things which you think give clues about the management style and culture of each.
- What are the implications of these philosophies for managers and their respective businesses in the future?

Management personality

In each unit we will be featuring a person who has made significant contributions to management thinking generally or in the context of the specific topic being covered. You are not required to have a detailed knowledge of these individuals, but the feature will help you to identify areas of management which you may like to review in more depth. It is always useful to be able to illustrate answers with evidence of your knowledge of the underpinning theory (Figure 1.7).

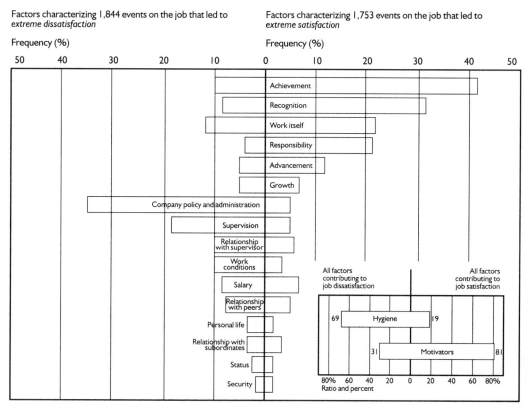

Figure 1.7 Herzberg's hygiene and motivating factors. Factors affecting job attitudes, as reported in 12 investigations

Frederick Herzberg: American Behavioural Scientist

A student of history and psychology, Herzberg was greatly influenced in his early work by a posting to Dachau concentration camp following its liberation. He became determined to look for answers to the question of what drove people to such human obscenities. He developed a focus on the prevention of mental illness as well as on care for the mentally sick. He came to believe that sanity requires as much professional attention to nourish the humanistic contant of character and ethics as in showing compassion for differences in personality. His theories have tended to emphasize strategies to keep the sane sane.

To assist in his work he compiled a bibliography of works on industrial psychology. Finding 'a paucity of conceptual thinking', he decided to fill the gulf. His goal was to keep people healthy in industry. His approach was: How do we keep the healthy from going sick?

A major conclusion was that managers need a high level of understanding, a broad education that allows them to see the interrelationships of sociology, psychology and the technical aspects of business. He is famous in management for work undertaken in the 1950s when he identified and separated two sets of work elements:

- People's animal needs – the hygiene factors.
- People's human needs – the motivation factors.

He found that sane people were made sick by the work they were doing, and this led to his theories of motivation and his breakthrough book *Motivation to Work*.

Herzberg's theories provide two challenges for managers:

- To recognize and serve individual's animal needs.
- To help them self-develop by targeting their inner motivations.

The hygiene factors are important, but not sufficient in themselves, since the most that can be expected from them is the 'prevention of dissatisfaction and poor job performance'. It is the motivational aspects which have the positive impacts and are now so standard in many organizations that the theoretical source has been forgotten. Flexitime, annual wage reviews, and cafeterias are all derived from hygiene theory. Appraisal, job enrichment and flatter structures come from motivational understanding.

Herzberg was among the first to encourage recognition that satisfying the client relationship was important to all workers. He is also responsible for identifying the essential facets of innovative people as:

1 Intelligence quotient.
2 Subject matter expertise.
3 Unconventionality.
4 Effectiveness in ambiguity.
5 Feeling the self.
6 Ability to separate motivator and hygiene values.
7 Control of anxiety.
8 Control of careerism.
9 Intuition.
10 Passion.

Key publications:
Motivation to Work, 1959
One More Time: How do You Motivate Employees? 1968
The Managerial Choice: To be Efficient and to be Human, 1976

SUMMARY

!

In this unit we have seen that:

- Managers are agents of the organization, charged with ensuring the delicate balance between its stakeholders and customers, a balance which is essential if the needs of both are to be satisfied.
- Management is a process dependent on the procedures, systems and structure which are developed to facilitate getting others to do specific tasks.
- The manager needs a whole range of business, personal and people skills as well as his or her specialist knowledge and competencies.
- Managers also need to have characteristics and personal strengths which enable them to operate and survive in an increasingly demanding and often stressful role.
- Identifying the necessary and ideal combination of knowledge and skills required for a particular management role is an important first step in developing an understanding of the role of managers and will be needed in the next unit as a starting point for:
  (a) A personal appraisal, necessary as a basis for further development of your own management skill.
  (b) Developing a management profile and job description – the baseline for selecting new managers.

Debriefing

Activity 1.2
You will probably have found that organizations vary in their understanding and use of the term. Some mission statements are crisp, others are lengthy. This is probably because of a

difference between managers' interpretation of mission and corporate objectives. The longer 'mission statements' actually carry what many prefer to see as corporate objectives.

This should not trouble you. The key thing is that management are working to a defined mission. You will undoubtedly find that organizations you work for will have singular terminology and procedures – you will have to adjust as your career develops and takes you through a variety of organizations and possibly across a range of sectors.

Activity 1.3

Certainly companies exist – they have a legal identity. They are separate from those who run them, however, and this must never be forgotten. When dealing with an organization it is actually the people with authority in the organization *at the time* that are your contacts. The organization, for all its logos and sense of purpose, is a shell within which people operate. Change the people and you are likely to change the organization.

Activity 1.4

There are many different activities which you may have included in your list. They are likely to vary a little in nature and descriptive terminology, according to the type and role of the manager of whom you were thinking. If you check our list you will probably find that most of the resource related activities that you identified can be categorized under one of these areas.

- *Audit* - literally taking stock of resources. Perhaps in the form of finished goods, people or assets. (Stock, human resource and financial auditing.)
- *Plan* - thinking through how the available resources can be employed to achieve specific objectives. Determining exactly how to deploy the resources.
- *Scheduling* - detailing the deployment of resources over time, e.g. a staff rota or delivery plan, or perhaps a timetable for a new project.
- *Budgeting* – allocation of resources in financial terms to allow for better control.
- *Control* - activities associated with performance review, feedback and plan modifications. Monitoring the effectiveness of resources as they are used up is an essential element of the manager's function.

Self-check 1.1

1 The marketing practitioner is a manager who specializes in activities and functions associated with the interorganization interface and its external publics. He or she will be responsible for some or all of the organization's marketing resources and will, amongst other tasks, provide information about the marketplace to help other managers make decisions about how best to satisfy customer needs.

2 The function of an organization is to transform scarce resources (factors of production) in a way which gives them added value – turning them into want-satisfying goods and services. It undertakes this activity in order to achieve its mission which means satisfying the needs of its stakeholders. In the private sector this is usually through making a profit.

3 Before any form of exchange can successfully take place it must be mutually profitable – both parties have to benefit from it.

4 Efficiency is about doing things the right way, getting the most out of the inputs used. Effective management uses the resources available to the greatest effect. Successful organizations must use the right way to do the right thing.

Activity 1.5

There are a number of possible skills and characteristics you might seek in your manager. Establishing detailed criteria for selection would entail not just a compilation of the list but some prioritizing and weighting given to each factor. You should also be able to see that, whilst drawing from the same broad list, the combination of skills needed by a more senior manager or a manager within a specialist function area, would be likely to produce a different candidate profile.

Mind maps

Many of our lists of skills and characteristics have been produced using a technique called 'mind mapping'. This powerful creative technique can be used very effectively to plan written work, take down notes, or as a technique for creative thinking. It encourages lateral and creative thinking by avoiding linear lists, and is a creative technique which can be used by an individual.

The basic rules for using mind maps are:

- Decide on the focus of the map. Write this in a small circle or box in the centre of the page.
- As each thought comes add a branch that is attached to the centre or to an existing branch.
- Reject nothing. Write down every thought and concept.
- Work out from the centre and follow a branch of associated thoughts until a new thought comes.
- Do not worry if the same thought comes up in several places – this just shows its importance and you can tidy the map up later.

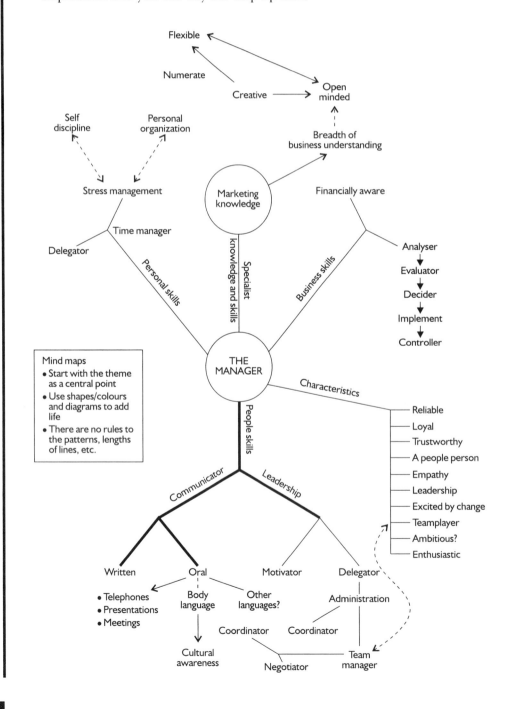

- Let the shape evolve. Never force a logic on the process.
- Use key words and print neatly on the lines. This forces discipline, and gives time for new thoughts to develop.
- Add colour, cartoons, or doodles as the mood takes you.

The result will be a more comprehensive list than from 'linear' techniques – and one that is produced faster and easier.

Mind mapping takes a little time to learn, and then a while to acquire confidence in its use. We promise that the time investment is one of the most important that you can make.

Managers of marketing, in particular, should work to develop their own 'creative toolbox' and mind mapping is as essential as a saw to a carpenter or a knife to a butcher. As tools of revision they are excellent, because each is unique, multidimensional, fun – and therefore easier to remember.

To learn more about mind mapping see:

- Tony Buzan, *Use Your Head*, BBC Publications. This includes detailed instruction on mind mapping, and also on learning, memory and speed reading.
- Hatton, Roberts and Worsam, *Solving The Management Case*, CIM/Butterworth-Heinemann Professional Series. This includes a worked example and also notes on other techniques of creative thought.

Improving management performance

OBJECTIVES

In this unit you will:

- Examine the need for developing the management resource.
- Consider the factors which influence management performance.
- Identify methods for management development.
- Undertake a personal skills audit.
- Consider methods for establishing development priorities.

By the end of this unit you will:

- Be able to assess management performance and diagnose problem areas.
- Appreciate the need for planned investment in management development.
- Appreciate the costs and benefits of alternative approaches to management development.
- Have a clear picture of your personal management strengths and weaknesses.
- Have produced a personal development plan based on specific improvement objectives.
- Be able to use job descriptions and skills audit information to advise on management development objectives.

STUDY GUIDE

Effective Management for Marketing is not intended by the Chartered Institute of Marketing to be a knowledge-based programme of study. There is considerable emphasis on the development of management skills and the examination will call upon you to demonstrate these in a number of ways. This unit is important because it will equip you with the tools to assess your own skills and to help you to develop your own personal improvement programme which can then be used as a basis for your own competencies development as you progress through the course.

You should allow 2 hours to work through this unit and a further 4 hours to fully complete the specified activities. You will need the following to complete your work on this unit:

- Your management skills notes from Unit 1.
- Any personal references, appraisals or performance feedback which you have available.
- A copy of your job description if you have one, *or* two job descriptions obtained by writing for details of advertised posts.

Examination failure is frequently due to a lack of examination practice rather than a lack of knowledge. Throughout this workbook you will find activities designed to help you develop not only the practical management skills you need in your work, but also the skills you need for effective examination performance. Do not skip over these – practice is critical to your success and will provide you with self-confidence supported by examples and evidence to help demonstrate your experience and skills in the examination room.

- Allow yourself enough time to thoroughly compete an activity or project. The times indicated are a guide only, if you need more time, take it, but be aware that in the examination time will be limited.
- Once completed, take time to compare your work with the answers or guidelines provided at the end of each unit. Identify any gaps or differences and make a note of any knowledge or skills on which you should be working.
- Do not expect to match the suggested answers perfectly. Management is an art, not a science. Therefore individuality in answers is to be expected. You should use management and marketing terms correctly. Where you refer to an underpinning theory it must be applied correctly and, usually, attributed to its source.

Explanations and definitions

1 *Appraisal*   Managers appraise their staff as a matter of routine. A formalized system of appraisal is designed to translate this informal act into one that is shared with the individuals who are being appraised. 'Performance appraisal' can be highly positive and developmental, or an ordeal which is meaningless at best and damaging at worst.

2 *Assumptions*   To assume is human – but leads to many problems. In particular, the assumption that others share your views and/or understand exactly what is in your mind. It is easy to say 'never assume', but much of life is only possible because of assumptions. On key issues, however, it is always better to check than assume.
   Remember: an assumption can make an ASS out of U and of ME.

3 *Attitude, skills and knowledge (ASK)*   These are the building blocks of every training and educational programme and class. All three are essential to learning, with attitude being by far the most important.

4 *Attitude*   An attitude is an internal state of mind which contains within it a predisposition to act. (Jackson) Marketers are familiar with the importance of attitude in their work. Human resource managers also spend a significant part of their time identifying and working with attitude. Attitude moderation and reinforcement are key areas of concern to all who work with people.

5 *Coaching*   A process in which a manager through direct discussion and guided activity, helps a colleague to learn to solve a problem, or to do a task, better than would otherwise have been the case. (BACIE – the British Association of Commercial and Industrial Education.) Coaching is an active learning situation where one individual assists another to develop identified skills. It is seen as a vital part of management development, but for many the pressures of time too often prevent coaching from being effective.

6 *Counselling*   This is a term which is commonly used by management in preference to 'mentoring'. Technically, a counsellor provides opportunities for discussion in neutral and psychologically safe circumstances. It is difficult for a line manager to counsel his or her staff because of the control they have over the individual. (Think of Counsellor Troi in Star Trek, the new generation. She is a senior officer, but out of line management and able to listen confidentially and respond to the human needs of crew members of all ranks.) We shall return to this issue in Unit 7.

7 *Learning contract*   This is a formal agreement entered into between student/trainee and the provider of the education/training. A learning contract can be for a whole

course of study, and/or for individual elements within a course. Contracts are valuable because they specify the commitment of both learner and tutor.

8 *Learning environment*   Also called the 'learning company', 'learning system', 'learning organization', and so on. These are comparatively new terms used to describe concepts which have been used for some time. In essence they all are used to indicate an organization which facilitates the development of all its staff, all the time, and is itself prepared to change to meet the changing demands of its environment.

9 *Management charter initiative*   An initiative launched in the late 1980s to encourage the on-going training and development of UK managers. Research had indicated a significantly lower average number of days per annum spent in training in the UK than in Germany and Japan. MCI introduced a hierarchy of learning for managers which is formalized in Certificate and Diploma levels and can lead to a Masters Degree programme.

10 *Management development*   Douglas McGregor describes two extremes in the approaches to management development. The oldest assumes that it is an automatic process – the cream will rise to the top. Nothing need be done by the organization except provide an opportunity and reward success. The second he calls the 'manufacturing approach', because organizations take active steps to create individuals with management talent. This approach leads to the use of such engineering terms as 'designing' a programme, and 'building' the necessary machinery to produce a supply of managerial talent. The original purpose can get lost in the mechanics.

11 *Mentoring*   Mentor was the servant of Odysseus entrusted with the care and training of Odysseus' son, Telemachus. Today mentors are seen as older, more experienced individuals who pass on the benefits of their experience to younger persons. Many experienced managers believe that the mentor relationships they experienced as juniors played a key role in assisting them along their successful career paths. It is common in management to use the term counselling in place of mentoring.

12 *National Vocational Qualifications (NVQs)*   The NVQs (SNVQs in Scotland) are competence-based qualifications. They test ability to do the job rather than academic ability. NVQs are widely available, and new subjects are being added as approvals are gained. The CIM is an Awarding Body, with the RSA, for NVQs in Marketing and in Sales. NVQs lead to Management Vocational Qualifications (MVQs) within the MCI.

Why invest in the management resource?

In Unit 1 we examined the changing role of the manager and his or her critical importance to the organization and its survival and success. If the manager is, in a real sense, the driving force behind the organization, responsible not only for the direction but also the pace and effectiveness of progress, then it is clear that the quality and abilities of that manager will directly impact on the performance of the team and the organization.

The concept of management investment is not an unusual one. Your CIM studies, and the time spent working through this book, are examples of your own investment in your personal management skills. Many organizations employ management trainees or trainee managers. Many offer programmes of management training and, increasingly, the importance of on-going management development has been gaining acceptance. This has been heavily promoted in the UK by the work of Charles Handy and the development of the Management Charter Initiative (Figure 2.1).

Clearly, the manager's skills are recognized as being too important to be left to chance. The best equipment, individual staff skills and work environment are not enough to ensure successful outcomes. Management is the catalyst that combines these elements and ensures that the desired outputs are derived from these valuable inputs. Investment in the management resource is therefore as fundamental as investment in capital equipment or new buildings.

There are a number of reasons which can be identified to support the contention that investing in management is necessary:

• The role and responsibility of the manager change as he or she progresses through the organization. New competencies are needed to perform satisfactorily in new roles.

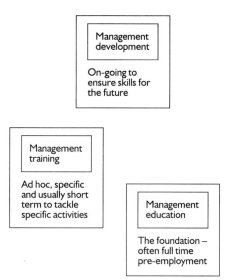

Figure 2.1 The building blocks of management investment

- The pace of environmental change is so fast that managers must constantly update and develop new skills to meet these new challenges and opportunities.
- Even in a static situation and role, improved skills will build confidence and improve performance – this usually translates into higher profits through lower costs or higher revenue.
- As Herzberg identified, personal development is a central motivation factor and is important in retaining the dynamic drive of the individual manager and the management team.

The pros and cons of investing in managers
As with all issues, there are two sides to the story. Spend 20 minutes and produce a list of the issues that support or reject the proposal that your organization should invest in management development.

                   Pros   Cons

(**See** Debriefing at the end of this unit.)

ACTIVITY 2.1

Creating the right environment

One of the responsibilities of the management team is to create an environment where the benefits of investment in management development outweigh the costs or its possible disadvantages. Senior management commitment is vital to ensure that a positive learning environment is created and maintained. A number of things can be done once senior management is committed.

- Evaluation of the improvement of a manager's skills by regular appraisal.
- Recognition of improvements and developments by giving managers the chance to demonstrate and use their new skills – and by providing promotional opportunities within the organization.

- Avoidance of 'inbreeding' the management team by encouraging new ideas, e.g. use of secondments, or cross-cultural work experiences with subsidiaries, suppliers or distributors.
- Encouragement of managers to recognize and develop the potential within their own teams and to provide an effective learning environment for them.
- Provision of frameworks and conditions which allow managers to recognize their own potentials and limitations, and to take responsibility for their own development.
- Resource provision – of both time and funding – to provide a menu of appropriate development and training activities.
- Provision to ensure that trained managers, returning from an MBA course perhaps, are encouraged to use their new abilities, and are *not* expected to remain in the same job using the same methodology!

A process for management development

Getting the environment right is only part of the picture. To be effective any investment must be planned, coordinated and evaluated. It is this process which ensures that development activities are relevant to the needs of both the individual and the organization and so uses the available investment to the maximum effect (Figure 2.2).

The process is straightforward.

1 *Evaluate* The starting point is a detailed evaluation of the range and level of attitude, skills and knowledge required by a particular role. This comes from the job description, supplemented by a job specification.

(**Note**: We shall examine the documentation in detail in Unit 5. For now take it that jobs are made up of tasks, and that a job specification itemizes the competencies needed to fulfil each task.)

Figure 2.2 What attitude, skills and knowledge?

2 *Audit* The competencies of each individual manager must be determined – usually through an on-going system of appraisal.
3 *Gap analysis* The variation between the competencies possessed and those needed is identified, and then prioritized.
4 *Implementation* A training programme is developed and implemented. Synergy will be sought by structuring regularly needed training on a systematic basis so that individuals can slot in where and when it is most advantageous for them and for the organization.
5 *Evaluation* Each individual training element should be evaluated by the manager undergoing training. The regular appraisal interviews (6 or 12 monthly) should evaluate overall progress.

The organization's overall training programme and policy must be evaluated at a senior level to ensure that it is achieving the overall objectives set (Figure 2.3).

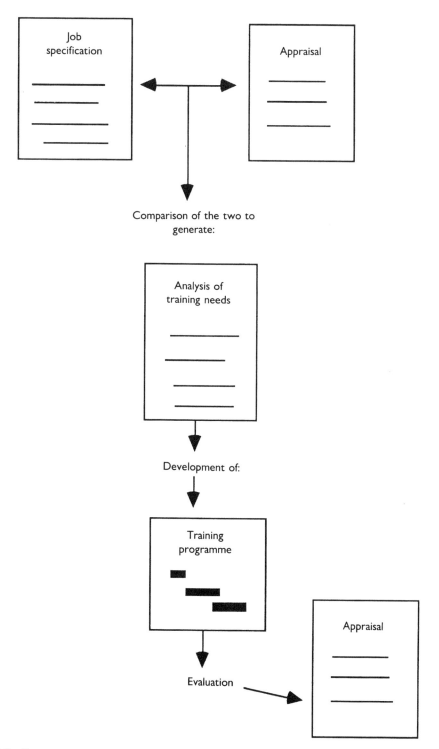

Figure 2.3 Process

Audit

There are almost as many ways of conducting management development audits as there are human resources managers to conduct them! An exaggeration, of course, but the area of attitude measurement is complex and subtle – as all marketers know. Assessment of the knowledge and skills levels is relatively straightforward, providing it is carried out objectively and one does not rely on opinion or the unsupported word of the manager who will find it hard to give a balanced judgement. (How do you know what you don't know?)

Attitude is the key to successful development. This has been said earlier but bears repeating because many coming new to management development focus on the observable elements of knowledge and skills. Attitude evaluation is known by a variety of names to make the process more psychologically acceptable. 'Management development priorities' may be evaluated, or the 'management approach'. This is the identical approach taken in marketing research depth interviewing – hardly surprising, because the techniques come from the same source, i.e. clinical psychology.

It is often more helpful to evaluate management development priorities in a group, where free discussion can be stimulated. The most common technique remains the same, however. An 'instrument' is used to help the individual focus his or her thinking. The results are scored and the outcome provides a basis for discussion. From the discussion an assessment of attitude can be made.

Extracts from two typical structured questionnaires will demonstrate the process (Figure 2.4).

EXTENDING KNOWLEDGE

Structured behavioural questionnaires designed to assess suitability for jobs, development need, etc., are readily available from any number of sources, from human resources texts to specialist consultancies. They are supposed to be proof against respondents who want to manipulate their results because the multi-choice responses check, double-check and cross-check to detect deliberate falsehoods. Unfortunately, many have grown up with these instruments and can quite easily achieve the response they require. The fact that they have been available for over 30 years without achieving widespread acceptance should indicate that they are held in considerable doubt by many HRM professionals. That said, the technique can be very useful, provided that it is in the hands of a professional who is trained and experienced in its use and it is never taken as the sole evidence on which to base a decision.

Alternative methods of analysis are more open-ended and easier to use. You need a way to get into conversation with a colleague, you don't want any threat to be perceived because none exists, yet you need to obtain some feedback on attitude. It is not easy! Questionnaires which provide you with topics or questions for you to consider and use in discussion *with* colleagues are a great help. Providing they are not attempting to be other than ways to get into useful discussion they do not have to be terribly deep. But they do need to be open-ended, and you must be prepared with supplementary questions to keep the conversation going. You should be aiming to contribute no more than 20% to the conversation. It is your respondent that you need to hear from.

Problem areas

- *Self-protection*   In dealing with people there is always the problem that they will colour their responses to what they think you expect. As marketers we know this to be a problem in marketing research – how much more dangerous are questions about *you* rather than your choice of soap powder! It is not surprising if truthful answers are hard to obtain.
- *Hidden agendas*   Somewhat akin to self-protection is the matter of hidden agenda. What does she think that he actually means and what does he think that she thinks that he actually means? Are people responding to the question asked, or to the question they think is being asked – or even to the one they believe ought to be asked?

Management development priorities

A series of 20 questions, the first three of which are shown.

Assess the extent to which you agree or disagree with each of the following statements and circle the appropriate figure. (0 – Strongly disagree; 6 – strongly agree.)

1 Low managerial effectiveness is a root cause of the present recession.

0   1   2   3   4   5   6

2 Management training contributes significantly to company performance.

0   1   2   3   4   5   6

3 Harassed organizations provide challenging opportunities for management development work.

0   1   2   3   4   5   6

The discussion that follows from the completed questionnaire commences with a grouping of results on a flip chart by the facilitator. It leads to an assessment of both the individual's and the group's views on the importance of management development, then to an action plan for their team and, finally, opens the way for individuals to accept their own need.

Management approach

This is designed to help managers review and assess the management style they prefer, and contrast it with the one they use. The result, obviously, is a training gap. It is a complex process, starting with 18 questions led into by quite formidable instructions.

Instructions

Many people relate to others in a number of different ways. Their approach or 'style' can vary, but the way they most usually behave or make other people respond can have a marked influence on their interpersonal relationships, whether as boss or subordinate. In this questionnaire are 18 self-descriptive statements, each of which is followed by four possible endings. These all relate to this work approach. Rank order the endings as they apply to you, and allocate accordingly in the blank spaces provided using the numbers 4, 3, 2 and 1. Allocate 4 to the ending that is *most like you* or best describes your own working situation, as you see it, most of the time. Allocate 1 to the ending that is *least like you* or your working situation. Allocate 3 and 2 to the remaining endings as appropriate.

Here is an example.

Most of the time at work I generally feel that I am:
   (a) good natured and friendly   (4)
   (b) hard working and dynamic   (1)
   (c) practical and thorough   (2)
   (d) enthusiastic and optimistic   (3)

Even if the statements that follow have two or more endings which seem equally like you (or not like you), please rank them 4, 3, 2, 1.

There are no right or wrong answers. The only correct answer is what you decide yourself.

1 I feel most satisfied with myself, when, in a problem work situation, I:
   (a) cooperate with other people and obtain their help.   ( )
   (b) accept the challenge and responsibility of leadership.   ( )
   (c) stick to the routine and procedures I know best and avoid unnecessary risk-taking.   ( )
   (d) adjust my ideas to fit in with the group or team I am working with.   ( )
2 In dealing with problem situations I find other people feel:
   (a) part of a team, well regarded and capable of being called on.   ( )
   (b) responsive and interested, confident about joining me in the work in hand.   ( )
   (c) justly and fairly treated, appreciative of my objective and consistent approach.   ( )
   (d) pleased and encouraged by my willingness to understand their point-of-view.   ( )

The scoring analysis for this instrument results in a management-style rating. It is a complex process, but the end result indicates the perceived weighting of management style between Helpful, Directive, Consolidative and Adaptive.

The scores give an indication of how the manager *intends* to behave, how he *actually does behave* and how others *perceive* him to behave.

Figure 2.4 Questions from typical structured questionnaires

• *Common understanding* Value loaded terms are very commonly used interpersonally. Descriptive terminology ('nice', 'warm', 'friendly'; 'awful', 'bossy', 'nosy') indicate areas for investigation, but they do not quantify. In any case, my 'nice' may be your 'lovely' – and where does that get us?

Assessing attitude, skills and knowledge
If you wanted to assess creativity you may structure a series of open questions that you will draw upon as needed. The opening has to set the tone. Use a scale of 1 (bad) to 10 (excellent) to rate each of these questions – and explain your ratings.

1 What do you think of as creativity?
2 Would you describe yourself as a creative thinker?
3 What creative problem solving techniques do you know of?
4 Which creative problem solving techniques do you find the most helpful?
5 Tell me about a problem you resolved with a creative solution.
6 In general would you consider yourself to be a lateral thinker?
7 What examples of creativity do you admire?
8 Who is your favourite creative person?
9 Why?

(**See** Debriefing at the end of this unit)

How are your management skills?
In Unit 1 you produced a list of skills and competencies needed by a marketing manager. Use this as a base to analyse your own personal management knowledge, skills and attitudes. Start by taking each of the characteristics in your list and creating a list of open-ended questions which could be used to encourage a colleague to discuss and analyse his or her skills in that area.

Use your questions and the strengths and weakness chart to help you assess your own competencies. Ask colleagues, use the notes from appraisals and other tangible materials where available, try to be as honest as possible and do *not* be too critical. If you can, ask someone who you know and trust to review your assessment.

Use a ten point scale – 5 is just below average, 6 is just above. With no mid-point you are forced to make a positive assessment on each criterion.

Strengths	Rating	Weaknesses	Rating

Training needs
When used by management this technique can reveal up to three levels of training needs:

1 *Organizational* These are needs identified as being general weaknesses within the organization and where training may be seen to be a priority. Action here could tackle a corporate weakness or be used to create a competitive advantage. It may, for example, take the form of language training for executives, customer care training, or IT familiarization.
2 *Occupational* Here the skill or knowledge gap is specific to a particular job or function. The need could be for training to equip the product managers to handle EC Regulations on advertising or to improve the sales research skills of the field sales team.
3 *Individual* These are particular ASK gaps which are perhaps unique to an individual.

Undertaking a complete training needs analysis is a time-consuming and specialized activity which would always involve the Human Resource Team and may require the use of external consultants.

Further reading
T. H. Boydell, *A Guide to the Identification of Training Needs*, British Association of Commercial and Industrial Education (BACIE)

Personal development plan
Now you have completed your personal management skills assessment you should be able to identify areas where you can develop your personal skills. These will be areas of existing strength on which you want to build, and identified areas of weakness which should be tackled. Take time out to review your profile and to establish a minimum of three personal improvement objectives to be completed whilst you are working for this examination.

Your objectives need to be specific and quantified – but they need to be realistic. If you want to develop personal presentation skills, for example, you could set an objective of making three presentations at work or college over the next 6 months. To strengthen your leadership skills you could offer to be the leader in a college syndicate group or in a work-related project during the next month.

My personal objectives are:

1 _____

2 _____

3 _____

Make a note in your diary now to review your performance against these objectives in 1, 2 and 3 months. Once you are satisfied with your improvement set yourself new objectives. Management is an activity which must be practised and constantly developed. You need to take responsibility for your own personal management development. In time it will become routine and you will wonder how you ever progressed in the narrow closed world of the non-evaluating person. If you do not consider that a non-critical approach necessarily leads to a narrow approach, you have perhaps identified a defensive attitude which could do with review.

Self-check 2.1
Take time to answer the following questions to help you assess your understanding of the material covered so far in this unit. You will find our answers at the end of the unit.

1 Briefly explain the difference between training and development.
2 Use the ASK headings to show the typically different approaches taken to customers by a credit controller and a sales person.
3 What do you see as the main rationale for using instruments as an aid to the identification of developmental priorities, etc.?
4 What special values might a team of external consultants offer in a training-needs analysis exercise?

Opportunities for personal development

It is one thing identifying the areas of skill and knowledge which need attention, it is another to actually take actions which will deliver the improvement desired.

QUESTION 2.2

Take 15 minutes to mind map the different methods and opportunities which are potentially open to a manager seeking to develop a particular competence.

You will identify a surprising number of options. Each, of course, has its own particular character, costs and benefits. Successful development is dependent on your finding the mechanism for development which matches your needs in terms of time, budget, effort and aptitudes. As you start on your personal development plan you will probably find that your first list of methods and opportunities can be at least doubled in size!

Compare your mind map with our list of training sources included later in this unit.

Learning styles

Much careful research has shown that a variety of learning styles exist. Each individual prefers to learn in a way that suits his or her personality and physiological make-up. Several models of learning style have been created and it seems that there are four overall categories into which learning style falls.

- *Activists* Enjoying the here-and-now, activists involve themselves fully and without bias in new experiences. They are open-minded, not sceptical, and this tends to make them enthusiastic about anything new. Their philosophy is 'I'll try anything once'. Their days are filled with activity, they revel in short-term crisis management. They thrive on challenges but are bored with implementation and longer term considerations.
- *Reflectors* Preferring to stand back and ponder experiences, reflectors like to observe from many different perspectives. They collect data from a wide range of sources and want to digest it thoroughly before coming to any conclusion. 'They are people who Look before they leap' and 'Leave no stone unturned'. When they act it is within a wide picture which includes the past as well as the present and other people's observations as well as their own.
- *Theorists* Wishing to adapt and integrate, theorists want to integrate observations into complex but logically sound theories. They think through problems in a vertical, step-by-step, logical way. They are keen on basic assumptions, principles, theories, models and systems thinking. Typical questions are 'Does it make sense?' and 'How does this fit in with that?' They prefer to maximize certainty and feel uncomfortable with lateral thinking.
- *Pragmatists* Keen on trying out new ideas, pragmatists positively search out for the new and take early opportunities to experiment. They return from management courses brimming with ideas that they want to try out at once in practice. They don't like delays, nor 'beating around the bush'. They respond to problems and opportunities as challenges. Their philosophy is 'There is always a better way' and 'If it works it's good'.

Much work has been done to create instruments that help individuals to define their own learning style – which is always a blend of the four basic categories but with a strong bias towards one or perhaps two predominant styles. These instruments are more reliable than those described for attitude identification because they are dealing with one aspect of an individual's psyche – and one where there is every reason to be open because the result cannot be seen to be threatening.

Once learning style has been identified it can be seen that some forms of learning are more suitable than others. Competency based learning would better suit an activist, whilst a traditional 'classroom' knowledge-based course would find favour with the theorist. To some extent there is need to tailor the teaching method to the learning style, but there is also need to widen the range of learning styles as part of an individual's self-development.

Learning cycle

Experience based learning operates in a cyclic manner. We Plan, Do, Review and Conclude (Figure 2.5). The four stages of the learning process correspond, roughly, to the stages of the cycle.

- Activists – Doing
- Reflectors – Reviewing
- Theorists – Concluding
- Pragmatist – Planning

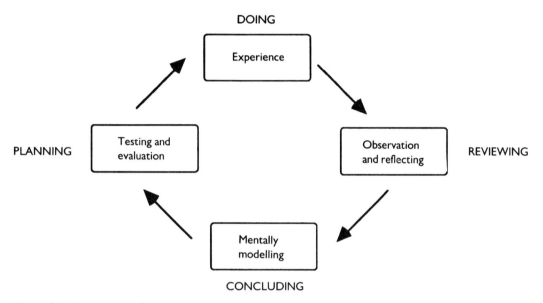

Figure 2.5 Learning cycle

What does this mean to the line manager?

- Developing a balanced learning style will help one to learn more effectively.
- Presenting material to meet the learning style of individual trainees is helpful to their learning.
- Grouping trainees with similar learning styles helps in material presentation (course content style) and short-term learning. It is not individually developmental.
- Mixing individuals with different learning styles in groups and syndicates widens the range of possible activities, and helps individual self-development long-term.
- As a manager, when training others beware of the natural tendency to use your preferred training style – you need to meet the needs of the trainee and so should work in their preferred learning style. We shall return to this issue in Unit 7.

Learning opportunities
In planning the learning for yourself and for members of your team it is essential to take individual motivation into account. Take 15 minutes and, for each of the four learning styles, list what opportunities are 'turn-ons' and what are 'turn-offs'.

Turn-ons Types and characteristics of activities from which most will be learned	*Turn-offs* Activities, etc., which are disliked and which will inhibit learning
Activists (hands-on people)	
Reflectors (pull out and think)	
Theorists (rationality and analysis)	
Pragmatists (tell me and let me try)	

(**See** Debriefing at the end of this unit.)

Consider which is your dominant learning style, and which is your least preferred. Then take steps over a 6-month period to structure your personal development so that you both:

(a) Maximize your short-term learning by concentrating on your preferred style.
(b) Commence long-term self-development by selecting specific learning opportunities to extend your learning style.

For maximum effect write down your assessment of your present learning style, and review the position at 2, 4 and 6 months from now.

Sources of training

Training is always formally organized even if it is informal in nature. 'Formal' and 'informal' describe modes adopted to meet trainees' preferred learning styles. It is therefore wrong to use 'formal' and 'informal' to describe 'organized' and 'casual'. Casual training should *never* be considered, it implies a lack of planning objectives and commitment which should not be tolerated.

Training can be provided in a number of ways and from a number of sources.

Open courses

These are courses where the participants are likely to be drawn from a number of different organizations and perhaps different functional backgrounds. They provide the opportunity for cost-effective training for an individual. Timing, level and length of the programme can probably be selected from a choice of providers. There are advantages in being exposed to the ideas of people from other backgrounds, organizations, industries and sectors.

Open courses are often blamed for sowing the seeds of dissatisfaction because course members naturally exchange information on benefits packages, and sometimes individuals are head hunted by those they have met on a course. Individuals can be exposed to ideas and approaches which are not recognized in their organization. Their attempts to implement the lessons of their learning can lead to frustration and perhaps resentment by colleagues and line managers.

Note: Concern over such matters as sharing information on benefits packages and acting as forums for dissatisfaction is a sign of an insecure management. If morale is high – which it is management's job to ensure – then concerns will turn to benefits. Others will be head hunted to join, and the forum will be developmental not destructive.

Closed courses

These are courses which are open only to the employees of the organization. They have a number of advantages in that content and level can be developed to meet the specific needs of the organization – although not necessarily the needs of each individual. The training programme can be used as a focus for team building, networking within the organization and as an opportunity for the marketing of corporate policy, cultural change, or to re-motivate a team.

Whilst usually more cost-effective, there is the problem in smaller organizations of having several people away from work at the same time. There is also the potential for dissatisfactions with the employer to be fuelled and spread.

Management education

Programmes of study for professional examinations such as the CIM or evening classes to extend your knowledge of a particular subject such as finance or HRM are readily available in most areas. They are usually cost-effective. Often employers will sponsor such programmes – paying the fees, offering study leave, and paying a bonus on completion. Such programmes are often built into the overall induction stage of a management trainee's development. More senior managers may be 'seconded' to gain an MBA or to attend an education programme at one of the large number of international business schools.

These opportunities can offer a breathing space away from the workplace where new ideas can be considered. Such time can be invaluable to the strategic managers who need an external focus and to actively seek new approaches and new ideas. These programmes will usually involve mixed groups and encourage cross-fertilization of views and experiences.

Other education courses

Extending knowledge and skills through evening classes in other areas such as languages or IT, or creative areas such as photography or drama, can all improve skills which are directly useful in the workplace, and are a cost-effective method of undertaking personal development.

Conferences

Whilst usually not facilitating any skill development, conferences are excellent forums for the exchange of knowledge and are often important to help individual staff keep up to date in technical or specialist areas. They are good opportunities for extending contacts outside the organization. Internal conferences and meetings are useful for such specifics as the presentation of new products or sales plans whilst at the same time building (boosting) team spirit and morale.

Secondments – internal

Managers are increasingly recognizing the wealth of learning opportunities which exist within their own organization. Secondments to other functional areas or divisions can improve communication, give experience of cross-cultural working or develop project team skills. Succession plans for potential senior executives will often involve a number of short contracts across the organization's areas of activity.

Improving understanding and company communication programmes of placement and attachment can be both cost-effective and valuable, but they do need to be developed specifically to meet the needs of the individual or the organization.

Think global!

For many years the multi-national organizations have had a global approach to management development. Senior managers are promoted to smaller countries to gain experience before taking a post in a large market. The Production Manager for Holland is sent as Production Director to Chile before taking post as Production Director of France. The UK Marketing Director has 2 years as Managing Director in Australia before returning to run the UK Company. Management Trainees are seconded to global head office before assignment to an operating company in a country deemed appropriate to their on-going development.

Secondment – external

Managers can considerably broaden their experience outside the organization through external secondment. If sponsored by a commercial employer it is often a short-term posting to a charity or voluntary organization because it is difficult to make a secondment to another commercial venture. Not-for-profit enterprises have no such problems, but their need is usually to host rather than seek secondment.

Similar benefits to formal external secondment can be gained by participating in not-for-profit organizations in your leisure time. Management responsibility can be taken within a local amateur dramatics or debating group. Presentation skills, and subject knowledge, can be boosted by taking up an evening class teaching post. Fund-raising groups are always in need of professional marketing assistance.

Professional group and institute meetings

These are an excellent way of keeping up-to-date with specialist areas, and are an effective forum in which to widen your network of contacts. CIM Branch Meetings will, for example, provide you with a wealth of case-study examples to illustrate your answers in the examination as well as the opportunity to meet fellow professionals. Contacts here (or colleagues at college) can open potential opportunities for job shadowing and mentoring.

Job shadowing

Working alongside an experienced manager – acting as a shadow by sticking close at all times – is an ideal way to gain experience of another's routine. It is an excellent way to broaden experience and to prepare for promotion. It also has great potential as a means of helping youngsters at school acquire a basic understanding of the world of work. More significant to managers is the opportunity to find out something of how managers in another functional area are motivated, how they think, and why they behave as they do.

Learning from your own job

Taking time to assess your own performance in a specific area can itself be an excellent way to facilitate personal development. Appraisals can be used to help focus this introspection and if you set and keep to a structured plan you will find that major benefits accrue. Considerable development can be achieved if you can work with a colleague to improve or develop a particular skill area. Many of the activities in this workbook will provide you with a focus for this personal development.

Mentoring

Having the guidance of an experienced manager can make a considerable difference to a junior's developmental progress. Mentoring need not be a formalized activity – in most cases it is not arranged by the organization. The less experienced person has the most to gain from mentoring, but the process is not one way, since the mentor will gain the benefit of a keen 'assistant'.

Setting up a mentoring relationship on one's own initiative requires understanding of the need for mutual benefit and the recognition – hard for some younger people to acknowledge – that the older hands have much to offer from their experience.

Coaching

Coaching involves one-to-one training which often extends over a period of time. It is as far removed from the 'sitting next to Nellie' approach as playing a sport is from watching it on TV. The one is active and developmental, the other passive and restrictive. A coach has to be experienced in training. 'Nellie' just has to know how she does her job.

The learner can be frustrated by 'Nellie', and also may learn the bad work habits that 'she' has acquired over the years. Job shadowing 'Nellie' for a time can be beneficial, but only within a planned training programme.

The media

Magazines, books, television and radio programmes can all provide sources for extending knowledge, keeping up to date and, in some cases, for skills development. Put your driving time to good use by searching out BBC Radio 4 on your car radio, and listen to training tapes on the cassette player.

> *Personal planning*
> Take the three personal objectives you established for yourself earlier. For each prepare a detailed plan identifying the methods you intend to employ to achieve these over the next 6 months. Plan to use a combination of methods and talk to your employer about training opportunities and to colleagues about job shadowing. As part of your development, aim to secure the trust and confidence of a mentor so that mutual benefit will be obtained.

ACTIVITY 2.4

Examination hints

The contents of this unit are extremely important to you whether you are working through continuous assessment or towards the formal examination.

For those working at colleges which are approved by CIM to evaluate your progress by continuous assessment, your personal development action plan or learning contract will probably be the benchmark for the assessment of your progress.

Those who will be assessed through the examination must prepare to answer questions which will require detailed knowledge on such topics as the *process* of skills audits or the mechanisms for managing your own learning. Practical experience in carrying through the activities and exercises in this unit – and in the course – will be invaluable.

Process questions are increasingly being used throughout the CIM Advanced Certificate and Diploma and you can be certain that they will feature strongly in this examination.

Process questions

Process questions are 'how to' questions. They require practical answers based on theoretical understanding and are replacing the traditional knowledge-based questions. Process questions place you in a situation and ask what actions you would take, or recommend. They ask you to show that you know the process of managing the topic.

Hints on answering process questions:

- Answer practically and directly. The examiner wants a report that could be actioned, not a theoretical appreciation of what might be done.
- Use theory to support recommendations – but explain it only if you are using it in an unusual or specially creative way.
- Quantify what you recommend.
- Keep your recommendations realistic and credible.
- Work in report format so that clear headings and subheadings provide an easy-to-follow path of recommended actions.
- Use flow charts and models to indicate the stages which have to be taken in sequence.
- Gantt charts and timetables add the important time frame to the action. Remember that the process of change – even of recruiting and selecting new staff – takes a longer time than one may think.

Look at the following scenarios. Identify the key issues/problems and recommend appropriate management development objectives.

Scenario one

The Deluxe Dolls House Company has grown from a cottage industry producing prefabricated dolls houses to a £5 million UK turnover employing 60 staff. The two supervisors who have been with the business since it started 8 years ago seem to be having a number of problems. Staff turnover and absenteeism have increased noticeably, and over the last six months both quality and reliability of orders being shipped have been below that expected. The company has tried training – one supervisor went on an expensive one week team management course, but complained it was all theory and not relevant to a business of this size. The other started a local college Certificate in Management Studies course last September. The first few projects were both relevant and valuable, but she left the course last month when the pressures of a couple of urgent contracts forced her to miss three classes in succession.

Scenario two

Your company has negotiated a joint venture contract with an Italian partner. Until now there has been no export business and generally there is no experience of working in a different culture. You have been asked to propose development objectives for the project team of 20 cross-functional managers who will be most involved at the early stages of this initiative.

Scenario three

J.B. Smith & Sons is a small chain of department stores located in the North East. Despite taking on an average of 20 management trainees annually, the turnover rate is high and, recently, first-line managers have had to be appointed from outside the company.

(**See** Debriefing at the end of thus unit.)

In this unit you have:

- Considered the reasons why investment in management develop-ment is worthwhile and have also identified the possible problems or limitations associated with it.
- Examined the role of job descriptions and job specifications and appraisal within training needs assessment and management development.
- Established that effective development must be focused and targeted on the needs of both the individual and the organization. You have started this process by undertaking a personal skills audit.
- Recognized that management skills must be learned and competencies practised, by establishing specific personal development objectives.
- Identified learning styles, and considered approaches that turn people on and also those that turn people off.
- Identified the alternative ways in which development or learning opportunities can be provided, and reviewed the advantages and disadvantages of each.
- Appreciated that a programme of personal development is crucial to your long-term career as well as to your short-term needs for success in your examination or continuous assessment.

Debriefing

Activity 2.1

Pros	Cons
• Managers are likely to be motivated and more loyal to the organization. Knowledge, skills and experience of the business are retained as a valuable resource	• It can lead to a self-sufficiency – the organization growing its own man-agers. This can be an unhealthy and inward-looking tendency. New blood brings new ideas and methods which can be of great value
• The organization is pro-active, plan-ning for the future by ensuring its managers are prepared for changing demands on them	• Considerable investment in training can be 'wasted' as managers move on to new organizations taking their new skills with them
• Development encourages confidence and a willingness to accept change	• Development and training can raise expectations which, if not fulfilled, lead to frustration and dissatisfaction
• Ensures that the organization gets the most out of the available resources	• Training is unfocused and does not target competencies which will improve work performance, and so is of limited direct benefit to the business

Activity 2.2

Too many of these questions are closed, and too many can be seen as challenges. No clarification of 'creativity' has been offered – many people think that only artists and musicians are creative, yet even a 'humble clerk' can be most creative in designing a simple system that cuts through miles of red tape.

	Our rating	Comment
1	6	Not closed, but 'what' is a challenge?
2	4	Centred on the person, good; but closed. Yes or No are the only answers.
3	2	Highly challenging. What if he or she knows of none? Especially if they are very creative without being aware of it.
4	8	'Which' is softer than 'what', but the question is trying for too much. Creative techniques are one question. Their use in problem solving is another.
5	9	'Tell me . . .' is a great opening. This would be a 10 question if we were certain that we had a common understanding of creativity.
6	1	Can we give this zero? 'In general' tells us nothing. We can almost all apply 'in general' to almost anything! What is lateral thinking, does the respondent know?
7	6	Shame about the 'what'. How about: 'Please help me to see why you admire creativity'.
8	8	Closed, but a great opening for the best supplementary question of all time . . . Why?
9	10	The best supplementary question of all time!

Activity 2.3

Individuals are motivated differently in learning – as in all else. For some it is best to set up a situation, let them loose, and then debrief and extract the learning points. Others are far more comfortable if they process the possible activities and identify the likely results before taking any action.

There is nothing wrong with either form of learning – provided that those who like to delay don't miss the bus whilst looking at the timetable nor that others get to the wrong place through leaping on the first bus that comes along.

The problem for tutor and learner alike is when a group is made up of a mixture of learning types.

Compare your thinking with the following which shows the kinds of situation that turn on and off, and the type of comment likely to be made in each situation. Note that turn-ons for some are turn-offs for others.

	Turn ons	Turn-offs
Activists	Trial in monitored test conditions 'Let's see if it sinks, and why.'	Discussions on possible results 'Let's work out what might happen.'
Reflectors	Programme of structured research 'We must explore all possibilities.'	Action not supported by understanding 'We are in a hurry for this information.'
Theorists	Programme of intellectually sound and structured research 'We need to know why it works.'	Use without an attempt to understand the rationale 'If it ain't broke, don't mend it.'
Pragmatists	Action with the minimum of preparation – learning by doing 'I know it works so let's find out how.'	Delay whilst actions are planned and potential results identified 'We are going to run tests before anybody is allowed to get in it.'

The opportunities you choose will depend to a large extent upon your learning style preferences. Recognizing what is likely to 'turn you on' – and turn you off – will help to ensure that you make the most of those opportunities

'Turn-ons'	'Turn-offs'
Types and characteristics of activities from which you will learn most	Activities, etc., which you dislike (and which may inhibit learning)

Activists ('hands-on' people)

'Turn-ons'		'Turn-offs'	
New experiences/problems	❏	Passive role (e.g. listening to lectures, observing, reading, etc.)	❏
'Here and now' *activities*	❏	Being asked to 'stand back'	❏
Drama, crisis, change, variety	❏	Having to assimilate or handle 'messy' data	❏
Leading roles, which give you high visibility	❏	Having to work on your own	❏
Freedom to generate ideas (without restraints)	❏	Planning what you intend to learn – and reviewing learning	❏
Thrown in at the deep end to tackle a challenging task	❏	Repetitive activities	❏
Involvement with others in a team	❏	'Theory' – or what you see as theory	❏
'Having a go'	❏	Precise instructions, with little room for manoeuvre	❏
		Too much precision, attention to detail	❏

Reflectors ('pull out and think')

'Turn-ons'		'Turn-offs'	
Opportunities to watch/think/chew over activities	❏	Being forced into the limelight	❏
Being able to stand back and observe and listen	❏	Having to act without adequate planning	❏
Time to think before you act	❏	Being forced to make 'instant' decisions	❏
Researching, investigating, probing	❏	Having to make decisions on insufficient data	❏
Being able to review your learning	❏	Cut-and-dried instructions	❏
Producing analyses and reports	❏	Time pressures	❏
Exchanging views in a low-risk, structured situation	❏	Having to make short cuts or do a superficial job	❏
Being able to make decisions without time pressures	❏		

Theorists (rationality and analysis)

'Turn-ons'		'Turn-offs'	
Being offered a systematic model, system, concept, theory	❏	Thrown into 'doing', without apparent context or purpose	❏
Exploring methodically relations between ideas	❏	Situations emphasizing emotions and feelings	❏
Questioning and probing basic assumptions and methodology	❏	Unstructured, ambiguous situations	❏
Being intellectually stretched, working with high-calibre people	❏	Having to act or decide without an underlying policy, concept or principle	❏
Structured situations with a clear purpose	❏	Being faced with a hotchpotch of alternative or contradictory methods (as in a 'once-over-lightly' course)	❏
Reading about or listening to well-structured, logically elegant ideas	❏	Subject matter which seems methodologically unsound	❏
Being able to analyse, then generalize reasons for success or failure	❏	Shallow, gimmicky subject matter	❏
Interesting ideas	❏	Feeling 'out of tune' with other participants	❏
Having to understand and participate in complex situations	❏		

Pragmatists ('tell me how and let me try')

'Turn-ons'		'Turn-offs'	
Clear, practical link with job: being shown techniques with practical advantages	❏	Apparent irrelevance, no clear link with practical needs	❏
Being able to try out/practise techniques with feedback/coaching from an expert who can do it himself successfully	❏	Organizer (or course itself) seems 'ivory tower'; 'all talk and chalk'	❏
'Models' you can emulate (a successful 'performer', a how-to film, examples, anecdotes)	❏	No practice or clear 'how to' guidelines	❏
		People seeming to go round in circles	❏
		Political, managerial or personal blocks to applying learning	❏
Opportunities to *use* learning	❏	Can't see a valid pay-off from learning	❏
Techniques you can use	❏		
'Real' problems, lifelike simulations to tackle	❏		
'Practical' activities (action plans, etc.)	❏		

Figure 2.6 Learning style preferences

Self check 2.1

1. Training is task specific, and usually short-term.
   Development is long-term, and individual specific.
2. A credit controller's attitude is governed by his or her experience of working mainly with customers who default. Their knowledge base is founded on financial management and their skills are sharpened by handling customers who are in financial arrears. The tendency, therefore, is to approach all customers as potential loss-making contacts and to require circumstances to prove otherwise.

   Sales people tend not to see the cash-problems side of customer contact. In fact they can sometimes be faulted for taking the customer's side against the organization! Their attitude is considerably affected by whether they have only sales or sales/profit responsibility. Skills are centred on getting the order and maintaining good relationships. Knowledge is customer/product centred.
3. Instruments are a vehicle that encourage individuals to take time out to focus on a given area. In themselves they are of limited value – it is the use that management makes of them that matters.
4. Consultants bring an external, non-political view. They are experienced and therefore should move faster, and probably with greater clarity. Their recommendations are not binding on the organization, and so internal managers can comment on them freely without any hidden agendas such as fear of upsetting the HRM manager.

Unit activity

Scenario one The problem here seems to be that the two supervisors' jobs have changed as the organization has grown rapidly over the last 8 years, but the management skills of the two people have not been developed in line with the changing needs of the job. It may even be that the two supervisors are no longer adequate to deal with the number of staff now employed. Clearly there has been recognition of a need for some staff development. However, in the first case, it looks as if the style of learning experience was not appropriate for the individual. He appears to have been an activist, more interested in doing, and therefore unable to appreciate the theoretical inputs from the course which he attended. The second supervisor appears to have been on a more appropriate course. One which was clearly benefiting both the individual and the organization. Unfortunately it seems that the organization did not give her continuing to participate the priority which it required. The objectives we would propose are:

- To undertake a detailed skills audit of the two supervisors and to identify with senior management the precise requirements of the jobs in the expanded company.
- To identify the skills gap and to recommend management training programmes suited to the specific learning styles and needs of both the individuals.
- The management development objectives are to have appropriate management development plans in place for both employees within 3 months, and within 18 months to have completed the management development activities necessary to enable them to perform their current roles effectively.

Scenario two The joint venture partner is not only located in a different country but probably has a different corporate culture as well. Managers from both companies are going to have to work effectively and build upon the strengths, experience and skills of both organizations. The objectives we would propose in these circumstances would be:

- To ensure that the 20 identified managers have an understanding of the differences of work within the Italian business culture and are familiar with the cultural norms and differences which they are likely to meet.

Note: this could involve familiarization visits to other companies who have experience of working within the Italian market, or team building and seminars held in Italy prior to the first joint venture meeting. The management may like to review the possibility of sending some, if not all, of the managers on an intensive language programme and also management skills in team building and working activities to ensure that everyone will be prepared and that the new joint venture settles to effective operations as quickly as possible.

Scenario three There could be a number of problems in this situation – possibly the management trainees who are being appointed are not of the right calibre for the job which they are being recruited for. Alternatively, the training programme is not relevant or stimulating enough to keep the trainees motivated and involved in the organization. Possibly there is inadequate communication with the trainees to encourage them to recognize the career prospects and opportunities for promotion within the organization. We would propose research to identify the cause of the high staff turnover and the reason why recent selections have not been able to be made from within the group of management trainees. To follow this up as necessary:

- With a complete audit of the skills needed by the first line managers.
- To review the recruitment and selection policy.
- Develop an induction and training programme which will ensure that future trainees develop the appropriate skills to an appropriate level within the organization.
- To review the method of training currently adopted and to identify ways in which more variety, new learning styles and a better range of experience can be included via formal training courses, project work within the organization, job shadowing, experience across different functions and departments within the store, monitoring and regular reviews and appraisals.

Peter Drucker: management writer, born in Vienna

Believed by many to be the person who 'invented' management, Drucker has been a prolific writer on management since his first book, *The End of Economic Man*, was published in 1939. *Business Week* have described him as 'the most read, most listened to, most regarded guru in management'. Tom Peters has said that 'Our debt to Peter Drucker knows no limit.'

Drucker's key achievements lie in his ability to identify and explain the issues that are at the heart of successful management. He was, for example, the first to:

- Define top managers as the keepers of corporate culture.
- Identify that the vision of the CEO is key to corporate success.
- Show that success comes from 'sticking with the basics'. That it all reduces to consumer sensitivity and the marketing of innovative products.
- Foresee the change to knowledge workers using computers, and to suggest a need for a radical revision to management thinking.
- Advocate mentoring, career planning and executive development as top management tasks.

Having rejected a conventional career as an investment banker because it 'bored him to tears', he emigrated to America in 1937 and, finding no philosophy of business, began to investigate it. He found that the concern was the factory floor – nobody had considered management. He invented the term 'top management' simply to fill a gap and, although he considers it a poor term, it has stuck. Management was taken for granted before Drucker began to ask challenging questions – and to provide pertinent answers.

Drucker himself will have nothing to do with his description as the 'inventor of management'. He says that the CEO who built the pyramids 6000 years ago knew more about management than any CEO alive today. Perhaps, he concedes, he is the man who discovered management – but 'at best as a co-discoverer and the most junior one'.

Others disagree and hold that no discipline of management existed before Drucker. There is no doubt that he has changed the face of modern industry – and from there his thinking has spread into all aspects of organizational management. He is responsible for, amongst others, decentralization, management by objectives, and the idea of customer-first strategies. All are now routine, but they were novel when Drucker began to write about them.

Key publications
The End of Economic Man, 1939
The Future of Economic Man, 1942
The Practice of Management, 1954
And many, many books and articles since.

Making the most of your time

In this unit you will:

- Examine the importance of time management to the personal effectiveness of the manager.
- Consider the need for prioritization and delegation.
- Investigate techniques for managing time in the context of a plan or project.

By the end of the unit you will be able to:

- Analyse how you use your own time and identify opportunities for improving the effectiveness of your time management.
- Recognize the symptoms in others who are having difficulties in managing time.
- Recommend strategies for people wishing or needing to improve their management of time.
- Understand the techniques of prioritization and work planning.
- Delegate work effectively to others.
- Plan a work activity or project and communicate that information to others.
- Understand the importance of time management in your examinations.

In the Effective Management for Marketing examination you will find that there is considerable emphasis on your ability to demonstrate practical time management (TM) skills. You may be required by the examiner to answer questions on methods of improved TM, and on helping others manage their time. You can expect to be asked to give an indication of your proposals for scheduling work and for managing the implementation of any proposals. You therefore need to undertake the activities and answer the questions within this unit to help you develop practical skills in scheduling projects and in managing your own personal time.

You should allow 3 hours to work through this unit and an approximately further 4 hours to fully complete the specified activities.

Whilst you are working on this unit we would expect you to be completing a personal TM record lasting a period of at least 1 week. This will be a basis for your own analysis and personal development in the area of TM. The details are explained in the first few pages of this unit.

Finding time in an already full working and home life is never easy and you need to identify opportunities for you to study without distractions. Make clear decisions about what activities you are going to give up in order to make room for study. Find and allocate specific study times in the week and try to stick to them. Perhaps you can find some study time whilst travelling to work or during the lunch hour. Remember that many people find effective study easier at earlier times during the day, working late at night may not to be so effective.

Several short bursts of study time are much more valuable than long unbroken stretches. Regular breaks are an essential part of effective learning because they allow your brain to relax and absorb what it has just been given. Try to make at least one break an active one. Get out for a short walk, even if it is just down the garden. This exercise refreshes you physically, and is in total contrast to the mental activity to which you are going to return. Plan your study sessions:

- Identify clearly what you going to do in each.
- Set yourself clear objectives.
- Allocate time to each activity.
- Vary the type of study method that you use.
- Plan at least three breaks in a 2-hour session.
- Do not go near an active television in any break!

Do not read and re-read textbooks and other study material. You have to take the content out of the material and establish it in your head. It is the process of *doing* that reinforces learning. Make your own notes, undertake the activities, practise question answering and, above all, put what you are learning to use in your 'real life'.

Explanations and definitions

1 *Accountability* Accountability can neither be assigned nor delegated, it must be accepted. (Sisk) A person accepts accountability as soon as responsibility is assigned and authority is delegated. (**See** *Delegation.*)

2 *Authority* Authority empowers a person to act for the delegator. (Sisk) In other words, to work with derived authority. Those delegated to must clearly understand what they are required to achieve, and the limits of their authority. If insufficient authority is delegated then accountability remains with the delegator. (**See** *Delegation.*)

3 *Contingency planning* A contingency plan outlines the steps that management would implement in response to specific adverse developments that might occur. The purpose of contingency planning is to encourage managers to give some prior thought to some difficulties that might lie ahead. (Kotler) Note that good times can be planned for as well as bad!

4 *Delegation* An organizational process that permits the transfer of authority from superior to subordinate. (Sisk) To be effective two factors must be taken into account:

- Responsibility must be assigned – it can never be delegated.
- Accountability is created when delegation is accepted.

In other words a manager who delegates can expect the subordinate to be accountable for results, but retains overall responsibility. Delegation is *not* an opportunity to pass on a problem. It is not a way to avoid responsibility – rather it is an acceptance of further responsibility, both for the person delegated to as well as for the factor that has been delegated.

5 *Fire fighting* A term in wide use to describe a management trait in which the person rushes from problem to problem, always unable to deal with the cause of the problems.

6 *Opportunity cost* (also known as *economic cost*) A measure of the economic cost of using scarce resources to produce one particular product or service in terms of the alternatives thereby foregone. (*Dictionary of Economics*.) For example, if resources are allocated to computer training they are no longer available for new computer software. If staff time is spent in meetings it cannot be used to answer the telephone.

7 *Pareto's law* Otherwise known as the '80/20 principle', Pareto's law is widely thought to apply to a range of situations in which most of the behaviour or value of one factor is deemed to depend on only a little of another factor. It is widely asserted, for example, that 80% of sales volume comes from 20% of customers; that 80% of profits come from 20% of sales; that 80% of problems come from 20% of the staff. A number of different strategic management applications are based on Pareto's law. Three of the best known are critical success factors, key variables and key result areas.

9 *Responsibility* All of the duties that must be performed in order to complete a given task. (Sisk) The obligation to accomplish assignments. (Kroontz) Responsibility relates to duties that have been specifically assigned. Once responsibility has been accepted it is for that person to achieve the task in the way that seems to him or to her to be the most effective and efficient. It follows that responsibility is only assigned to trusted members of staff. (**See** *Delegation*.)

9 *Return on time (ROT)* When making a cash investment it is normal to consider the return on investment (the ROI). In a similar way, it is possible to estimate the ROT. Calculate what you are costing per hour – include *all* costs (salary, NI, pension, benefits, office space and equipment, car, expenses, etc.). Do the same for the individuals in your team, and for the team as a whole. You may be very surprised! When you have the facts you are able to make more effective judgements. Should a person costing 10 pence a minute be used to research telephone numbers in the main library, or is it better to pay the charge made by British Telecom?

Time – the great constraint

Management time is not only scarce, it is also a very expensive resource. The current changes in organizational structure, especially the delayering of middle management, has left a smaller number of senior managers responsible for the whole range of activities that take place within an organization. Management writer Charles Handy underscores the changing pressure on manager's time and the changing demands which are being made on managers. His prediction is that half as many managers will be doing twice as many activities for three times the pay – an attractive forecast for those employed. It appears they will be paid well, but the increased workloads will mean that TM will be critical to individual success, and even survival, in this tougher work environment.

Time for everyone is limited. There are only 24 hours in the day and 168 hours in the week. Managers have only so much time available in their working lives and in their working weeks. There is only one way to get more productivity from the manager and that is to help him or her make more effective use of the time available. Managers have the responsibility for their own time and also of the their team's effective use of time.

There is a further dimension to the issues associated with TM that needs to be taken into account. Poor TM is one of the single biggest causes of stress amongst managers. Poor performance, personal ill health and even breakdowns can result from the pressure felt by a manager who suffers from a work overload, or is not in control of his or her activities. Worry about failure to meet deadlines or the expectations of senior managers can lead to increased pressure, which results in poorer performance, which increases the pressure – and the downwards spiral is self-perpetuating unless action is taken to halt it.

Unfortunately, one gets trapped in this spiral without appreciating what is happening, and therefore an individual may not call for help until it is far too late. It is for line managers to keep a close eye on the workloads and pressures of all in their teams – especially on the most conscientious since they are the most likely to take on too much.

In humanitarian terms the case for good TM is obvious, but it can also be justified in hard-nosed pragmatic terms. Investment in people must pay off just as must any other investment. People under stress are not likely to perform well, and people off sick are a great cost to the organization. Hard work is one thing, overload quite another. We expect machinery to break under excessive use, and we mark the safe working load on our equipment. Yet many do not realize that they, and their staff, have the equivalent to a safe working load. It is a common fault to regard those who break under the strain as in some way defective, and so people will strive too long before it all becomes too much. We would not let this happen to equipment – why let it happen to the vitally more important people resource?

It is the responsibility of every manager in the organization to ensure that those staff working in his or her team are not suffering from stress caused by poor TM or a lack of TM skills.

It is hardly surprising that CIM attach considerable importance to TM. It is a crucial management area having impact on the:

- Personal effectiveness of the individual.
- Performance of teams within an organization.
- Effectiveness of the management team as a whole.
- Overall effectiveness of the organization.

Thus TM is highlighted within the CIM syllabus for this paper. But even more importantly than helping you prepare for the examinations, the ideas included within this unit will be of immediate benefit to your own performance, and your own long-term health.

ACTIVITY 3.1

How do you spend your time?

Produce a list of the types of activity which you undertake during a normal working week. Your list will probably include things such as waiting time if you visit clients, meetings, writing letters and reports, and so on. Keep the list general, but make sure it is as full as possible.

Compare your activities with the range of typical working activities given in Debriefing at the end of this unit.

Your list should also include things you do in your non-working time because one type of time cannot really be divorced from another. Just as you can spend pound coins on food, drink and entertainment as you choose, so you can spend your hours. The coin does not change if it is used for a bus fare or a bar of chocolate. Your hours do not change with the use you put them to.

Your extended list will give you a clearer picture of how your are balancing the three factors of work, home and time for yourself (Figure 3.1).

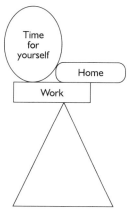

Figure 3.1 There is a need to balance the time required for work, home and yourself

An audit of your time

The only way to make a more effective use of resources is to start by knowing what is currently available and how these are now used. In the case of managing your time you can do this by keeping a detailed diary for a period. You need to know which activities are actually taking up your time. The list which you created for the last exercise will help you provide a focus for this activity. You need to review what you do against the time taken to do it.

The specimen Manager's Time Sheet provided at the end of this unit can be used to monitor a week of activities. Photocopy the page and use it as a basis for recording the activities which you undertake during the week. If possible, get others to do the same exercise so you can compare the results. (It is best to create a page for each day, and then *each evening* make a summary on the master sheet.)

Keep your time sheet with you throughout the week and keep a track of activities as you undertake them during the day. Do not rely on completing it from memory.

- Make an assessment of how important you feel that each activity was to you on a scale of 1 to 10.
- Think about whether or not someone else could have undertaken the activity equally well and indicate who in the column provided.
- Think about how important you think the activity was to others, perhaps the others in a meeting that appeared of low value to you, to other departments or other functions, again on a scale of 1 to 10.
- Importantly, make a note of any interruptions, phone calls, disturbances whilst you were undertaking each activity. Try and note not only the number of these but also their duration.
- In the final column make a note of anything special or specific which you think will help you when you are analysing the amount of time spent on that particular activity. This might be related to the effectiveness of the time spent or the amount of time it took, e.g. it took you longer or less time than you had anticipated, you achieved more or less than expected. You will find this column useful when you are analysing the use of your time at the next stage.

Time analysis

When you have completed your time sheet for a week you are in a position to analyse how you actually spent most of your time. Use the Work Analysis chart given at the end of this unit to examine the nature of the activities, how much time you spent on those activities and, finally, to analyse the percentage of your time which that particular activity represents over the week. Add the work activities appropriate to you to the list.

Once this activity is complete you can ask pertinent questions about how you spend your time. For each activity logged you can ask:

- What would happen if I did not do this kind of activity?
- What would happen if this activity was not undertaken at all?
- Am I spending too long on it?
- Is this activity preventing me from undertaking more important tasks?
- Could someone else do this activity equally well?
- Am I undertaking the activity effectively?

Does Pareto's principle apply?

- Are you spending 80% of your time on 20% of your activities?
- Perhaps 80% of your most productive work is done in 20% of your time?
- Are 20% of your staff (or customers) taking up 80% of your time?

> Use the Pareto principle to help you identify problem areas and opportunities for rearranging your priorities. (Do not, of course, expect to find an exact 80:20 split. It may be 70:30 on occasion – frighteningly, even 90:10!)

Opportunity cost

Each of the activities a manager undertakes needs to be considered in terms of its opportunity cost to the business. What is the benefit involved in you undertaking this activity and at what cost? What else would you have been doing had you not been tied up with that particular activity? Was the short-term decision to train the most beneficial in the long-term? If not, how could the training have been re-scheduled? For example, time spent training junior staff may be more profitably spent meeting with new clients – what is the opportunity cost of rescheduling the training?

The art of delegation

The last two activities have already led you to identify aspects of your work which are taking up valuable time and yet could equally well be undertaken by others. Effective TM depends on managers being able to delegate effectively. Delegation is not a management activity which comes naturally to everyone; it is an art which has to be learned and a skill which needs practice.

Why delegate?

If you are constantly short of time, find yourself fire fighting and struggling to fit in all the activities that are required of you both at home and at work, you are perhaps already only too well aware of the potential benefits of delegation. Delegation is necessary for the effective running of an organization for a number of reasons:

- In large and complex organizations managers cannot undertake all the tasks themselves.
- Delegation frees up senior management time for senior management duties.
- Junior team members profit from being given the responsibility of undertaking delegated tasks.
- Delegation creates interest and is therefore important in the motivation of other members of the team.

Herzberg led the way to our present understanding that motivating factors are extremely important to long-term morale. Effective delegation is a major motivating force for senior managers who find they are free from niggling worries, and for the juniors who are stretched, fulfilled and helped prepare for a more senior post.

Why the reluctance to delegate?

Newly promoted or newly appointed managers often find it difficult to delegate tasks which they have undertaken themselves. Partly this is fear of letting go, partly a natural pride in the belief that they can do the job better than anyone else, partly an avoidance mechanism that allows them to justify any difficulties of coping with their new responsibilities.

Experienced managers can also be reluctant to delegate. This reluctance can come from a range of sources:

- *Lack of confidence in staff capability* If the manager feels that the only way to get a job done right is to do it him or herself, then the tendency will be to not delegate. Junior staff, not given the opportunity to learn, will never be able to do tasks effectively and the manager's perception will become a self-fulfilling prophecy.
- *Fear of failure* Responsibility and accountability cannot be delegated and so managers may feel that the short-term need for success outweighs the long-term need for staff development.
- *Active discouragement* Delegation may be seen by top management as work avoidance rather than good management policy.

- *Poor control* Delegation is difficult without good control and communication systems. Delegation is routine in very structured organizations such as the military where clear command and control structures are built into the framework of the organization.
- *Team membership* Becoming actively involved in the day-to-day operational activities of the group allows the manager to feel they are still one of the boys or girls! There is a definite step to be taken when one is promoted. Out of the work group – but not out of the team.
- *Satisfaction* Dealing with the day-to-day demands of the job can be more immediately rewarding and satisfying than strategic planning for the long-term security of the team, department and organization.

Overcoming the problems

Overcoming the problems of delegation requires a number of positive actions:

- *Commitment* Senior management must be committed to delegation. They must lead the way by example, and must show that they know it takes time for experience to be acquired.
- *Staff calibre* Recruited and promoted staff must be of a calibre that enables them to undertake their designated tasks, or they must be trained effectively before being required to perform to the required standard.
- *Control and communication* Efficient and effective systems must be in place to ensure that everybody knows what is to be done, and performance expectations are clear. Implicit within control is the requirement that feedback be prompt and directed to the responsible managers. Exception reporting ensures that this is a positive aid to effective management.
- *Authority* Staff must have the authority to take action. Guidelines must be explicit. A newly appointed manager may have the authority to commit the organization to a limit of £100 – with experience this may be extended to £250 ... £1,000 ... £5,000, etc. It should also be clear under what circumstances a matter should be referred to higher authority.

Lateral delegation

Normally we think of delegation as a downwards activity. There is no reason, however, why a manager should not delegate in any direction he or she wants to. It is not normal to delegate upwards in an organization – but if you ask your boss who is going to a sales office to check something out are you not delegating? A moment's thought will show that it is quite normal to delegate to one's colleagues, and to accept delegation from them in return. Sometimes we call it 'doing a favour', but this it is often full-blooded delegation.

ACTIVITY 3.4

When to and when not to delegate?
In two columns write down all the reasons why and occasions on which you think it would be appropriate to delegate and all the occasions when and reasons why it is not. Spend 15 minutes on this activity and compare your list with our thoughts in Debriefing at the end of this unit.

Effective delegation – Key points

- *Identify* Select a person who has the right skills, experience and personality to perform the task effectively.
- *Resource* Make sure that *all* the necessary resources are available to undertake the task effectively.
- *Brief* Make certain that the individual:
    (a) Understands the task required.
    (b) Knows precisely the performance levels and indicators which will be used to judge the effectiveness of the activity.

(c) Is willing to undertake the task and accept responsibility for it within the scope of the delegated authority.

(d) Knows when to refer a matter upwards.

- *Keep a distance* Do not interfere, do not fuss. Respond to requests for assistance, but do not take the task over. Allow more time to the less experienced, and tighten expectations as confidence is gained.
- *Depersonalize* Accept that the job will be done differently by each individual. Judge on results not process. Only rarely is there a fixed process that *must* be followed.
- *Supervise* Stay in touch, without interference. Evaluate through the feedback and reporting system.
- *Review* Review progress with the individual. Use review sessions to develop, not to criticise!

Urgent or important?

The ability to establish priorities is an essential skill of the effective time manager. Many managers are constantly prevented from getting to the important work because of the urgent. They spend their time fire fighting. Fire-fighting managers rush from one emergency to the next. The unplanned and the unexpected can keep management focus on operational and tactical problems. Clearly, in business, as in life, not everything can be planned. A crisis on the production line, problems with an order, a change in the exchange rates, failure of a supplier to deliver an essential raw material, and staff suddenly taken sick are all examples of unexpected events which can prevent managers from undertaking their planned daily activities.

The manager has to take great care to ensure that activities which call for immediate attention, which appear to be urgent, are in fact important to the long-term well-being of the organization. Often the apparently urgent is fairly insignificant when analysed and considered carefully. Urgent issues can cause managers to lose focus and can be distractions which prevent the important issues being tackled effectively.

Urgent issues are often far easier to delegate than are important ones. It may take a little time to ensure that the delegation is effective, but is time well spent if it is less than it would take to do the job. Managers must learn to prioritize their work. This starts with a clear analysis of what has to be done, and an assessment of how important and urgent the various activities are.

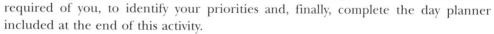

ACTIVITY 3.5

In-tray exercise

Having been away from the office for a week on a TM training seminar, you have returned to find that your in-tray includes the items listed below. Allocate yourself 20 minutes and use the time to analyse the tasks required of you, to identify your priorities and, finally, complete the day planner included at the end of this activity.

You are to assume the role of Marketing Director, the day is Monday, 9 March, and the company is UK Engineering Limited. Your PA is Jenny Rowlands.

1 *Memo*

   To: Marketing Director
   From: Managing Director

   Strategy Review Meeting
   Please note that I have rescheduled this meeting from the 18th to 2 p.m. on 11th March. I hope you will be able to complete your strategy review for presentation at that time.

2 *Note*

   The Personnel Director will be calling by at 11 a.m. to discuss the job specification for the new sales reps post. Pete, Sales Manager.

3 *Phone message (4.30, 5 March)*

   Northern Sales Manager will be on the site this afternoon, showing round the Buyer and MD of Smith & Co. She has been trying to win their account for 3 months and would appreciate you joining them for lunch 1.00–2.00. JR.

4 *Competitor analysis*

Monthly Report – Executive Summary.

- Key competitors have been using price promotions very effectively over last month. Estimated we have lost 3% of market share as a result.
- Forecast they will keep pressure on margins – to compete we need to act quickly. The sales team need briefing with new discount parameters by Weds. for this month's sales push.

5 *Help!*

We got an urgent order worth £10,000 on Friday from a new client.

Production say if we take it our regular order from Johnson's can't be guaranteed on time. That's worth £70,000. The sales rep thinks the new customer could become a big regular account. Production need to know what you want them to do before 9.30 a.m. Jenny.

6 *Reminder . . .*

The attached proofs of the new brochure need to be checked and back with printer by tonight if we are to have them for next month's exhibition. Jenny.

7 *Message (8.25, 8th March)*

MD has asked you to join him for lunch to discuss your approach to the Strategy Review. He is treating it as a high priority issue. Have said you'll be there. JR.

8 *Confidential*

To: Marketing Director, UK Engineering

Dear . . . .

We have been regular clients of UK Engineering for almost 6 years and I am writing in disgust at the way your Accounts Dept. appear to have arbitrarily changed our normal credit terms from 60 to 30 days.

I was most unimpressed with the way your accounts staff dealt with my employees. I have to say that regretfully we are actively reviewing our contract with you.

A B Smith

Managing Director

9 *Confidential memo*

From: Personnel Director

To: Marketing Director Date: 4 March

Ref: B Jones, Promotions Manager

It came to my attention during your absence last week that Brian was in local pub for an extended lunch on at least two occasions. He missed an important meeting one afternoon. As you know drinking during the working day is strictly against company policy. I trust you will deal with the matter urgently.

(**See** Debriefing at the end of this unit.)

Prioritize

Recognize that both the urgent and the important tasks have to be done. Tasks which have both high and low priority need to be undertaken, otherwise low-priority jobs will become urgent or important in their own time. The problem comes when managers try to do both urgent and important tasks, undertake too many of them at the same time, and fail to complete any of the tasks effectively. The tasks which need to be done are not *either/or* tasks. They all need attention. The flexibility for the manager lies in who is going to give attention to the task under what degree of priority. In other words, there is the potential for delegation, and for a decision on how to slot each task into the diary.

Successful managers handle a variety of activities and projects by devoting themselves to one thing at a time. This allows them to work efficiently and effectively by reducing the number of distractions and increasing their levels of concentration. Once tasks have been identified as having a high priority they are the ones that need to be done first, however difficult they may be. The temptation to leave a difficult task until an unspecified later time does not make it go away – it remains as a niggling distraction to worry about!

The ABC priorities approach encourages managers to allocate tasks to a particular category.

- A tasks – the most important to the management function of planning, decision making and controlling,
- B tasks – those which the manager must do personally, or which can only partly be delegated.
- C tasks - targets for delegation. Minimal time requirement on each, but overall time investment may be reasonably large.

In addition, there will be the routine and mundane tasks that are necessary for simple maintenance of the status quo. Contacts with maintenance to get a leaky window fixed, for example.

Time allocation must be dictated by circumstances. In a typical day a manager may allocate time to undertake one or two of the A priority tasks, an hour to B tasks and one hour to C tasks. By undertaking A tasks during times when interruptions and distractions are kept to a minimum, the manager is able to work in the most effective way. Given proper planning it is possible to clear time in a schedule, to divert calls to a trusted deputy and to work free of interruptions.

The good TM manager schedules the day into blocks – some of which are for the staff, some for privacy. It takes very little time for people to realize that a manager is available at certain times, and to hold everything but the genuinely urgent and important until then.

Self-check 3.1

Take time to answer the following questions to help you assess your understanding of the material covered so far in this unit. You will find our answers in Debriefing at the end of this unit.

1 What characteristic would you expect high-priority tasks to share?
2 What actions would you suggest to a colleague who was having difficulty in meeting deadlines at work and therefore in accomplishing the activities required by his line manager?
3 In what circumstances can delegation not be a staff motivator?
4 How would you explain the difference between urgent and important tasks?

Contingency planning

Managers need not always be unprepared for the unexpected. One cannot be prepared for the unthinkable – but everything that can be conceived of as possible can be prepared for. Whether it is cost-effective to prepare contingency plans is a management decision. There is no question that contingency plans can always be made. Some events are so predictable that contingency plans should be in place, and updated regularly.

Possibly the most famous situation where the lack of contingency planning is known to have brought down a company is the case of the *Herald of Free Enterprise*. She was a roll-on roll-off car ferry which sank with serious loss of life in Zeebrugge harbour. The cause of the disaster was crew failure to close the watertight door before setting sail – an entirely predictable occurrence. With no contingency plans the owners were caught entirely unprepared. Their proven inefficiency in ensuring the safety of their passengers plus their ineffective public relations handling of the situation resulted in the collapse of what had until then seemed a most successful company.

We are used to preparing for contingencies:

- You plan to have a party in the garden, but book the local hall in case the weather is bad.
- Driving to Greece you would carry a tool kit, spare parts, reserve fuel – and probably take out AA, RAC or EuropAssistance cover.

At work we should take similar precautions:

- Revised price lists at different levels of tax may be calculated in anticipation of possible Budget changes.
- Press releases can be drafted ahead of an event so that each of the possible results is covered.

Effective prioritization – a checklist

- *Organize* You must have a clear picture of what work you have in progress and what the deadlines are. You must be able to identify new work which has come on line, and be aware of pending correspondence and requests from other managers.
- *Take time* Each day take time to assess the work which you must complete – categorize and prioritize it. Plan which activities will be tackled urgently. Establish performance objectives against time for each of them. During the day tackle some activities in each of the categories A–C.
- *Delegate* Force yourself to delegate some of the activities to others who have the appropriate skills and expertise. Make sure that they have the resources to undertake these tasks and that there is an established system of feedback.
- *Review* At the end of the day take time to review your progress. Identify tasks not completed and leave them clearly marked for attention on the next day.

ACTIVITY 3.6

Evaluating you own time management
Take some time now to review your assessment of your personal TM which you undertook at the beginning of this unit.
  Carry out a SWOT analysis on your TM activities

S | W

O | T

Now use your swot to help you produce two quantified objectives which you can work towards in improving your TM:

1 _____

_____

2 _____

_____

Hints and tips on time management

There are many ways to improve your management of time. Some only save a little, others save a lot. In total it is surprising how much time can be saved with just a modicum of thought backed up by self-discipline. You will find the following list useful when briefing others.

Personal issues:

- *Aim to delegate*   Force yourself to prove that you *can't* delegate, not that you can.
- *Control your time*   Book appointments and duration. 'We'll meet for 20 minutes from 10 a.m.'
- *Don't be frightened to let go*   Work finds its way to the effective manager, so don't worry that you'll be out of a job if you delegate.
- *Don't be possessive*   You are not the only, or probably the best, person to do a particular job.
- *Don't panic*   Little is so important that it can't wait an hour or so.
- *Handle once*   Develop the confidence to complete a job. Don't let it go through your hands twice.
- *Information*   Ask for information to be translated at source. It is easier for accounts to present their data in the form you need than for you to translate it.
- *Praise generously*   Most people criticise. You will find yourself surrounded by happy and effective people if you give praise generously and genuinely.
- *Respond effectively*   There is no need always to reply formally. Hand write a response on the original letter and return it. Copy it first if you need a record. With faxes this method is especially effective.
- *Speed reading*   Courses are available. These key principles will get you started:
  - (a) Always run a pointer (a pencil will do) along the lines as you read. It adds over 50% to your speed.
  - (b) Read the summary. Skip through the remainder.
  - (c) Start from the index and dip into a book to see if it is relevant, readable and of value.
  - (d) Text books are for reference, never for reading.
  - (e) The Managing Director's requests are not automatically urgent. Check with his or her Secretary if in doubt.
- *Visit, don't host*   As a visitor to another's office you have more control over your time.

Team issues:

- *Ask for pre-briefing*   Before a meeting ask for brief notes of the key points to be put on paper.
- *Avoid overstaffing*   This leads to work creation, and created work is hard to get rid of when staff levels fall.
- *Identify the time wasters*:
  - (a) Regular events such as an end of period rush to meet budget can be smoothed by applying consistent pressure throughout the period.
  - (b) Individuals who waste time must be dealt with smartly.

- *Meetings – others*:
    (a) Be well prepared so you can be brief, direct and achieve your objective(s).
    (b) Don't go if you don't have to.
    (c) Don't speak if you have nothing to say.
    (d) Don't complain and then do nothing about it.
- *Meetings – yours*:
    (a) Avoid them as far as possible.
    (b) Cancel a regular meeting if there is nothing to discuss.
    (c) Construct an original agenda for each.
    (d) Invite only those who are needed.
    (e) Circulate notes quickly to all who need them – whether at the meeting or not.
    (f) Start on time, finish on time.
- *Motivate* Encourage staff to think through a problem to save you time. Respond to queries with 'Yes we have a problem – what do you think we should do about it?' Then, if necessary, ask 'How can I help?'
- *Organize*:
    (a) Don't face an open door – distractions!
    (b) Keep desk top clear.
    (c) Keep an Action List of jobs to do.
- *Set time hurdles* Train your team's gatekeepers to ask 'Shall I interrupt?' rather than granting immediate access.
- *Stand up* Meetings are shorter when participants are kept standing!
- *Substitute* Do you personally have to go? Why not one of your team?

EXTENDING ACTIVITY 3.1

Add your own tips to the list given above. You will find them invaluable

The time management of others

Managers must ensure that their team is working in the most effective and efficient way and is getting the most out of the work time available to it. Adopt a return-on-time approach.

Groups of people working together fit onto a continuum that has two extremes:

- Where the members of the team work as individuals – there is little sharing of activities, or responsibilities, little team work and, therefore, no synergy.
- Where the team work as a collective at all times.

Without synergy a team is wasting a valuable resource; but too much discussion and debate in an attempt to come to a consensus decision is pointless and wasteful. The management task is to steer the team between these two extremes, i.e. to encourage individual activity and acceptance of responsibility whilst facilitating and enabling the group to work effectively together as a team whenever that joint effort will be beneficial.

EXTENDING KNOWLEDGE

As a training exercise two teams were given the same task. To decide upon the colour used in the redecoration of their training room. The teams met once a week for 3 months.

The managers from commercial companies had a freshly painted room in their third week. The managers from education and social services never did decide on the colour they wanted.

Recognizing time management problems
Take 15 minutes to complete the mind map we have started below.
Identify the 'failing to manage time' symptoms and characteristics you
might identify in your team or that might apply to individuals within the
team.

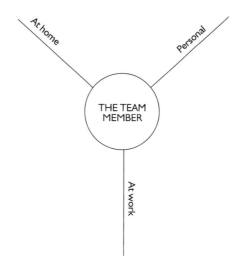

When you have completed your mind map turn to Debriefing at the end of this Unit
and compare your thoughts with ours.

Auditing the time skills of a work group
Stage 1 (allow 60 minutes)
Prepare a brief report to your senior manager clearly laying down your
recommendations for reviewing and analysing the effective use of time
within an identified team or work group. Think about the alternative activities and
methods of collecting information which would enable you to:

- Make a judgement on the quality of TM skills:
  (a) Within the group as a whole.
  (b) Of individuals within the group.
- Identify areas of weakness.
- Make recommendations for improving TM effectiveness.

Your report should clearly identify the alternative methods of collecting information to
ensure the fullest picture possible is gained.

Stage 2 (allow yourself an amount of time that you consider sufficient, but not
generous)
Identify a specific group, perhaps your team at work or a group of people who you work
with in a social or leisure context. Try to implement the recommendations in your
report by undertaking a TM audit. Prepare a report on your findings.

Whilst you are undertaking this process, be sure to identify the most useful methods of
collecting information and identify any problem areas in undertaking this activity. This
information will provide useful illustrations for you to use during the examination.

Managing the time dimension of a plan

During the examination you can expect to be asked to give an outline of a timetable for proposals you are making in answer to a specific question. Managers should be aware that effective plans must be based on quantified objectives expressed over time. It is these two aspects of quantification which provide the framework for control and the measurement of performance. You will find that the requirement for a timetable or schedule of activities is equally critical in many of your other CIM examinations – at Diploma level, they are routinely expected, and the examiner is unlikely to remind you of their need.

The steps involved in developing a timetable are:

1 Where are you now and what is the deadline?

2 What has to be done?:
  (a) Identify the steps which must be completed before the deadline.
  (b) Break the tasks down into each of the elements involved in the process, e.g. the creation of a new brochure may involve the identification and selection of an advertising agency as well as all the steps involved in the origination, production, approval, proofing and distribution of the finished item.

3 What is the best order?
  (a) Put the identified steps in order and allocate each a forecast time allotment.
  (b) Identify which of the activities can be:
    • Done simultaneously.
    • Are dependent on the outcome of a previous stage.
    • Can be delegated to others.
  (c) Plan each stage against the time available – remember to allow some spare or slack time as a contingency.

4 Review:
  (a) Does the schedule work?
  (b) What are the critical points?
  (c) Are there any opportunities to save time?
  (d) Which are the key control points that you will use to monitor progress?

Your timetable or schedule should be a logical sequence of the stages and tasks which need to be undertaken if the deadline is to be met. All staff who are undertaking any part of the activities need to be given realistic time frames and adequate notice to allow them to manage the rest of their workload effectively.

The Gantt chart

Gantt charts allow a simple visual presentation of a schedule. They are especially useful to managers because they make it easy to communicate stages and time frames to other members of the team. They are also very useful in examinations because they can be drawn quickly to convey key information effectively to the examiner.

To produce a Gantt chart:

• Identify the time frame for the complete schedule.
• Identify each activity that must be completed within the schedule.
• For each activity estimate:
  (a) The time it will take.
  (b) When it must be completed.
  (c) When it can/should commence.
    Note: Differences between possible start date, duration and required end date will be identified, and must be reconciled.
• Create a horizontal bar chart to show the activities against time.

A completed Gantt chart is shown in Figure 3.2.

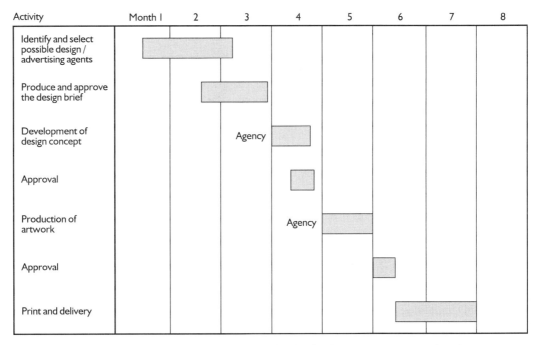

Figure 3.2 A Gantt chart: a schedule of activities for developing a new corporate brochure

Planning
You have been put in charge of organizing the preparation for a major national exhibition. This is scheduled to take place over a period of 4 working days and is to open in exactly 6 months time. The stand space has now been booked, as has accommodation for the staff who will be working at the exhibition. Prepare a schedule of the activities which will need to be undertaken to ensure that presence at the exhibition is a success.

(**See** our Gantt chart in Debriefing at the end of this unit.)

Network analysis

Where the problem is more complex than can be coped with by using a Gantt chart there is need for network analysis. The critical path method (CPM) and the programme evaluation and review technique (PERT) are two network techniques that have each been developed to meet the needs of what has been called 'an age of massive engineering'. They were designed to make highly complex projects manageable, and are now available to PC users.

Both CPM and PERT became generally available in 1959, after both had proven their worth. PERT was developed by the US Navy and first used in submarine development. CPM was designed by DuPont, also in the USA, to reduce the down-time required for plant maintenance.

Four conditions have to be met in order to use network analysis for planning and control:

- There must be a clearly recognizable end-point (objective). One-of-a-kind projects, such as the building of a railway terminus, are suitable.
- There should be a series of clearly defined events, that are separate but interrelated and lead up to the completion of the final project.
- There must be a time established for each activity.
- There must be a starting point that is recognizable – the signature on the contract to commission the new terminus would be ideal.

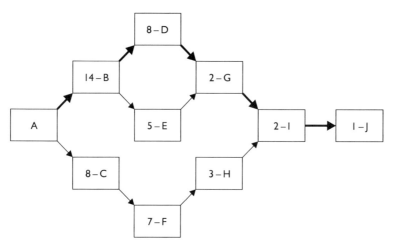

Figure 3.3 An abbreviated and simplified form of network analysis

Figure 3.3 shows a simplified network. Each square represents an event. The number indicates the days it will take to complete. Events, as such, occupy no time – they are simply milestones. The letters identify each event and would be explained in a legend. The arrows indicate the sequence of events and the heavy arrows show the *critical path*. The critical path is the longest route in time from start to finish and provides a focus for management action. Only if one or more events in the critical path can be shortened can the project be shortened. Network analysis is dynamic in form and so, obviously, if an event's time is shortened another path may become critical.

PERT differs from CPM in degree rather than kind. Both share the same benefits:

* A high degree of planning is forced upon management, with the result that plans are objective, structured and flexible.
* The critical path focuses attention on events of current significance.
* Inter-relationships are shown more clearly than with any other management tool.

Time is the most scarce resource of the student in the examination room. The limits imposed by a 3-hour examination are always demanding but cannot be changed. The need to manage time effectively, whilst always important, is crucial in this particular examination because the examiners will be looking for specific evidence of your effective management competencies. You need to think through the requirements of the examination and plan how you are going to manage your time effectively long before you get into the examination room.

As with all your Advanced Certificate and Diploma examination papers, except the Case Study, you will be faced with two sections. The first is a compulsory section which is worth 50% of the marks and should therefore take up 50% of the time available (i.e. 90 minutes). Do not waste time dithering about which section to tackle first – make up your mind beforehand and do not waver!

The second section of the examination paper will require you to answer two questions in the remaining 90 minutes. Thus there are only 45 minutes a question, and this must include time for reading through the question, planning your answer, and checking through your work! The maximum actual writing time will be 40 minutes – more likely closer to 35! You need to use time effectively. This means avoiding waffle – use report format or the format specified, and answer each question directly.

As was emphasized in the Study Tips section in Unit 1, practice is essential if you are to present effective answers to questions against these sort of time constraints – take every opportunity to practise. This is not simply a matter of working in fits and starts in an ad hoc way. You need to find time to practise under examination conditions, which means writing and planning your answers in the same time frame you will be allowed in the examination room.

Without constraining yourself make sure that from now on you take a note of how long it takes you to complete the activities which are indicated in the units. Compare your times with those which are suggested. Identify which aspects of your work need speeding up in order to be effective in the examination room.

Look at each of these scenarios in turn and try to identify or anticipate the possible TM issues which they might entail. What recommendations would you make in each situation? Compare your thoughts with ours given in Debriefing at the end of this unit.

Scenario one

Established 8 years ago, J. Shah's business has grown from a single retail unit to a small chain of ten speciality craft shops located in city centres across the region. Each shop has a manager, but stock selection, ordering and marketing decisions are all made by J. Shah and her assistant. She is considering further expansion, but performance indicators show that sales levels and profits from a number of the shops have fallen, or are below forecast levels.

Scenario two

Jayne Burrows is the Buildings Manager for a large national service company. Following a decision to relocate the head office to a site some 10 miles away, she has been given responsibility for coordinating and managing the move. What does she need to do to ensure that the relocation goes smoothly?

Scenario three

Darren Phelps is the newly appointed Marketing Manager for a fmcg manufacturer. His team of five customer coordinators and a field sales force of twelve have recently been reorganized and are the slimmed down remains of a department which used to number nearly thirty. Morale is clearly low. There is little evidence of team work. No-one in the department seems able to cope with their new responsibilities and increased workloads.

Charles Handy: management educator, born in Ireland

After graduating at Oxford University, Charles Handy worked with Shell International both overseas and in the UK. It was at Shell he discovered his love of teaching. He became involved in the establishment of London Business School in 1965 and 2 years later began to teach there. His early interest was in the power of mathematics and the computer, but he was introduced to organizational behaviour at Massachusetts Institute of Technology and it is in that area of management thinking that he is renowned.

Handy described his first book, *Understanding Organisations*, as a textbook about organizations not a book about business. In it he says 'I would encourage anyone else to burn this book after reading it and start to write their own – it is the only way to really own the concepts'. (NB: The principle underpinning this advice is extremely valuable to anyone coming new to a subject – it is essential to make concepts and understandings your own, take them from any source, but adapt them to your individual needs.)

Handy has extended his interests beyond the field of business organizations with publications on schools and voluntary organizations. In his book *The Gods of Management* he used the analogy of the Greek Gods and the characteristics of various organizations. It is, however, his more recent works which have focused on the future and the training of management and for which he has gained wider recognition.

In 1984 he wrote in the *Future of Work* about how work was changing and he followed this with the *Making of Managers* which researched the international comparisons in management education. In *The Age of Unreason*, he encourages organizations to treat employees as individuals rather than 'human resources'. The results of this work were a catalyst for a number of UK initiatives to improve British standing and achievements in this field.

Handy stresses that the people who have thought 'unreasonably' have had the most profound impact on twentieth-century living. The great successes have come from discontinuous 'upside-down' thinking. (Possibly what de Bono calls 'lateral thinking', see Unit 11.)

The future, he predicts, will be one of 'discontinuous change' which will require a fundamental change in people's thinking. The steady course of development is no longer valid. No longer can we be guided – blinkered – by the past. It is for managers to lead the way.

Key publications
Understanding Organisations, 1976
Future of Work, 1984
The Age of Unreason, 1989

SUMMARY

In this unit we have seen that:

- Time is a valuable, critical and finite resource both for the individual and the organization.
- Developments in organizational structure mean that the manager of tomorrow is likely to have to undertake more tasks than the manager of yesterday. Therefore TM is becoming a critical success factor.
- For the individual manager the ability to prioritize work and delegate activities to others in a planned and coordinated way is fundamental to effective TM.
- The manager is responsible for ensuring that the time resource is effectively used by his or her team. The manager must be able to recognize the symptoms of poor TM both in the individual and in the team, and be able to make recommendations and take action for improvement.
- Projects and plans have to be undertaken over a specific time period. Careful scheduling and planning of projects are required to ensure that deadlines are met. This is another important dimension of the manager's TM responsibilities.

Debriefing

Activity 3.1

The activities listed below represent those which might occur in your list of the kind of activities which you undertake during a normal week:

At work	*Other*
Meetings	Travelling
Interviews	Eating
Training	Sleeping
Presentations	Time with family
Visiting customers	Time with friends
Visiting suppliers	Watching television
Dealing with staff queries	Cinema/theatre
Dealing with staff problems	Reading or other leisure pursuits
Checking	Evening classes and study
Supervising	Sports
Planning work	Shopping
Dealing with customer complaints	
Handling correspondence	
Recruiting new staff	
Preparing reports	
Answering phone calls	
Collecting moneys owed by clients	
Visiting operations or production facilities	
Analysing management information	

Activity 3.4

When to delegate	*When not to delegate*
• The subordinate has the capabilities needed to undertake the task required.	• The staff member requires training before being competent to be left with the responsibility for this activity.
• Staff are being developed for promotion or broader responsibilities.	• There is an inadequate system of control and communication.
• The parameters of the delegated authority are clear.	• The task requires confidentiality or tact, perhaps involving a security or disciplinary matter.
• Others in the team have knowledge and skills more relevant to the task.	• The activity is critical, very high risk or 'politically sensitive'.
• The manager trusts the person and believes he/she is capable, and suited to the task in hand.	• There are inadequate resources available.

Activity 3.5

1 This links with items 3 and 7. The MD and the Northern Sales Manager ask you to join them for lunch. It seems reasonable to assume that your work on the strategy review has not yet been completed, if it has even been started! A 2-day deadline is clearly not going to be adequate for you to undertake such an important piece of work.

   The MD may well feel that contact with an important new client takes precedence anyway. (Urgent against important.) Suggest you contact the MD's office first thing to:

   (a) Ask for a rain check on the lunch invitation and try to arrange a meeting early tomorrow to discuss the strategy review. You could also suggest the inclusion of one or two of your team members who may be able to make a useful contribution to the work in this area.

   (b) Reschedule your presentation of the review to later in the week or early next week to allow sufficient time for this work to be undertaken effectively. This activity, whilst important, is clearly not urgent and some time flexibility would obviously be advantageous to both yourself and the organization. Better for this piece of work to be done thoroughly and well, than rushed and not completed properly.

   (c) Your PA has committed you to the MD's lunch. Probably he or she did not know of the conflicting invitation, but should they have committed you in any case? Your response to this will depend upon your management style, the length of time your PA has been with you, and your assessment of his or her level of experience and training needs.

2 Suggest that this is delegated to the Sales Manager – and that you are briefed on decision.

3 This is important and clearly urgent. Potential business for the company takes priority over nearly everything else and we would therefore want to meet the client. If lunch seems too much, or if the MD won't agree to your request for a rain check, then a quick phone call to find out if it would cause any problems if you joined them for a rather briefer time, e.g. during their tour in the afternoon or possibly at the end of the day when you could handle any other questions.

4 This looks both urgent and important. We are losing business and clearly need to act quickly. Delegate one of the team to undertake any necessary background work and collect the relevant information. Call an urgent meeting of the key people involved in strategic pricing decisions and implementation of change for this afternoon.

5 Also about business and equally urgent. Clearly we do not want to upset or lose a long standing and large account but at the same time we do not want to lose the opportunity of winning new business by failing to meet their needs on a first request basis.

   A personal visit to the Production Director is likely to bring the fastest resolution and identification of the alternatives to ensure no misunderstandings between these two functional areas. We would suggest a visit to his office about 9.15 to discuss any possible flexibility. Perhaps moving some staff to deal with the urgent order – identifying if the whole of the large order need be late – what proportion of it could still be made available? If necessary ask the relevant Sales Executive or Sales Manager to speak to one or both companies to identify the possible areas of leeway in delivery, but recognize that you, the Marketing Director, will have to make a decision on priorities after securing the necessary information.

6 Clearly it is important that this brochure is got out although there are a few weeks before it is needed. Delegate the proof-reading and checking to other team members with the appropriate skills and experience in this area.

7 We have dealt with this in item 1.

8 This important letter needs an urgent response. The first thing to find out is what happened within the department. Delegate the background research to one of the team members and schedule a report-back time in the late morning. The intention is that you will positively respond to the client before the end of the day.

9 Clearly a disciplinary issue which needs to be handled directly and discreetly by yourself. Call Brian for a meeting in the late morning, discuss the problem, try to identify the causes, agree a course of action with him, and remember to thank and update the Personnel Director this afternoon.

Self-check 3.1

1 There will be a limited time available. In addition there will be one or more factors such as:
   • The task has great significance or impact on either the staff or the organization.
   • The action will have an impact on the quality of customer care.
   • The chances of winning or retaining business are involved.

2 We would advise a colleague to take time to undertake an audit of how he or she is currently spending his time, e.g. by completing a week's Management Time Sheet or diary. Review his or her attitudes to and ability to delegate, and to take time daily to plan and prioritize his or her activities.

3 • When delegated authority is not clear and the parameters for performance have not been set.
   • When staff do not have the skills or the expertise to undertake the delegated task.
   • When there are inadequate resources, including the time available to staff.
   • When the line manager is not available to give support, advice and help if it proves necessary.

4 'Important' and 'urgent' are not mutually exclusive – some important tasks are urgent. However, as a general distinction between the terms, *important* is to do with the potential impact or value that the activity or decision will have on the business, whilst *urgent* indicates a lack of time available for an activity that must be completed.

Activity 3.7
See illustration on p. 63.

Activity 3.8
An exhibition schedule will typically look like the illustration on p. 64.

Unit activity
Scenario one TM is a particular problem for small entrepreneurs who have grown the business. Usually they fail to at the same time grow the structures, systems and personnel necessary to manage the increased workload. It seems that J. Shah is suffering such problems. She has only one assistant, and we are not clear what level of responsibility or ability the assistant has. She has not sought to delegate much of the management activity to the individual store managers. Low profits and low sales could be result of a number of factors:

   • Possibly poor morale and interest from the store managers who are not given the responsibility that they might welcome.

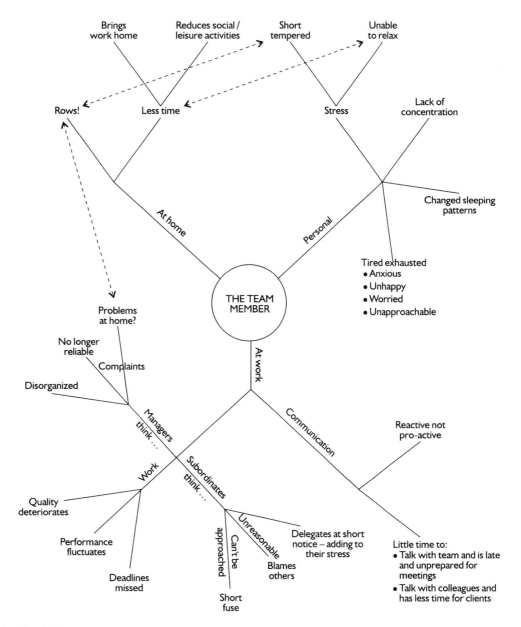

Brings work home   Reduces social / leisure activities   Short tempered   Unable to relax

Rows!   Less time   Stress   Lack of concentration

Changed sleeping patterns

At home

Personal

THE TEAM MEMBER

Problems at home?

Tired exhausted
• Anxious
• Unhappy
• Worried
• Unapproachable

No longer reliable

Complaints

Disorganized

At work

Managers think …

Communication

Reactive not pro-active

Work

Subordinates think …

Quality deteriorates

Unreasonable

Delegates at short notice – adding to their stress

Little time to:
• Talk with team and is late and unprepared for meetings
• Talk with colleagues and has less time for clients

Performance fluctuates

Can't be approached

Blames others

Deadlines missed

Short fuse

Activity 3.7

- A failure to use managers' local knowledge to identify customer needs and match stock levels and marketing activity specifically to meet those needs.
- Further expansion of the store chain is likely to exacerbate the problem, making J. Shah less and less effective. We recommend that:
  (a) There is a complete review of the organizational structure.
  (b) Staff training is provided to create an effective Assistant Managing Director who is able to take on some of the central role.
  (c) Possibly the stores will be large enough to actually allow for the appointment of a buyer and/or marketing coordinator or executive to take on some of the Head Office responsibilities.
  (d) Review is undertaken with the store managers so that one can work with them to both build their skills and identify the areas of activity which they would be able to take responsibility for. Set each of the stores specific sales and profit targets and delegate budget authority to the store managers.

Scenario two A major logistical project which needs careful planning. We would recommend that Jayne identifies a group of people who could become a project team from across the Head Office functions to act as communication links and to work together on undertaking the various aspects necessitated by the move. Their first job is to brainstorm a list of all the activities which need to be undertaken, from producing change of address cards, arranging

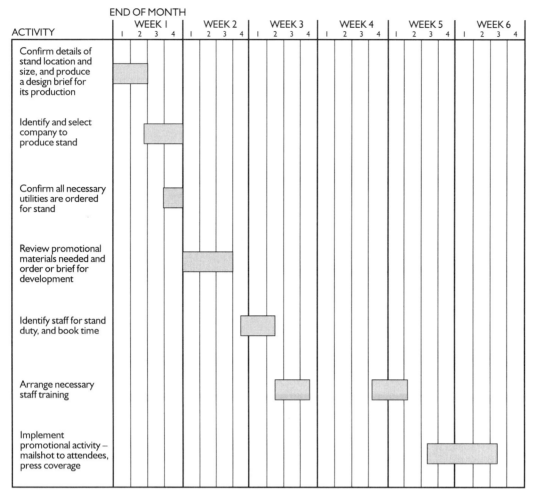

ACTIVITY	END OF MONTH WEEK 1				WEEK 2				WEEK 3				WEEK 4				WEEK 5				WEEK 6			
	1	2	3	4	1	2	3	4	1	2	3	4	1	2	3	4	1	2	3	4	1	2	3	4
Confirm details of stand location and size, and produce a design brief for its production																								
Identify and select company to produce stand																								
Confirm all necessary utilities are ordered for stand																								
Review promotional materials needed and order or brief for development																								
Identify staff for stand duty, and book time																								
Arrange necessary staff training																								
Implement promotional activity – mailshot to attendees, press coverage																								

Activity 3.8

Day Planner

Monday 9th March	Things to do tomorrow
9.00	
10.00	
11.00	
12.00	
13.00	
14.00	Delegated
15.00	
16.00	
17.00	
18.00	

Manager's Time Sheet

Day: ....   Date: ....

Time	Activity	How important? (Scale 1–10)	Could someone else do it?	Was it valuable to others? (Scale 1–10)	Interruptions or calls? (No. and duration)	Comments
7.00 7.30 8.00 8.30 9.00 9.30						
10.00 10.30 11.00 11.30 12.00 12.30						
13.00 13.30 14.00 14.30 15.00 15.30						
16.00 16.30 17.00 17.30 18.00 18.30 19.00 19.30						

Work Analysis: Hours spent per day:

Work type	Monday	Tuesday	Wednesday	Thursday	Friday	Weekend	% Total
Meetings							
Correspondence							
Phone							
Waiting							

telephone lines, and selecting moving firms, through to counselling and discussion with individual staff members to ensure that the move is going to cause individuals no undue hardship. Once identified, all these activities should be allocated a time frame, and be put into a logical sequence with contingency time allowed. Then the different activities can be delegated to specific individuals and departments within the organization. Jayne needs to establish a master timetable with clear control indicators which are monitored regularly to ensure that the plan is working effectively.

   Note: Take care to distinguish between questions which ask you to 'plan' the activity and those which ask you 'how' you would go about the problem – a 'how' question is an example of a process question. The latter are becoming increasingly popular with the CIM examiners.

Scenario three   Possibly two problems here. Morale is low. Perhaps not only because of the higher workloads, but also as a result of the reorganization and the recent redundancies and staff changes which have been made and perhaps not communicated in as positive a way as they might have been to those left behind. Individuals are perhaps not yet familiar with their new responsibilities, and the first thing we would suggest Darren does is to review job descriptions, performance indicators and requirements from each of the individual staff members. Secondly, suggest that there are some team building activities identified which would help the new group to form and establish a tighter teamwork ethic. An audit of the group's TM skills and performance (as undertaken in Activity 3.2) would help to identify any weaknesses and provide a basis on which Darren can begin to make recommendations for change and improvement. Tight control is going to be necessary to ensure that the group continues to perform effectively during this difficult process of change.

The manager as a communicator

In this unit you will:

- Analyse the elements of the communication process.
- Assess the manager's role as a communicator.
- Review the mechanics and styles of different communication methods and opportunities.

By the end of this unit you will be able to:

- Appreciate the critical role of the manager.
- Identify weaknesses in your own and other peoples' communication skills.
- Make recommendations for improvement in these areas.
- Plan effectively for communication in a number of typical business settings.
- Set up, participate in, or chair meetings.
- Ensure that meeting time is effectively used.

STUDY GUIDE

Your communication skills will be evaluated by the examiners throughout their assessment of your paper. Every question will require you to communicate clearly your recommendations and/or evaluation of a particular situation.

You will also see from the specimens included in this workbook that the examination questions are set in specified scenarios. You are required to do everything from planning a presentation to writing a memo or drafting a report.

This unit is therefore very important to you because it will provide you with the basic framework and skills not only to improve your own communication performance, but also to prepare you for the specific contextual requirements of the examination questions. You should allow yourself 3 hours to work through this unit and a further 2 hours to fully complete the specified activities.

You will need the following to successfully complete your work on this unit:

- A selection of communications examples collected from your own office or from an organization with which you are familiar. Ideally, this should include a number of letters received from other organizations, a sample of standard letters sent by your department or organization, a selection of memos sent and received by yourself and, if possible, one or two examples of formal reports produced within the organization. Keep these, as you will be using them again for an activity in Unit 10.

Whilst there is considerable emphasis in this course on the development of skills, clearly there has to be underpinning knowledge before you are able to develop a particular competence in any area of activity. The examiners will be looking for you to demonstrate that knowledge within the context of the examination questions. Remember that the work which you are doing, the notes that you produce, and work files that are created whilst studying for any particular programme, are examples of communication to yourself.

Think about your needs as a reviewer of your own work before the examination. You will need to use your notes for revision purposes and so every effort should be made *now* to make sure that they are effective and clear. This will make revision as easy and straightforward as possible. Think about the way in which you lay out your work files, make sure that material is well indexed and that it is clearly referenced back to the textbooks or workbooks which you are using.

A useful hint is to produce a series of index cards containing key notes about particular topics or providing checklists and frameworks for particular plans and activities. These are easy to file and make excellent revision cards.

Also think about the presentation of your notes. We have already introduced you to mind mapping. Mind maps are extremely memorable – particularly if they are personalized. Use cartoons, diagrams – anything which helps the notes to stand out as different. You will find that mind maps are an excellent way to take notes at a meeting but also to take study notes and as a basis for revision of topics.

Before moving on to work through the rest of this unit, spend 5 minutes reviewing your materials from the first part of this course, identify the strengths and weaknesses in your own presentation style and make decisions now about ways to improve this aspect of your study.

Explanations and definitions

1 *Jargon* A mode of speech only familiar to a group or profession (*Concise Oxford Dictionary*). Commonly 'jargon' is used in a derogatory fashion because it is technical and shuts out those who do not understand it. However, it is of key importance within a profession such as marketing because it allows precise and subtle meanings to be transmitted and received. Promotion, PoS and DMU are examples of marketing jargon, which we find invaluable. Within marketing, therefore, always use jargon, and never apologise for it. If you introduce jargon from another area always specify the meaning.

2 *Perception* The process of recognizing or identifying something. Usually employed as 'sense perception', when the thing we recognize or identify is the object affecting a sense organ. (*Dictionary of Psychology*). Perception therefore applies to stimuli detected by any and all of the human senses. Conceptually the term can extend to the 'sixth sense' – intuition – which draws upon our internal bank of knowledge and experience, preferences and beliefs and attempts to relate the incoming signals to a body of present knowledge or experience, etc.

3 *Verbal and non-verbal communication* 'Verbal communication' refers to the words used in communication. They may be written or spoken. 'Non-verbal communication' (NVC) refers to all other aspects of the communication, from 'body language' through to paralinguistics (the tone and timbre of the voice, the pace of speech, pauses, etc.).

Both terms are commonly misused. 'Oral' communication is what most people intend to communicate by the word 'verbal'. NVC is used as a blanket term for every signal other than speech. There is no requirement to become deeply involved in the very detailed classifications of human communication. Simply note that, on occasion, you need to be precise – when you mean spoken communication either say so, or use the term 'oral communication'. When speaking generally it is easiest to adopt the common usage – which we shall do throughout this course unless there is a specific need to clarify a point.

Effective communication – a critical skill

Communication is a core skill critical to all managers, but very specifically a requirement of every effective marketing practitioner. The ability to plan and produce professional communications is essential:

- Weaknesses in either written or oral presentations detract from the quality of both the work of the individual and of the organization.
- A lack of confidence in the making of formal presentations can be a significant cause of stress amongst managers.
- A lack of, or ineffective, communications within the team or the organization causes a loss of motivation, synergy and direction.
- Misunderstood instructions, poorly organized meetings, and ineffective communication in all its forms are major causes of waste in very many organizations.

Clearly, time and physical resources invested in improving the quality of communication activity within the organization can be critical in its effects on:

- The image of the organization to external audiences.
- The morale and motivation of people within the organization.
- The effective use of the valuable time of employees within the organization.
- A reduction in the stress and an increase in the confidence of managers representing the organization, both internally and externally.

The manager – the communication hub?

All managers have a critical role to play in the communication activity of the organization. They are at the hub with messages passing through them, up, down and across the organization (Figures 4.1 and 4.2). The quality of communication within the organization is

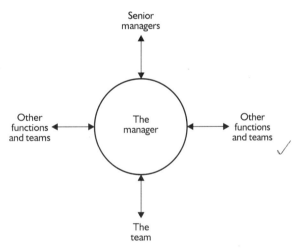

Figure 4.1 The manager as a communication hub

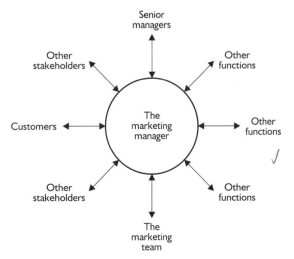

Figure 4.2 The marketing manager at the hub of communication activity

only as good as the weakest link within the communication chain. In this critical central role it is easy to see why it is so important that the manager has to be a particularly strong link.

Marketing managers have another critical dimension to their communication role. They also act as the exchange point for communication between the organization and its customers. Frequently, marketing will also be responsible for managing the communication flow through public relations activities and corporate promotions of stakeholders in the business from the financial community and shareholders to pressure groups and the general public (Figure 4.3). To be effective in this central communication role the marketing manager must:

- Appreciate the importance of communication.
- Be able to send and receive messages effectively.
- Have the skills needed to identify weak links in the communication chain and the knowledge needed to put identified problems right.

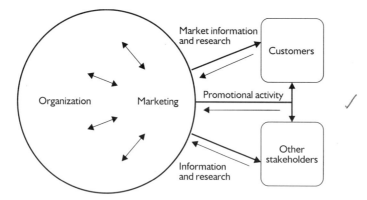

Figure 4.3 The marketing manager as a communication centre between the organization and its external audiences

A review of the rest of the CIM's examination programme is further evidence of the importance of communication to the marketing manager:

- Certificate students study a course in Business Communication, emphasizing the practical skills of communication in the business world.
- Advanced Certificate and Diploma students take examinations in external communication at operational and then strategic level.

Talking to the customers
Take 15 minutes and produce a list of the way in which your organization communicates with its customers.

Compare your list with ours in Debriefing at the end of this unit.

The communication process
The simplistic model of communications shows a sender in direct communication with a receiver. This, it is quickly realized, does not work very well and a reason is sought, through feedback. Direct questions can be asked, body language can be read, the sender can modify and try again (Figure 4.4).

A more developed model of the communication process shows that many things are happening other than the simplistic sending of a message (Figure 4.5).

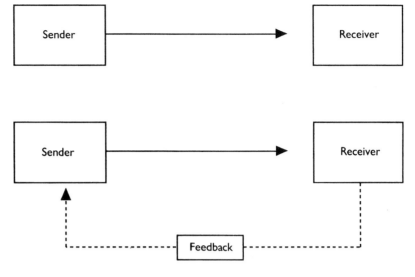

Figure 4.4 Simple models of communication

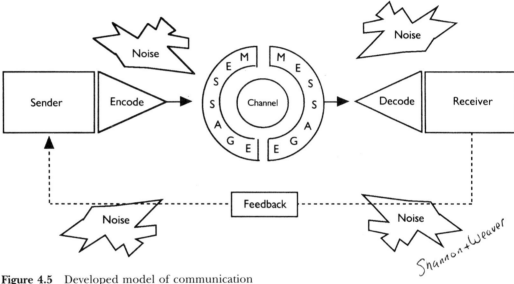

Figure 4.5 Developed model of communication

- *Sender* The sender is working from within his or her own frame of reference, and is guided by his or her own perceptions and understandings. It is necessary to transmit the fullest understanding of what the sender intends, and this intention is a mental construct. As we do not have telepathy we cannot communicate directly, and so are forced to progress in stages.
- *Encoding* Technically a code is simply a transposition of a message from one form to another. We are concerned with business communication and so our choice of codes is narrowed to verbal and visual.
  - (a) Verbal codes include our choice of language, not simply English or French, etc., but also the particular form, (US Legal English perhaps). All forms of all languages have their jargon, which must be used correctly.
  - (b) Visual codes include factors such as images and colour. It is well known to many that white reverses significance from the joy of weddings (US and Britain) to symbolize death (Asia). Selecting a visual code that can be understood by the receiver is perhaps more important than getting the verbal code correct. (As we shall see.)
- *Message* The actual content of the message has to be constructed from the code. What we want to transmit has to be put in a form in which it can be transmitted along the channel we have selected. The message channel selection is very closely related, since if no channel exists we cannot transmit the message, however striking it may be.
- *Channel* The channel is the medium which carries the message. If in writing, it can be a letter, report, memo, scribbled note; it can be transmitted through an electric or electronic medium and emerge as a cable, telegram, fax; it can go directly from

computer to computer; it can reach the receiver through public media such as television. Whichever channel is chosen will have an effect on the message, for each channel, each medium, has its own image and positioning. Not very long ago the arrival of a telegram was dreaded. Within the experience of the majority of the British public only bad news was transmitted by telegram! If the message is to be oral then the choice of channels varies from the directly personal – face-to-face – through the personal – by direct contact without the benefit of sight – to the impersonal – one-way communication through radio, television, etc. Obviously it is important to confirm that the receiver has access to the selected channel and can read the encoded message.

- *Decoding* A simple reversal of the procedure so that what was coded comes out as was intended. Unfortunately it doesn't always happen – as those who have tried to set up a complex piece of equipment whilst guided by instructions written in sixteen languages by a Japanese firm will know. Things can also go seriously wrong because of a lack of basic concepts. The French have no word for leadership – the Russians none for freedom. In both cases it is more than the word that is missing – the underpinning concept is totally absent also. They can also go wrong through mistranslation. 'Out of sight, out of mind' was translated to 'invisible idiot'. There are too many examples – and so just one more. This time to do with the literal interpretation put on to a group of letters. 'Nova' was chosen as the global name for a car. Great marketing – except that in Spanish nova means 'no go'!

- *Receiver* Hopefully the receiver will receive the message through an appropriate channel and decode it accurately but, for any one of many reasons, fail to take any notice and fail to take any action.

- *Feedback* The importance of feedback is clear. The sender has to know that the message has been received, correctly decoded, understood, and acted upon. If any of these elements is missing the communication has failed. Therefore the feedback procedure must be carefully thought through in advance so that weaknesses, as well as outright failure, are detected and diagnosed.

- *Noise* The term 'noise' refers to any and everything that can destroy or detract from the communication attempt. Everything from poor selection of the code(s) through faulty equipment, to a distracted receiver who acknowledged but then forgot to take action.

Note: When working on communication within the promotional or sales communications practice papers you will find a need to understand the communication process in far more depth. For our purposes this general introduction is sufficient.

Problem analysis
Examine each of the following scenarios and identify the problems. Compare your findings with ours given in Debriefing at the end of this unit.

Scenario one
The customer on the telephone is very upset. He has missed the opportunity to have his staff attend a product training day which your organization sponsored last week. Your assistant cannot understand the problem. The customer was sent the full details with their monthly statements, as were all your key accounts, at least 3 months ago!

Scenario two
You are somewhat surprised to hear from the Credit Manager that your assistant did not attend an important meeting earlier today. He tells you that he could not attend as he had to get a budget review onto the Marketing Manager's desk by 10.00. He left a note on the Credit Manager's desk before he left the office late last evening.

Scenario three
You could not see your Sales Representatives personally when they were in for a meeting last week and so you sent a copy of a memo to each of them emphasizing the importance of accurate and complete expense returns. This was all part of a general

tightening up on expenses that has taken place company wide. The feedback you have received indicates that in this instance it has caused great resentment. At least two of the Sales Representatives have spoken to the Personnel Manager to ask if the memo was an official warning!

Scenario four
The evaluation forms completed by the trainees at the end of a training programme indicated quite clearly that the session your assistant had presented was the worst of the day. The feedback identified that the material was not understood and its importance not recognized. Many claimed it was an irrelevant session.

The senses in communication

When asked which is the most important sense, most who are new to the topic respond immediately – sound. They are wrong! The most important communication sense is vision. In normal communication circumstances where one can see and be seen the amount of the message carried by sight is a staggering 75%. Only about 20% is carried by sound.

Note that we distinguish sound from speech. This is because a large part of visual interpersonal communication is lip reading in synchronization with the speaker. Thus people really can 'hear' better with their glasses on! An adage that has stood the test of time sums the matter up perfectly:

What he hears he forgets,
What he sees he remembers,
What he does, he knows.

'Doing', of course, involves many more senses – all of them in most situations. Thus, if you can motivate action from those you are trying to communicate with you have a far better chance of your communication being remembered. Why do you suppose we are constantly asking you to engage in activities? Why is this a workbook and not a textbook?

Incidentally, and finally, when reading a textbook you are actually 'hearing' the text rather than 'seeing' the material. That is why most people prefer books with pictures, charts and diagrams. Likewise, you can help the examiner's 'reading' of your exam paper by including suitable visuals.

Guidelines for improved communication

Sender

Take time to think about who you are, the role you are adopting as the sender and, importantly, how that role is perceived. Are you perhaps representing the organization? Is your role therefore formal or perhaps authoritative? Are you perceived by others to be difficult or uncooperative? Their image of you will influence the way in which any message received is decoded and interpreted.

You need to be clear of the exact purpose of the communication. What response are you trying to ellicit? What do you need to achieve? The method of communication you select will be affected by your objectives. If you want to inform or persuade, or inform and persuade, your approach and style will need to differ if they are to be appropriate.

Who is your intended audience? Are you sending the message to the right person or people? Do you know about your audience? What are their needs, their interests and their requirements? If communication is to be effective it usually requires a considerable amount of 'receiver research'.

Encoding

Remember that the language you use in your message has to be appropriate to the audience. The use of jargon, the problems of translation and interpretation if working with receivers from another culture or country, are potential problems which need to be considered.

In *The New International Manager**, Guy and Mattock provide an 'action guide for cross-cultural business'. In it they stress the need for managers to learn what they term 'overseas English'. Their research is extensive and it shows very clearly that the English spoken where it is not the native tongue differs markedly from that in the English-speaking countries. They recommend that managers who are serious about trading internationally should learn 'overseas English' and use it extensively. Some examples:

- Actually   – *at the moment*, as in 'They are reviewing the situation actually'.
- Aggress   – *attack*, as in 'He aggressed me and so I walked out'.
- At last   – *lastly* (with no overtones), as in 'And at last it is time to . . .'.
- Competent – *well qualified*, as in 'The surgeon is competent to operate on you'.
- Dismiss   – *resign*, as in 'She had an argument with her boss and dismissed the company'.
- Nearly   – *approximately*, as in 'One metre is nearly one yard'.
- Yes   – covers a range of meanings from 'You are absolutely right and I agree' to 'I am listening and reserving judgement'.

It is also important to remember the hidden elements of your message encoded in body language if you are making a presentation or meeting face-to-face, and implicit in the use of visuals, colour and style in all forms of presentation from memos to posters.

Message
This must be as clear, simple and unambiguous as possible if it is to be effectively received. It has to be capable of transmission in a form suitable to the selected channel of communication.

Channel
This must be appropriate to the target audience and to the type of message and the objectives set. The audience must have access to this channel and it needs to be cost-effective and appropriate. Detailed or complex information is more appropriately sent by fax than over a telephone. Detailed financial information, facts and figures of all kinds, may be more appropriate in a report than delivered as part of an oral presentation. Certainly, when presenting orally it is important to supply copies of the key material. If the audience has to make notes as they listen you are dividing their perception, and damaging your message.

Decoding
This is always done against a background of noise, which can be as simple as traffic outside the window or a dirty telephone line, or as subtle as an unwillingness to consider a challenge to a cherished belief. Conflicting messages could be received – this is particularly true within an organization where the informal 'grapevine' may be saying something different from the formal communication from senior management.

The 'hidden agenda' is an expression that has recently come into common use. It refers to the way in which people 'read between the lines' of any message and perhaps take a different view from that anticipated and intended. If a message is to be sent to a large number of receivers, perhaps to a whole customer base, then it is sensible to test the message with a sample audience to see how effectively it is decoded. In other circumstances the sender must rely on the quality of the feedback to give an indication of how effectively the message has been received and understood.

Feedback
It is all too easy to send messages and then walk away without checking that they have in fact been transmitted effectively, i.e. received in the form intended, with the required results initiated. Feedback provides a control, allowing the message or its format to be adapted and retransmitted if necessary in order to ensure its effective delivery. It also provides you with information so you can continually develop and improve your communication skills. It helps

* Published by Kogan Page

you to identify when communication has gone wrong and to analyse the cause of the failure. Feedback provides the basis for the constant improvement of individual communication activities and of the communication structure within an organization.

Feedback does not always come automatically. Often it has to be sought formally through evaluation and questioning. It can be measured informally through checking people's response in the form and number of questions that they ask, or do not ask, and their body language and general attitude during a meeting or presentation. But the final check in terms of feedback is: did you achieve your objectives?

The one true measure is to observe what the receiver does and discount what he or she says they will do.

Some wonderful work is done in the world of advertising. A 28 second commercial will be designed to impact on the target audience at the right time and in the right way. It may be designed for subsequent reduction to 10 or even 5 second reinforcement advertisements that carry the essence of the whole message. Stills from the film may be used in the press, on posters and at point of sale and packaging. The soundtrack may run on radio and in-store.

Some 'classic' commercials are remembered long after the campaign has finished – perhaps even be passed through the generations. Persil doesn't wash whiter – but for many the commercials that said it did are still alive. Guinness is not good for you – Beanz no longer Meanz Heinz – but millions of teetotaller bean haters still remember the advertising, and they were not even in the target audiences!

Self-evaluation

Continuously reviewing the communication process must become routine if a manager is to be effective. But self-evaluation is not an easy exercise even for the most experienced communicator. As soon as you embark on a serious attempt at evaluation it is almost certain that you will be found to be at fault. You will not score a perfect 10 on every scale! It is human nature to avoid criticism, and so many try to avoid evaluation because of the potential ego damage. This is an area where firmness is required in self-discipline before you can require evaluation of others. It is too easy for a manager to evaluate, and not to be evaluated.

Non-verbal communication

We speak with our vocal organs, but we converse with our whole body (Abercrombie).

Non-verbal communication (NVC) is technically known as 'kinesics' and is far more important than most people recognize . It has been popularized by Desmond Morris with his works on Man Watching and Body Watching which are concerned with showing the signals that we constantly emit, and how they are read in different cultures.

We are to some extent already experts in NVC, although most of us respond only at the subconscious level. Most are unaware that they are constantly sending, receiving and acting upon important signals. Those people with good interpersonal skills, and who are effective communicators and negotiators, have learned to become conscious receivers of non-verbal messages and to deliberately use NVC to reinforce their oral messages.

How well do you interpret non-verbal signals?

1 Look at the following people sat at a meeting. What can you tell about their attitudes from their body language?
2 How might you be able to tell if someone disagreed with you?
3 How do you interpret people's time keeping?
   (a) A manager arrives 15 minutes late for a presentation to a key client.
   (b) A sales representative arrives 20 minutes early for a meeting.
4 Do other cultures place the same interpretation on time keeping?
5 In face-to-face communication how would you interpret:
   (a) The other person looking at their watch.
   (b) Nodding.
   (c) Physical contact with you.
   (d) Direct eye contact.

Communication in business

The effective manager must be aware of the different requirements of each of a number of different situations and settings. He or she must be able to select the appropriate format for a particular objective, and plan and implement the delivery of communication effectively.

Informal communication – a note

Not all communication in the workplace is formal in nature. Much information is exchanged informally. The grapevine is often an important source, keeping employees and colleagues informed about what is going on.

Facilitated through social interaction, informal networking is positively encouraged by many organizations who see informal channels across the organization as simply opening up new communication opportunities. It helps the organization get things done on the 'I know a man who can . . .' principle, and it can encourage flexibility and cross-fertilization.

Managers must recognize, monitor and influence informal communications – they must not be ignored. Misinformation and rumours can lead to de-motivated staff and generate an atmosphere of suspicion and non-cooperation between work groups and teams.

When managers are seeking to implement change and to sell new ideas to staff they are well advised to plug into the informal communication networks. Identifying the key influencers in these networks is an important first step in any internal marketing activity.

Formality in business communication

There is a tendency to think that business communication is formal communication. This is not so, although decisions taken and agreements made must be recorded formally. The process of reaching decisions, and entering into agreements may rely extensively on informal communication.

A formal meeting may well put the seal on a deal, but often there will be much informal contact outside the meeting. A decision to increase production will be formally confirmed, but only after informal discussions to check that it is both possible and acceptable.

The key is to understand when formality is required, and at what level.

ACTIVITY 4.4

How formal is formal?

For each of the following business communication activities, indicate on a scale of 1–10 which you think are the least formal (1) and the most formal (10). You will find that circumstances will affect your answer, so think through the potentials of each activity before coming up with a response.

Activity	*Ranking*
(a) A business lunch	—
(b) A memo	—
(c) A telephone call	—
(d) A contract	—
(e) An annual general meeting	—
(f) A report	—
(g) A client presentation	—
(h) An appraisal interview	—
(i) A disciplinary interview	—
(j) A staff briefing	—

(**See** Debriefing at the end of this unit.)

Getting started

As a general rule, the more formal the approach the more preparation and planning will be required. However, in any communication you would start by answering three questions.

- What are your objectives?
- Who is/are the receiver(s)?
- What are their needs?

In some situations it will require considerable research to answer these questions. In others it will be more obvious.

At the beginning of this unit you identified how your organization communicated with its customers. Over the next week make a point of observing and talking to others with a view to assessing how effective that communication is.

Prepare a report indicating your key findings and making at least four recommendations for improvement. Review these with your line manager or colleagues.

Hints:

- Try calling your own organization. How well is your call answered and your query handled? (If your voice is well known get a friend to call while you listen on an extension.)
- Try the same activity with your competitors. How do you compare?
- Collect samples of the leaflets, literature and letters sent out. Is there a clear house style, from logos and typeface to writing style and manner? What impression does this give the customer? What impression would it give you if you were the customer?
- Are brochures and instruction materials clear, well laid out and professionally presented?
- Review internal documentation and reports. How effective are they?

Self-check 4.1

Take time to answer the following questions to help you assess your understanding of the material covered so far in this unit.

1 Why is it good practice to write a difficult letter today, but delay its despatch until tomorrow?
2 What could go wrong in each of the following situations?
   (a) You leave a message with your boss: 'Unless I hear to the contrary by 17.00 today I will take action as outlined.'.
   (b) You fax an urgent, but confidential, document to a client.
   (c) You complete a sealed bid and put the envelope through the office franking machine.
3 Why is it good practice to confirm agreements in writing? Why does this sometimes cause antagonism?
4 In planning communication what is the central, key need that must focus your plan?

(**See** Debriefing at the end of this unit.)

Business communication – a review of the options

In this section of the unit we will be considering ways in which the various communication options can be planned and undertaken more effectively.

To phone or not to phone?
Key forms of communication with colleagues in other sections of the organization are the:

- Telephone.
- Internal memo.

Produce a list of the advantages and the disadvantages of using each. Then work through this section of the unit and add to your initial thinking. Finally, compare your assessment with ours provided in Debriefing at the end of this unit.

The telephone

For many of your customers the telephone will be the most direct access to the company. How the phone is answered will be a critical aspect of the customer care which your organization is perceived to give to its clients. Calls will come in, of course, not only to the marketing department, but through the switchboard and to other employees.

It is because we are all so familiar with using the telephone that the need for telephone skills training and improved techniques of using the telephone are so easily overlooked – and this despite the fact that many of us will have direct experience of the frustrations, the aggravation and the disillusionment often experienced when trying to communicate by phone. You will have researched how effective your organization is – and will know what action is needed.

Using the telephone effectively

You have probably been using the telephone for years, and so the idea of learning how to use it may seem strange. But as a marketing manager you will be responsible not only for how you use the phone yourself but, importantly, how the telephone is used by others in the organization. In any case, have you grown a little careless in your own telephone technique?

Planning the telephone call

Telephone conversations are two-way conversation that are often unstructured. This casual approach is endemic because of the ease with which one can stretch out an arm and pick up the telephone. It pays considerable dividends to restrict this automatic process – to plan each call before making it.

Even the shortest of calls benefits from planning to ensure that you achieve your objective. Before starting a call make sure that you know to whom you want to speak, and what your objectives are. Make a list of the information or the points that you wish to cover. Have available any correspondence or information which you may need for reference and be prepared to make a note of any answers which you are given. This sheet of notes should be dated and timed – and do not forget to add this to the file of relevant documents.

If you are leaving a message with a third party, a secretary, receptionist or assistant, it is important that it is simple and very clear. Complex messages simply will not get through. Often it is better to fax a note of your needs or the information that you wish someone to have. This adds the benefits (and disadvantages) of written communication.

Good telephone techniques are a matter of applied common sense. The basic rules are:

- Be brief – but not so brief that the message cannot be understood clearly.
- Be polite – this is not only important when dealing with external callers. The image and reputation of your department can be influenced by colleagues feeling that they are interrupting, getting in the way or not welcome.
- Speak clearly and slowly – this will maximize the chances of your messages being understood.
- Take the initiative – particularly when handling messages for people who are not available. Try to help the caller with their problem. This concern will come across as helpful and caring: important attributes within any marketing department.

Answering machines

These are so routine in the US and the UK that we may not appreciate that they are still gaining acceptance in countries that are not as developed. This is easier to grasp than the fact that in some countries they are meeting resistance because the culture requires that contact be courteous and personal.

Your machine

Set up your outgoing message so that it is courteous and clear. At home it can perhaps be as crisp as 'Hi, I'm out – you know what to do.' In the more formal world of work this casual approach will not do.

Your message has to:

- *Identify* The organization, department and/or person.
- *Thank the caller* Common courtesy requires your thanks, and the time allows the caller to register that he or she is dealing with a machine.
- *Establish contact* During a working day your message may apologise for your absence. After working hours no apology is needed because you are adding a benefit which the caller will appreciate. Therefore you should have at least two outgoing messages. It is best to have two tapes, and switch them at night and in the morning.
- *Instruct* It is infuriating to be told to speak after the tone and then find that the machine emits five short beeps and one long one! If the message tape is restricted to 30 or 60 seconds, then for goodness sake say so, or callers will be cut off mid-sentence. Specify what information you must have. Is the telephone number enough? Do you want the address?

Needless to say (?) you must always clear the tape as soon as you return to the machine, and each caller's needs must be attended to.

Others' machines

You should not be surprised to be greeted by an answering machine, and so you should be prepared. Know what minimum you need to say in order to achieve your purpose. Brevity is a considerable virtue, especially as you may be on a 30 second tape.

You have to make it easy for the receiver to deal with your call. Therefore:

- Identify yourself early. Name and phone number.
- Speak very clearly. Spell even the most simple names.
- Say concisely the minimum you need to communicate.
- Say what action you expect to follow.
- Close with your name and phone number.

It is not helpful when people call in and give their details very fast and then go on to their message. Sometimes a tape has to be run to and fro several times before the details can be taken from it. You cannot prevent this happening to you – but you can prevent it happening to those who you call. Remember – it benefits you if you make it easy for them!

EXTENDING KNOWLEDGE

The telephone can dominate a situation. For some reason buried deep in our psyche we cannot leave a ringing phone unanswered. Answering machines take some of the strain, but in an office if the phone rings we answer. It may not always be convenient to speak, but convention forces us to respond.

It is good manners, and good sense, for the caller to start the call with an enquiry if it is convenient for the receiver to talk at that time. Not only does this show courtesy, it also allows time for the receiver to collect themselves and 'switch out' of what they were doing. If it is inconvenient for the receiver to speak then fix a time to call back. That is far better than forcing a conversation on a receiver, who will resent the intrusion even if he or she is too polite to say so.

Written communication

Written communication has the advantage of offering a time lag between the sending and the response. This allows both sides to think through and revise their messages in order to ensure greater clarity. The fact that there is also a record of the communication means you must be careful to write exactly what you mean – there is no immediate chance for clarification nor modification.

The choice of words is important as they carry the 'tone' of the communication. Careless selection can give unnecessary offence or cause misinterpretation. Language and style are the 'body language' of the written communication.

Letters

Letters are for external communications. They are the main formal contact with customers, suppliers, agencies, and so on. They must be properly addressed, and laid out in a style that is crisp, clean and a credit to the organization.

You cannot control the circumstances surrounding the arrival of your letters, nor the mood of your receivers. A letter could reach its destination at a time of pressure, with your receiver in a foul mood following a domestic problem. You would probably postpone a meeting – but you cannot hold the letter back! Therefore try extremely hard not to use phrases that could be misinterpreted. A friendly style is acceptable – a jocular style is not recommended!

As a manager you need to be aware of the style and format of written communications being sent to customers. It can be a useful and illuminating activity to monitor all the correspondence generated by your team in a week. Try talking to a close client and ask to review their file on your organization ... what impression does the variety of written documentation create? Is there a clear house style?

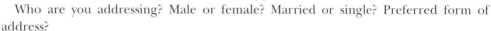

Addressing

It can be extremely difficult to address correspondence so that it does not give offence. Address conventions have changed markedly of late, with traditional styles giving way to today's approach.

Who are you addressing? Male or female? Married or single? Preferred form of address?

- J. Smith, Esq.
- Mr J. Smith.
- John Smith.
- J. Smith, Esq.

- Mrs/Miss/Ms

- Dear Mr Smith.
- Dear Mr Smith (with 'John' added in ink)
- Dear John.
- Dear Smith. (A form of address now falling out of use but indicating a privileged relationship. As from a Director when issuing a mild reprimand to a valued junior.)
- All fraught with problems, since each person has her own view on the style she prefers.

The accepted approach is to address using the style adopted by the correspondent:

- Dear Mrs Smith.
- Dear J. Smith.
- Dear Mrs. Jane Smith.
- Dear Ms Smith.
- Dear Jane Smith.
- Dear Miss Smith.

It is worth taking the time to find how a person likes to be addressed because 'nothing is sweeter than the sound of our own name'.

Take your sample of letters addressed to your organization. Critically assess each:

- How clear is the message?
- Do you know what response is expected?
- What impression does it give of the sender? Of their organization?
- How could it be improved?
- Which is the:
  (a) Best?
  (b) Worst?
  And why?

It is only by taking time to consider and review both your own communications and those of others, that you will find the basis for positive development of these skills.

The written report

Report writing is particularly important to the working manager. It is also a required skill if you want to do well in your CIM examinations. In Analysis and Decision, report writing is mandatory – no report, no pass!

Reports must written in 'business English' and be crisp, clear, and come to some definite conclusion(s) upon which action can be taken. Depending upon the management seniority and role, it is necessary for the writer to *specify*, or (more usually) to *recommend*, action.

Developing the style takes practice, but once acquired the process becomes automatic. The key rules are:

- Always head a report with the name of your organization.
- State to whom it is addressed, from whom it comes, and give the date.
- Head the report, e.g. 'Public Relations Plan for 199X/9X'.
- Number and subnumber sections and paragraphs within them.
- Head sections if appropriate.
- Introduce the subject of each sentence and paragraph early. Do not make the reader search for it!
- Use capital letters for appendices.
- Present contents in a logical order.
- Include diagrams, graphs and tables only if they have positive value. Never without thought!
- Include recommendations for action – that are written as intention against time.
- Refer to any appendices within the body of the report – 'See Appendix A'.
- Indicate when the report concludes, e.g. . . . / Ends.

The memorandum

A memorandum is an *internal* written communication. Its purpose is to communicate effectively. No salutation is required. Style is similar to a management report – although calling for actions(s) may not be appropriate. A typical examination requirement is: 'Draft a memorandum on the role of an Account Executive in an advertising agency'.

Note: 'Draft' because often junior managers are regularly required to draft memos for their seniors. The requirement to draft does *not* diminish the requirement for quality. It does not imply that slipshod work is acceptable.

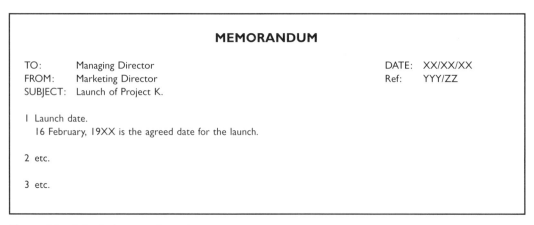

MEMORANDUM

TO: Managing Director   DATE: XX/XX/XX
FROM: Marketing Director   Ref: YYY/ZZ
SUBJECT: Launch of Project K.

1 Launch date.
    16 February, 19XX is the agreed date for the launch.

2 etc.

3 etc.

Figure 4.5 A typical memo format

The key rules are:

- Use the organization's style – often memos are preprinted. In an examination, head your answer 'Memorandum'. There is normally no need for an organization or department name.

- Style is similar to that used in management reports.
- Indicate the conclusion by '. . ./ Ends', or by signature over your printed name.
- A typical memo format is shown in Figure 4.5.

Effective oral presentations

Of all the forms of communication it is undoubtedly the personal presentation or talk which creates the most stress in individuals. Being asked to stand up in front of an audience of 5 or 500 can be equally daunting and requires considerable preparation. Meticulous planning is needed for you to create the image you want and to achieve your objectives without the cost of a nervous breakdown!

The rules for preparing a presentation are essentially the same as for any other communication activity. You need to find out about the audience:

- *Who and how many?* The level, grade and number of the people whom you will be presenting to.
- *Knowledge and expectations* Their existing knowledge of the subject area. What they expect and need from you.
- *Purpose* Their understanding of the overall intention of the activity.? Is your responsibility to inform or to instruct? Is it to persuade or inspire? Are you to entertain and amuse? Are you to do *all* of these?

Before planning a presentation you need to find out the facilities and resources that are available. Are there visual aid facilities, such as overhead and/or slide projectors? Is video available? Will you have a flipchart and/or a white board? Will all of these be seen effectively by the audience?

A presenter should always try to visit the venue in person to check out the acoustics, the facilities and the room layout before the presentation. This is not always possible in the business context, particularly when presenting at a client's venue. It should *always* be possible, however, to secure some basic information about the facilities available and the type and size of room. Even a phone call gives a minimum level of knowledge.

It is professional to enquire what will be available. Even if asked to visit a client's senior management you should never hesitate to enquire formally and politely about the facilities. Remember that the directors to whom you are presenting are themselves presenters – they would enquire about their venues, and will respect you for doing the same.

You should find out how long you have to make your presentation. The basic rule is that the shorter the amount of time the more intense your planning and preparation need to be. It is much harder to do an effective presentation in 10 minutes than in 2 hours.

Planning presentations – the basic rules

- *Time* Must be managed – by you. *Never* present without a clock or watch that you can see easily; preferably one that the audience cannot see. Putting your wristwatch on the table or lectern allows you to see it without the audience noticing.
- *Structure* Must be clear. Your logic must be in terms that your audience will understand.
- *Questions* Decide whether you will take questions as you go, or prefer to have them at the end. Often it is best to delay them. If so, you must give the audience a reason – 'Please hold questions until the end because I think you will find that many will be answered as I go along'.
- *Introduction* Possibly the most important part, since it must be attention getting and lead the audience into the meat of your presentation. It is better to plan this word-for-word, and practise so the flow is entirely natural. This ensures a positive start, and helps you control your nerves which are always at their worst for the first few sentences.
- *Humour* Jokes are best avoided. They are for after-dinner speeches. Build in some light-hearted moments, and if you can get laughs naturally, fine. Striving for humour is almost certainly going to detract from the overall impression – and failed humour damages your self-confidence.

- *Middle*   Package your main messages in digestible chunks, and support them visually. Illustrate with oral examples in addition to any visual aids such as a flip chart or slide projector.
   (a) Never show off with too much technical detail or factual information.
   (b) Use broad numbers as indicators and provide the detailed information in separate handouts, appendices or reports.
   (c) Keep the messages simple and straightforward, keep to the point. Use visual aids to reinforce, to build interest and to communicate trends and general information clearly and effectively.
- *Questions*   Indicate when you are ready to take questions.
- *Conclusion*   Your opportunity to leave the audience in exactly the state of mind your objectives dictate. All conclusions should be planned, and carefully rehearsed. You have the chance to go back over errors in the middle, but never in your conclusion. It is better to be brief, and always use clear body language to signal the end. (Step back. Put your notes down. Take your glasses off. Sit down. Something definitive.)

Planning presentations – the technique

As with all management activity you must have written objectives to achieve. Only when these are ready can you begin the process of planning the presentation in detail. The 'planning frame' given at the end of this unit provides the heading and columns that you need in order to structure your presentation.

The process is:

- Prepare your presentation verbatim. You may need to do this by actually writing down every word, or by dictation and transcription. This stage will pass with experience – but you will still find that you need the overall structure in mental draft before you can make an effective plan.
- Structure your material into main points and subheadings.
   Reduce each point from several sentences in your draft to key words and phrases that act as aide-mémoires.
- Determine which visuals will best support the key points you need to make.
- Create illustrations to support and bring the key points alive.
- Indicate your expected time for each topic.
- Calculate your overall time need.
- Add additional material so you have 10% more than you think you will need – as a contingency against under-running.
- Draft the questions that you expect to receive – and their answers.
- Transfer your key notes to postcards or A5 sheets.
- Number these key note cards, perhaps link them loosely with a treasury tag – then if (when!) you drop them they will remain in order.
- Arrange for the visuals to be produced.
- Rehearse – especially your opening and closing – which must be smooth and confident.
- Revise your plans, as rehearsal helps you to tighten up your thinking.

After the presentation review its degree of success. Make notes while the experience is fresh. Keep your presentation notes and visuals for subsequent use.

1   *Visuals and illustrations*   A visual is a physical picture, model, diagram or graph. An illustration is an oral description that brings the visual alive – makes it more memorable.

   - A visual of a telephone could be illustrated by saying 'Imagine a cable that is as thin as a human hair, can stretch from Land's End to John O'Groats and carry the entire peak conversation of the USA on Mother's Day'. Then you could move on to fibre optics, what they are, how they work, etc.

2 When presenting you are the leader in the room. You have the dominant position, which people in the audience have conceded to you. They are ready and willing to follow your lead.

- Always be positive. Never apologise for a late start, lack of visuals, etc. Take these disadvantages in your stride, the audience doesn't care about your problems!
- Expect equipment to be missing, or to go wrong! Always have contingency plans – be ready to switch to a flip chart if the projector breaks; carry spare pens so you have a range of colours; have a pack of tissues to clean a white board if the rubber has gone missing. As you gain in experience you will find that your list of essential personal equipment grows ever longer – you may need that electrical screwdriver and spare fuse only once in 10 years, but when you need it, you *really* need it!

ACTIVITY 4.6

Visual aids
Consider these three visual aids. Identify the strengths and weaknesses of each and produce a checklist of the characteristics of an effective visual aid. Compare it with our thoughts given in Debriefing at the end of this unit.

A. Planning presentations:

1. Agree your subject –
   – identify the key points you want to include.

2. Spend time thinking about a good style –
   – an interesting approach or angle.

3. Identify material examples to illustrate your theme.

B. Presentation Hints

Before

- *Practise*
- *Nail those Nerves*

During

- *Use prompt cards – not notes*
- *Monitor audience response*

C. Effective presentation

You need to know:

- Purpose

- People

- Points

Effective use of meetings

Meetings with senior managers, with team members, for interviews, for appraisals, for discipline; meetings with suppliers, with customers and with contractors; meetings for discussions; meetings for decision making, meetings for the exchange of ideas . . .. Turn the pages on the diaries of most managers and you will find them filled with meetings for a variety of purposes and with a variety of people. They can be on a one-to-one basis or significant numbers of people may be involved. They can be formal or informal. The one characteristic of all meetings is that they hold the potential to represent an expensive waste of managers' time.

Note: Specific types of meetings, e.g. negotiations, individual staff meetings, appraisal, and job interviews, will be handled in more detail in later units.

Take the time during this week to review your diary for the past 4 weeks. Identify how much time you have spent in meetings. The time log sheet which you kept for the last unit should be a help in doing this. What percentage of your time was spent in meetings and how much of that was effective? Could the objectives of each meeting have been achieved in some other way? Could better planning for the meeting have reduced the amount of time that it actually took?

Which meetings do you find of value? Which do you look forward to? Are they the same ones? Which ones do you wish you could avoid? Why can't you?

True or false?
Decide which of the following statements about the work of groups and meetings are true and which are false.

1 The camel is said to be the result of a committee trying to design a horse.
2 People are generally more committed to decisions which they have been involved in taking.
3 Different minds on the same problem are sure to create synergy.
4 Groups are often less risk adverse in their decision making than are individuals.
5 Meetings slow down decision making.
6 Meetings provide a useful forum for the exchange of ideas and information, but achieve little else.
7 Improved technology and communication make face-to-face meetings increasingly unnecessary.
8 Meetings called on a Friday afternoon will finish more quickly that those called on a Monday morning.
9 In general, managers do not take enough care when selecting members to attend a meeting.
10 The best decisions are always those which come from a consensus of opinion.

(**See** Debriefing at the end of this unit.)

Over the next week identify an opportunity when you can attend a meeting as an observer. This may be in the context of work, or as a member of a social club/group or community activity such as a residents' association, parent/teacher group or one of the many council committee meetings which are open to the public .

Use the opportunity to analyse the effectiveness of the meeting.

- Make a note of the controllable factors:
  (a) How many people?
  (b) What kind of environment?
  (c) Facilities and information available to them.
- Monitor the interactions.
- Is the Chair* the focus or the facilitator of the communication?
- Do all members participate?
- Record instances of specific group roles and behaviours, and which members are involved. Typical behaviours are:
  (a) Creative/idea generation.
  (b) Information seeker.
  (c) Information giver.
  (d) Elaborator – expanding on ideas/modifying them.
  (e) Coordinator.
  (f) Summarizer.

Chair of meeting

- Who in the group was:
  - (a) Mediating?
  - (b) Diagnosing?
  - (c) Evaluating?
  - (d) Seeking group consensus?
  - (e) Setting the pace, confirming?
- Were there incidents of unhelpful behaviour?
  - (a) Non-participation?
  - (b) Anger?
  - (c) Side-tracking?
  - (d) Non-cooperation?
  - (e) Other?

Produce a brief summary indicating how effective you felt the meeting was, and make recommendations for improving meeting performance in future. If possible share these with the participants or the Chair.

* We are using the non-sexist term 'Chair' to indicate the person controlling the meeting.

To avoid duplication we shall leave meetings at this time, but return to the skills required for effective management of meetings under such topics as teams and roles which we cover later in the workbook.

Make certain that every examination paper which you take for the CIM – but most particularly this one – clearly demonstrates your personal communication skills.

- Work needs to be well and clearly written.
- Answers need to be planned carefully and presented logically.
- Use diagrams and illustrations to help communicate complex information.
- Use colour to highlight your work.
- Avoid red and green which are the examiner's colours.
- Use a ruler to underline key points and headings and to draw diagrams.

Professionally presented work can be worth several extra marks, often enough to turn a marginal paper into a pass. Make sure that you produce work which does credit to the quality of your thinking. Don't let careless or lazy presentation damage your quality!

Remember that white space sells – do not overcrowd your work. Help to make the examiner's job of marking your paper as easy as possible.

You have been asked to give a presentation to a local sixth form college on 'Management as a career'. The audience of 'A'-level students is expected to number about sixty. You have been given 60 minutes including time for questions. Use the planning frame given at the end of this unit to prepare your presentation. Plan your presentation and compare your plan with our suggestions given in Debriefing at the end of this unit.

Tony Buzan: originator of much conceptual understanding of how our brains function, born in London in 1942

The originator of mind maps, the self-enhancing master memory matrix, the group/family/ work/study technique, and new concepts in brain functioning relating to the process of change and metapositive thinking, Buzan is also the founder of the International Brain Clubs and Buzan Centres.

Buzan emigrated to Vancouver, Canada in 1954 and graduated from the University of British Columbia in 1964. He achieved double honours in Psychology, English, Mathematics and the General Sciences. Returning to England in 1966 he worked on Fleet Street, also editing the *International Journal of MENSA* (the high IQ society). Since then he has published 10 books (nine on the brain and learning, and one volume of poetry). His books have been translated into 20 languages and his best-seller, *Use your Head*, has achieved world-wide sales of more than a million copies. It is a standard introductory text for Britain's Open University.

Tony Buzan has featured in, presented and co-produced many television, video and radio programmes, including the record breaking Use Your Head series on BBC Television, the Open Mind series for ITV, and the Enchanted Look for Thames TV. He is adviser to royalty, to governments and to multi-national organizations. He is a regular lecturer at leading international universities and schools.

A stimulating and innovative tutor, Buzan continues to break new ground with his pioneering work in understanding the processes of brain function – what makes him unique, however, is his intuitive and inspirational ability to translate theoretical understandings to practical use. He teaches thinking and memory techniques that enable people to understand the true capacity of the human brain, and to realize and develop many of the abilities that normally lie dormant.

His mind maps, in particular, are of key value to creative managers, and Buzan's work should be linked with that done by de Bono (see Unit 11).

Key publications
Use your Head, 1974
Make the Most of Your Mind, 1977

In this unit you have:

- Identified the critical role of the manager in the process of ensuring effective communication within the organization.
- Reviewed the importance of the good communicator, recognizing both verbal and non-verbal communication signals.
- Identified the importance of NVC in all communication – but especially when the communication is cross-cultural.
- Examined the manager's communication requirements and the skills needed to achieve successful communication.
- Established the framework for effectively planning communication activity in a number of business settings.
- Identified possible problem areas which can result in a breakdown of the communication effectiveness, and made recommendations in a number of scenarios for tackling communication problems.
- Appreciated that improved communication activity requires both an analysis of the current performance and planned and coordinated investment for improvement of the situation.
- Appreciated that practical evidence of communication competence will be essential for your success in this examination.

Debriefing

Activity 4.1

Types	Examples
Corporate literature	Annual reports, newsletters
Public relations	Pro-active and reactive
Promotional literature	Brochures, leaflets, price lists
	Advertising and sale promotion
Packaging	Labels, instructions, simplicity, effectiveness
Electronic	Fax, telephone, EMail, data link
Paper based	Business correspondence, direct mail, invoices and statements
Personal	Sales teams, delivery staff, service engineers
	Presentations and meetings
	Factory visits

Activity 4.2

Scenario one

The message has to reach the right audience (receiver). Information on product training would have been needed by the marketing department or the sales manager. Instead it has almost certainly ended up in the waste paper bin of the accounts department, to whom the monthly statements would have been sent. Better targeting of the communication in the first place would clearly have prevented this problem. But so would a proper feedback system – a telephone call to the key accounts to confirm their interest or lack of it would have helped identify this problem early.

Scenario two

It looks as though the Credit Manager did not receive the feedback. He may be at fault for not having checked his messages on his desk or possibly the message was left in the wrong place and it got lost in other paperwork. The problem of 'noise' intervention is a frequent one in business. It would have been far better to have made positive contact. Now there is need to repair some damage to personal relationships – and to discover what was covered in the meeting.

Scenario three

This is an example of choosing the wrong method of encoding a message. The formal style of a memo has encouraged the individuals to decode the message as a serious and personal issue that affects their continued employment! Choosing the appropriate method and manner in which messages are transmitted is an important aspect of communication decision making.

Scenario four

The problem here was perhaps in a lack of preparation and planning for the presentation. It looks as though the audience was not clearly identified – nor perhaps, were the objectives of the presentation. Feedback was clearly not taken during the presentation because the body language and the general lack of interest should have given a clear indication that all was not well. The approach and/or message could then have been amended.

Activity 4.3

1 These are classic examples of body language which may often, but not always, be interpreted as we describe. Be careful not to judge on appearances, but develop the habit of routinely monitoring behaviour so that you can adjust your communication style and evaluate the response.

    A *Arms crossed, sat back from table, looking angry/cross.*
        Every indication of disagreement, withdrawal from the discussion, possibly frustration at not being able to express the views held, or expressing them to an audience that fails to react as expected. The need is to encourage this person back into the meeting,

if possible. If not, then to make personal contact as soon as possible after the meeting to identify the problem(s).

B *Sat gazing out of the window, doodling, attention not on the meeting.*

It would seem that the body is present, but the mind has gone away! Is this your fault? Is the meeting wandering off the point? Are you waffling? It can be difficult to recover an absent mind without making an issue of the contact but, unless you want to exert firm discipline, it can often be achieved by swinging the discussion around to an issue that you know is of concern to the absent mind.

C *Happy, nodding, looking directly at speaker, sat close to table, attentive.*

The classic signs of somebody in close agreement and paying careful attention. Eye contact usually indicates trust, it certainly shows that the person is alert and taking part.

D *Head down, not meeting direct looks, looking at table.*

The classic explanation is of shyness. Perhaps the person is feeling out of their depth. Gentle encouragement is called for, but without demeaning the person. Careful, because any 'demeaning' will be viewed from the perspective of the person and they might see a contact very differently from how you intend.

2 • Disapproving look.
  • Silence in response to questions or request for comments.
  • Shaking of head.
  • Someone anxious and wanting to break into the conversation or make a comment in order to put their differing view.
  • People who sit opposite you in meetings may well be in opposition to the stance which you are planning to take. Those who support your views and role appear more often to sit on the same side or close to you.

3 (a) The manager's late arrival, unless preceded by an apology, may be interpreted as a lack of interest and, therefore, as perceiving the client to be unimportant. The manager can be seen as rude and/or arrogant. His behaviour is certainly discourteous and likely to damage relations between the company and the client.

(b) Early arrival indicates that the sales rep. has taken the appointment seriously. He is indicating that his time is less valuable than the client's. Early arrival should not be accompanied by any pressure to bring the meeting forward.

4 Time has different meanings in different cultures. In some parts of the world late arrival would not be interpreted as rude or discourteous. In others there is strict protocol that must be observed. It is vital to research the cultural differences in behaviour and body language which can be more significant than verbal language. The language barrier will be blatantly obvious but offence through non-verbal signals can be given without being realized.

5 (a) The other person is late for another meeting, wishes to draw this meeting to a close, is bored – or perhaps just wants to know the time!

(b) In the UK, nodding would symbolize agreement and permission to continue. In India the same signal indicates disagreement. The need to research non-verbal signals can be seen to be very important before embarking on intercultural business.

(c) Physical contact is sought in many cultures. In the Midi region of southern France one crosses the road to greet people – and shakes elbows if the hands are dirty! Middle Eastern custom is to negotiate closely, almost nose-to-nose. Northern cultures prefer to 'keep their distance'. You have to know the culture of the other to interpret the message.

(d) Direct eye contact is usually a sign of support, openness and trust between the people involved. If as a speaker you make direct eye contact with members of your audience you are likely to be seen as confident and trustworthy. You will also know that individual members of the audience are taking positive interest.

Activity 4.4

Your list will depend on your perceptions and experience, but you can see that there is scale of formality, ranging from activities such as contracts and AGMs with a legal purpose and dimension, to telephone calls or chats, with no written record and an informal style.

Ranking

(a) 4–7   The purpose of the lunch will dictate its level of formality.
(b) 4–8   Usually less rather than more formal. But memos can contain instructions.
(c) 1–6   Casual chats (1) have a place in developing relationships. Otherwise, a phone call should be structured, and in this sense formalized.
(d) 10   Contracts must be highly formalized.
(e) 10   The AGM is of key importance and must follow a clear structure.
(f) 6–10   Reports are intended to initiate action.
(g) 10   Content can and often should be light, and fun, but the underlying purpose is extremely serious and structure and control are essential.
(h) 8–10   Purpose is highly formal. The method should be friendly and relaxing.
(i) 10   It is crucial to follow procedure to the letter.
(j) 4–8   'Briefing' implies guidance rather than direction. Daily briefings can be less formal, but still need to be got out of the way efficiently.

Self-check 4.1

1 'Sleeping' on a problem often puts it into a different perspective – also you may have written in haste and without due care and attention, especially if you were cross, or otherwise emotionally disturbed by the situation to which you are responding.

2 (a) Negative permission should never be tolerated. What if the manager never saw your message? If action has to be taken then the only choices are to seek an alternative manager with the necessary authority; go ahead on your own initiative, or miss the opportunity.

(b) Faxes are open communication – anyone can read them if they happen by.

(c) Sealed bids must be anonymous. Your franking, if it identifies your organization, will cause the bid to be rejected unopened.

3 Written confirmation ties down the details and prevents misinterpretations. Annoyance can be aroused for a variety of reasons from 'Don't you trust me' to 'I wanted to leave it loose so I could interpret it in my favour later'.

4 The key, central need is the need of the receiver of the communication. Unless they are motivated to listen, you are wasting your time.

Activity 4.5

Telephone

Advantages

- Speed.
- Immediate feedback.
- The two-way nature enables clarification and checking to ensure that the messages have been received and understood.
- More personal and friendly, allowing social networking across the organization and the building of team links between individuals.
- Allows direct access to how the receiver feels about a particular issue or activity.

Disadvantages

- Intrusive.
- No automatic written records.
- Messages may be forgotten with no record to act as a reminder.
- Need for immediate response allows little time for consideration and review.
- Oral communication is potentially subject to more misunderstanding and ambiguity than when information is put in writing.

Memo

Advantages

- Provides a written record.
- Allows detailed information to be included and clearly explained.
- Provides an opportunity for the receiver to consider and then act upon the information provided.
- Fast and less formal than letters and reports.

Disadvantages

- Can be interpreted as formal and unfriendly.
- Does not facilitate the creation of networks across the organization.
- No opportunity for clarification of contents.
- Information content may be limited and inadequate.
- Potentially perceived as routine/ unimportant. Memos lack the status of other forms of communication.

Activity 4.6

Of the 3 visual aids reproduced in this activity:

- A is more like a page from a textbook. It includes too much detail, is difficult to read and is typewritten.
- B is better – three clear bullet points and some use of visual presentation.
- C is even better – key points which can be expanded in the presentation.

Checklist:
- Never use type-written or badly hand-written copy.
- Keep the points simple and brief. Their purpose is to reinforce your main points.
- Be creative in presentation and layout. Boxed titles, bullet points and use of more than one colour all help to make visual aids more valuable as communication tools.
- Where possible use graphs, cartoons, diagrams and pictures to add memorability to your presentation.

Remember that the quality and the professionalism of your visual aids will reflect on the professionalism of yourself and your organization.

Activity 4.7

1 *True*   There are many similar sayings and deeply held beliefs that support the idea that committees and meetings have, over the years, been seen to confuse issues and to result in silly compromises.

2 *True*   Even where people have not agreed with the final outcome they are likely to be more motivated and feel more responsible to a decision which they feel they have taken part in making.

3 *False, unfortunately*   The idea would be that the different minds will generate synergy, but if the group is not working cohesively then the opposite may well happen.

4 *True and false!*   Shared decisions seem to allow individuals to take a greater risk than they might on their own. Clearly this is a two-edged sword in organizations which are themselves risk-adverse. Group decision making can challenge this pattern of behaviour, but undue risk taking is not necessarily a good thing for the organization.

5 *True, generally*   Meetings can delay decision making because it takes time to call them and the output is not always conclusive. However, because meetings bring together a range of different people with different inputs and knowledge it can be a quicker process than allowing individuals to work on specific issues that result in a joint decision.

6 *Often true, sadly*   Too many meetings provide a valuable function of ideas and information exchange but achieve little else. Well-run and well-managed meetings with clear objectives, can result in important benefits.

7 *True, probably*   EMail access, video conferencing and improved telecommunications generally should be reducing the number of face-to-face meetings. However, much of this technology is still to be fully accepted. In any case, there will always be a need for one-to-one or group meetings where NVC signals can be interpreted.

8 *True, probably*   It perhaps should not be true, but human nature is such that it is likely to be. If a short meeting on a Friday afternoon is effective why have long ones at other times? Planning for a Friday on the grounds of shortness only means that the meeting is out of control. Late in the week is normally a bad time for meetings for other reasons – people are tired, and like to clear their desks ahead of the weekend.

9 *True*   Individuals summoned to meetings are too frequently an ad-hoc bunch selected because of their functional expertise, the areas they represent or their availability. To be an effective team the group members should be considered in terms of their role, their characteristics and the contribution they can make to a particular group. Personality and style should be taken into account. The objective is to find a cohesive group that will work together effectively.

10 *True*   Consensus decisions are a good thing – but they do not happen very frequently. The objective of a meeting is not always to get everyone to agree, but to ensure that all points of view have been considered and the best decision made in the light of that information. The Chair may well use the meeting as a forum to listen to other people's ideas and then to make up his or her own mind. Alternatively, the majority view may hold. In essence there is nothing the matter with either of these styles of meeting management.

Unit activity

- You should have a structured and logical plan which breaks down into key points.
- These key notes should be capable of transfer to postcards or A5 sheets which should be numbered.
- Your introduction and conclusion should be worked out in detail.
- You should have a time estimate for each stage.
- You should have a note of the equipment you will need.
- Your visuals should be imaginative – they must carry your message clearly and without 'noise'. Therefore any visuals must be an integral part, and not simply tacked on and intrusive.
- You should have a range of illustrations that will appeal to 'A'-level students.
- The questions you expect should be drafted – together with their answers.

PRESENTATION PLANNING FRAME

Aim:

Opening:

Middle points:

Support materials:

Close:

Summary:

Presenter's Notes:

Handouts:

Visual aids:

Tools for forming the team

In this unit you will:

- Examine the need for teams and the potential problems of building teams.
- Be aware of different team roles and be able to identify how teams can be helped to work more effectively.
- Investigate how to identify gaps in the skills of a team and how to use this knowledge as a foundation for recruitment.
- Be aware of the process of recruitment and selection.
- Understand the importance of training programmes and training plans.

By the end of this unit you will be able to:

- Recognize the possible problems affecting group performance.
- Plan a team skills audit.
- Recommend ways of enhancing team performance.
- Translate identified gaps for team weaknesses into job descriptions, and job and personnel specifications.
- Manage the recruitment activities for a new marketing team member.
- Plan and manage the selection process.
- Use information from the selection process as a basis for training programmes.

Managers need to understand what makes a team successful:

- What dynamics may be at work within a group.
- Why individuals sometimes perform better when alone rather than when involved in a team activity.
- Why a group of individual experts or specialists does not necessary make a successful team.

You have probably already started to examine the dimensions of human behaviour from the point of view of the marketer needing to understand customer behaviour. There is as much need to understand the behaviour of people in work as there is to understand the behaviour of customers. The knowledge gained from the one activity is useful in achieving the other.

This unit is devoted to identifying how best to make teams more effective and how to build teams through recruitment and selection. We suggest you allow 3 hours to complete the work within this unit and a further 4 hours to complete the specified activities.

You will need the selection of job advertisements collected for Unit 1, and the references and job descriptions you used in Unit 2. These should be updated with current examples, if necessary. For one post you should have a copy of the job description, job specification, personnel specification and the job advertisement – perhaps for a post currently being offered within your own organization?

Management is a practical activity and to develop competencies and or to answer credibly in an examination requires the individual to have been involved as closely as possible in the actual activities being described. Most of us have been through the process of recruitment and selection from one side of the desk, but it is important that the manager understands the process from both sides.

Whilst working through this unit it is recommended that you involve yourself with the practical issues involved in team building, recruitment and selection. Observe the process if you can, but certainly seek out managers with practical experience and find out how the process, which seems straightforward, actually works in practice. Remember that management style varies considerably – so locate several managers with different approaches to secure a rounded view.

You will find that doing these activities will help to speed up your learning process and will reinforce the knowledge and understanding which you are gaining as you progress through this workbook.

Preparing for the examination is rather like preparing for a job interview. You need to make yourself aware of the examiner's requirements – and you need to prepare yourself in order to demonstrate the attitude, skills and knowledge which are expected of a successful candidate. The examiner's requirements are made clear through the syllabus, tutor guidance notes and a report on each examination. These are supplemented by articles in *Marketing Success*. It is your responsibility to identify the areas which you need to develop more fully in order to do well in your examination. Within this workbook you will find all the help you need – except for the necessary research into each examination paper as it is set, and reported upon.

Do not concentrate your efforts on the areas and activities which you find enjoyable or in which you already have a level of competence. Build on your strengths of course – but develop the general level of understanding which you will need to succeed in the exam and in management. Managers need a broad competence across all the areas and activities for which they are going to be responsible.

Explanations and definitions

1 *Instrument*   In the training and HRM context an instrument is any device which can be used to achieve a training or evaluation objective. Thus a structured questionnaire is an instrument, as is an ice breaking team exercise used to help a group to form.

2 *Job description*   Also called a 'job definition'. A broad description of a job or a position at a given time (since jobs are dynamic) formulated during job analysis. It is a written statement of those facts which are important regarding the duties, responsibilities, and their organizational and operational interrelationships.

3 *Job specification*   A statement of the activities which comprise the job. It records the knowledge and skills needed to complete the job satisfactorily, not necessarily those to be present in a successful applicant for the job.

4 *Personnel specification*   An identification of the personality, aptitudes, skills, knowledge, attitudes, qualifications and experience required in a candidate for a specific job.

5 *Recruitment* The process of identifying the personnel requirements of a particular vacancy, devising an application procedure, commissioning and/or placing advertising as needed to attract suitably qualified applicants.

6 *Selection* The process of choosing between applicants attracted by the recruitment process in order that a candidate who best meets the requirements of the Personnel Specification is appointed to the job.

7 *Training plan* A detailed plan showing the stages of training required and achieved by individuals. Usually developed by team, within department, and used as the basis of both training planning and budgeting.

8 *Training programme* An analysis of the ASK factors needed in a job holder if the job is to be done satisfactorily.

What is a team?

A team is a collection of individuals working towards a common goal or objective. They recognize that they are part of the same team because they have shared values and goals. Currently there is much interest in the use and importance of teams within organizations. Today's more flexible management structures depend on bringing people together to work in groups – as project or task teams for short periods. Then individuals are expected to reform with others to focus on another task. Many individuals can find themselves the members of several teams simultaneously, and possibly having very different roles within each.

Just a group of people?

Fundamentally a team is 'just a group of people'. A company is 'just a group of people'. A department is 'just a group of people'. A sports club is 'just a group of people'. But are groups of people automatically teams? Of course not!

Teams form around a need to achieve a common objective. In the case of a company the uniting force is the mission of the business and its corporate objectives. A departmental team will have more specific task objectives and a unique vision of its role within the organization as a whole. A sports club may focus around sporting excellence, or the social dimension. Perhaps there will be several subgroups within a club – if each has a different set of priorities, major problems can arise.

ACTIVITY 5.1

Acme Sports & Social Club has a cricket and a tennis section that share the same ground. The tennis courts are to one side of the cricket pitch, and all members share the same pavilion, which is well equipped with modern changing rooms, a large meeting room, and a well-stocked bar which serves snack meals.

Within the tennis section there are three groups of members:

- Those who play at County standard and want to retain their position as one of the top clubs in the country.
- Those who play for exercise, fun and an opportunity to meet people.
- The beginners, who are learning the game.

The cricket section has no ambition to be a top club. Their membership is concerned with:

- Social activities.
- Exercise and fun from playing.
- The need to manage enough teams to ensure that all who want to can play.

Consider how the groups within the tennis section may focus, and how they may interrelate. Where they might have common purpose, and where particular team interests lie.

(**See** Debriefing at the end of this unit.)

The major difference between a group of people and a team is in the implied cohesion and therefore effectiveness, when a group of individuals becomes a team. In this sense a team can vary in size with the smallest being two people and, in the broadest sense, any number of people who make up an organization. Effective teams, however, cannot exceed a size where they break down into subteams which have goals that differ from the overall team's brief.

There will be both formal and informal teams within an organization. A formal team will be the directors and representative stakeholders who comprise the senior management team. The sports society may have several sections and teams which will be semi-formal since they are organized within the organization and, therefore, have its active or passive support. An informal team may develop on individual initiative around the focus of a common interest and will not be known to the organization or, if it is, will have no official standing or recognition.

As a manager you may be given the responsibility for two distinct kinds of formal group:

- *The command group*, where you are designated leader with the authority to plan and coordinate the activities of that group and have responsibility for the quality and quantity of the outcome.
- *The task group* (or project team). You may or may not be designated as leader. The group may be encouraged to work together to decide how best to organize their activities in order to fulfil the task or project.

Informal arrangements, less hierarchical in nature, are becoming increasingly common as the number of 'knowledge workers' increases and the number of managers required to command them decreases. When working with task groups it is common to find individuals within several teams, and for them to have a different role in each.

Who is in the team?

Question: How many people are there in a football team?

Answer: More than 11.

The football team is not just the 11 players who take to the field on a Saturday afternoon. A moment's thought shows that the team can be extended to include all those associated with the prime task of winning matches. Thus a football team can be extended in stages:

- Eleven players who start the match.
- Two substitutes.
- Two or more others in the first-team squad.
- The manager

- Assistant manager.
- Team coaches.
- Physiotherapist.
- Doctor.

- Locker room staff.
- Coach driver.
- Team administrator(s).

- Members of the second team and juniors.
- Paid administrative staff running the club.
- The Directors of the club.

- Officers of the Supporters' Club.
- Voluntary staff acting as Stewards.
- Members of the Supporters' Club.

- Supporters, generally.

For the majority, the manager of the team is clearly identified as the excitable person based in the dugout at the side of the pitch. What most fail to realize is the extent of the task. Premier League teams play only forty-two league matches in a year – 63 hours of activity. Adding in other games such as the FA and League Cups may increase the publicly active hours to about 100.

Success and failure are quantified very clearly by the team's position in the competitions – too much failure to achieve and the manager will be looking for a new job. Football management must have one of the highest and most public staff turnovers of any management activity. Yet the work of the manager is never seen by the public – he is judged simply on the results that he achieves through his players in those 100 hours. Truly, management achieves through people!

What makes a successful team?

Bringing groups of people together is one thing – turning them into a successful team is clearly something quite different. A word of warning! We have mentioned earlier in this workbook that the manager in steering the people resource is working between two extremes – dealing with the problems of groups who will not work at all as individuals but instead prefer to share, rather than take individual, responsibility for their actions.

The ability to work in teams is becoming an increasingly important dimension of successful employment, as organizations are now requiring people to be flexible about the groups within which they work. Traditionally, individuals tended to spend a great deal of their working life with the same group of people, normally as part of the same command team within the hierarchical structure of the organization. There was plenty of time to get to know one another and to build long-term working relationships. Careers were hierarchical also, and the expectation was of an almost parental relationship with the organization taking responsibility for each individual's welfare through their career and also their retirement.

In today's more fluid and flexible matrix style of organization, with its flattened hierarchies, project teams may come together for part of a working week. They may work together intensively for only a short period of time, but individuals will be expected to create relationships and perform, perhaps with different roles in a variety of teams, over a fairly short period of time. In order to do this effectively everyone needs to understand the dynamics of team forming and building – and be aware of their own strengths and weaknesses, as both a team leader and a team member.

The importance of the individual

This increased emphasis on the team and team skills should not be taken to the extreme of encouraging people to think that the only effective work that can ever be accomplished is within a team. For certain individuals and for certain tasks individuality is the most effective approach, provided that the contribution can be integrated effectively in the requirements of the group as a whole.

As always, the two extreme positions are equally untenable. An organization with no teams is not maximizing the value of the people resource – an 'all teams' approach is adding complexity and denying the flash of individual brilliance which can be such an effective trigger.

Establish teams when and where the team approach is likely to generate the results which are required. Encourage individuals within groups to undertake specific functions and individual tasks and to bring back their contributions and findings to the group. Do not smother initiative by procedure!

What makes a successful group?

The simplistic definition would be the team which achieves its objective(s). But this simplistic approach fails to take into account the resources which are used up in the process. So we require groups which not only work efficiently but also effectively. We need to be concerned with what is done and also how it is achieved. This approach also depends on the assumption that the objective(s) set for the group were appropriate in the first place (Figure 5.1).

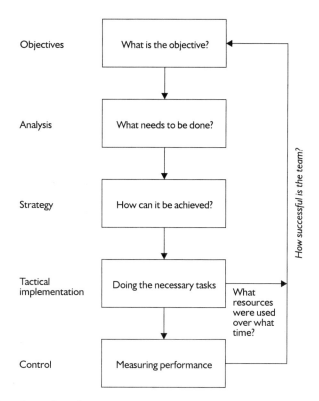

Figure 5.1 Analysing the task and team success

- *Objectives* To analyse task and team success it is necessary to break down the task into a number of stages which have a reflection in the normal planning framework. The team needs to start with clear objectives, it needs to know what it is expected to achieve. Only with the objectives in place is it is possible to analyse what needs to be done in order to achieve the objective(s).
- *Analysis* The alternative approaches to the task must be identified, evaluated and decisions made regarding the most appropriate approach given the resources available and the time constraints.
- *Strategy* As a result of this analysis the team will able to determine a strategy – a statement of how the objectives will be achieved. This strategic statement is extremely important because it ensures that the whole team is aware of the approach which will be taken. The team must know where it is headed, and the route that has been selected.
- *Tactical implementation* The tasks required to achieve the strategy must now be identified and allocated to individuals within the group, as appropriate. It is during the implementation stage that resources will be consumed and time will be taken. One measure of the efficiency of the operation can be to assess results against budget.
- *Control* The organization is concerned to control individual groups, but the team should assess its own performance and identify areas of activity which need improving if the group's performance overall is to improve. The organization will normally evaluate through budgetary control supplemented by discussions with the team leader. Group self-evaluation can take many forms, from the unstructured to the extremely formal. It is for the group leader, working from his or her management style, to determine the degree of formality. Once again there is danger of being either too structured or too loose.

How teams form

Groups can be seen as developing through four stages, referred to as forming, storming, norming and performing (Figure 5.2). In environments where individuals are brought together for short periods it is important that they are aware of these stages and take an active part in helping the group to move forward through them.

STAGE	CHARACTERISTICS
1 Forming ↓ Team building activities can help to speed up the process	A new group, individuals are unclear about their roles and each other
2 Storming ↓ Flexibility is needed to allow role changes and the group to 'shake down'	Groups, as they get to know each other, often go through turbulent times. The leadership or objectives may be challenged. The group may change in shape
3 Norming ↓ Gaps in the team skills and resources should start to be apparent at this stage	More familiar with each other and the objectives, the individuals start to settle down. There is a greater shared understanding and agreed procedure
4 Performing ↓ Monitoring feedback will help identify areas of weakness which can be tackled	It is only at this stage that the group has really become a team, capable of delivering targeted objectives

Figure 5.2   How teams develop

- *Forming*   Many team-building exercises and activities have been devised to help a group to form. These are designed to break the ice, to introduce team members to each other, and to help them identify the roles which they are likely to take. Social interaction can help to speed up this process and many organizations take teams away from the work environment for a time (perhaps a day or a weekend) to encourage the development of rapport. Many of the innovative areas of adventure training have been developed to encourage and speed up the process of team building.
- *Storming*   Individuals bring their own value judgements and priorities to the group. Almost inevitably there will be disagreements, some of which can be of major importance. Usually, however, these are relatively easy to solve because they are so clear and specific. Of far more long-term danger are the subtle differences which do not seem important, but which can fester over time until they either explode or – probably worse – never come to a full head but detract from the group's performance. Sexism, racism, ageism – these and other 'isms are typically problem areas that must be monitored and dealt with early.
- *Norming*   Group standards of behaviour and of expectation are established. Street gangs adopt uniforms, styles of dress, and even body markings such as tattoos, as indicators of group membership. Work groups do not (normally!) go this far, but successful groups have accepted standards and expectations that are created from within.
- *Performing*   Groups often develop a social dimension – their members like being together. This can be a powerful force to enhance performance if it is channelled in that direction. It can also distract from performance, and even lead to slower working so that the group's existence is extended. It is important that a group monitors its own performance and that the performance is also monitored by others. Complacency is an ever-present risk – particularly in an established team where the group appears to be performing well, is achieving its objectives and is possibly acclaimed as a winning team. Managers must be vigilant to identify areas where either the team or individual performance needs further development and where areas of weakness exist. Action must be taken to maintain the group at a high performance level. **Note**: criticism is likely to be counter-productive, since the group will respond by self-protective withdrawal.

Staying successful

It is easier for a team to become successful than to stay successful. This is due to one or more of a range of factors. Examine the list below, supplement it from your own experience, and note the actions you would take as a manager in each circumstance.

Problem	*Actions*
• Motivation of the challenge to succeed is diminished.	
• Complacency develops.	
• Routine sets in.	
• Familiarity/friendship deters challenges.	

(**See** Debriefing at the end of this unit.)

A blue chip company, which must remain nameless, rushed a new pack on to the market in the UK. The motivation was purely personal – a major competitor had been first on the market in America, and the US management had been roasted by corporate management. The British management were not going to make the same mistake.

The launch was successful, corporate management were complimentary – and then the complaints began to come in. The package was defective, and the contents had deteriorated! All stocks had to be withdrawn, at a considerable loss. Corporate management were *not* told of the failure.

At the subsequent enquiry all functions were represented. No fault was found. In turn each admitted their errors and, in turn, others said 'Yes, but . . .'. 'Yes, but you couldn't have known'; 'Yes, but we ought to have double checked'; 'Yes, but it was as much our fault'. After an hour it was agreed that valuable lessons had been learned, and the matter was closed. (Which is why the firm cannot be identified. Corporate management still do not know of the debacle!)

The manager–leader

John Adair's *Action Centred Leadership* model has been widely adopted as a basis for modern-day management/leadership training. He contends that working groups of teams have three needs (Figure 5.3):

- To achieve the common task.
- For team maintenance.
- Those which individuals bring with them into the working situation.

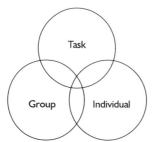

Figure 5.3   The Adair model of action-centred leadership

Adair represents each need by a circle, and the circles overlap. Thus each contributes something to the others. Equally, if one of them is not handled effectively it will detract from both of the others.

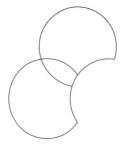

Figure 5.4   If the manager loses sight of any segment there is damage to the other segments

Given that the three areas of a manager's concern have a mutual interdependence, it follows that the greater the area of overlap the more effective the operation.

Leadership and management are conceptual in nature. Each individual will lead and/or manage in their own style. It seems to many currently practising managers that 'leadership' is of more value than 'management' – especially the forms of management that are bureaucratic and administrative in nature. Certainly managers who can lead with talent are harder to find than are supervisory managers. We shall return to leadership in Unit 6.

Self-check 5.1

Take time to answer the following questions to help you assess your understanding of the material covered so far in this unit.

1 In about 30 words show the relationship and importance of the ASK factors to management.
2 How can group and subgroup dynamics work for and against task achievement?
3 In troubled times what do team members look for in their manager?
4 List the four stages of group development. Show why each is important to the manager.
5 Use the Adair model to assess your perception of three different managers of whom you have personal experience. (These can be from any part of your life – work, social, domestic.)

(**See** Debriefing at the end of this unit.)

Effective groups

To be effective, groups need a wide range of roles and skills within them. These are supplied by the individuals that make up the group and it is very possible for one person to contribute under several headings. It is this mixture of roles and skills that makes each group individual and gives each its unique dynamic.

Every member of the group is also an individual in their own right. They bring to the group their own personality, characteristics, aptitudes, attitudes, values and objectives. All will have a 'personal agenda', but some will be more likely than others to reduce the effectiveness of the group for personal agenda reasons.

Each team member will have a tendency to adopt a particular role within the group. Human relations specialists have produced methodologies to help individuals identify the team roles for which they are most suited – and to which they are most inclined. Typical role models are: coordinator, dominator, critic, note-taker, caretaker, and distracter.

Typical skills include coordination, creativity and problem solving. There is need for some to have the determination to stick with a given problem, for others to sense when it is time to move on. There need to be positive contributions from opinion givers, and from cynics who ask questions and demand clarification. There needs to be input from the maintainers who ensure that activities are still targeted to achieve the objectives, and there need to be note-takers who ensure that actions are allocated to specific individuals and that a record of decisions is kept.

Group dynamics

As the manager of a group you need to:

- Select the members to form a group.
- Manage the group dynamics.
- Recognize when to change, extend or reduce the group.

In order to be an effective group manager you have to become a people watcher. Behaviour must be observed, analysed, understood and the understanding acted upon. (In Unit 4 you covered the essential people skills, which you must constantly work on developing through practical experience.)

ACTIVITY 5.3

Observing groups in action

Find an opportunity to sit in on a team or group meeting. Perhaps within your own organization, but preferably with an unfamiliar group. (You will tend to have already formed opinions about the roles that close colleagues adopt and they may alter their behaviour knowing that you are observing.)

Monitor the way in which this group gets on with the task in hand:

- Is the objective clearly understood?
- Is it accepted by all?
- Are strategic decisions made, then restated and clarified?
- Are implementation decisions clearly made, and allocated as responsibilities to individual members?
- Are control measures identified and agreed?

Devise an observation form based on the outline given at the end of this unit to help you monitor the contribution of the individuals in the team. Can you identify:

- The role(s) taken by each individual?
- Individuals level of commitment and, perhaps, their personal agenda?
- The skills brought to the meeting?
- The skills missing from the meeting?

What actions would you recommend be taken to improve the performance of the group?

(**See** Debriefing at the end of this unit.)

Team skills audit

An important stage in management and personal development is to identify the current ASK factors in yourself and your team members. Many instruments have been devised and are readily available to assist with this process. The regular and routine assessment of competency encouraged by the Training Plan (see below) is also of considerable value.

Two typical exercises are shown below

Team analysis

Under each of the headings which follow, decide which statement best describes the way the team operates:

1 Firstly, as an individual.
2 Secondly, as a group.

	Circle as appropriate	
	Individual	*Group*
Objectives		
The objectives of the team activity were:		
Completely clear	a	A
Very clear	b	B
Clear	c	C
Fairly clear	d	D
Not clear	e	E
Relevance		
The relevance of the activity has been:		
Complete	a	A
High	b	B
Fairly high	c	C
Moderate	d	D
Not clear	e	E

Using a similar format the instrument deals with:

- Time utilization.
- Participation.
- Tolerance.
- Frankness.
- Commitment.
- Overall appraisal.

Note: This evaluation is intended for use to focus thinking, and to indicate areas of individual and group strengths and weaknesses.

As with all such tools the value lies not in the completion but in the use made of the analysis by the manager or trainer.

To discover your reaction to your job

Please answer each question to show how you feel. Do this by placing an 'X' at the point on each scale between 0 and 5 which best describes your opinion. For example, if the answer scale for a question were like the one shown below and the answer lies in your opinion, between 'Quite a few' and 'A great many', put an 'X' as indicated.

None	Very few	A few	Quite a few	A great many	All
0	1	2	3 ✕	4	5

The following areas are covered using scales such as:

Almost always; Very often; Fairly often; Not very often; Almost never.

and

Almost none; Very few; A few; Quite a few; A great many; Unlimited times.

- How often have you felt unable to use your full capabilities in the performance of your job?
- How many functions on your job do you feel are relatively unimportant or unnecessary?
- How many opportunities do you feel you have to make worthwhile contributions?
- How often do you feel that your job is one that could be dropped?
- How much say do you feel you have in deciding how to carry out your job?
- How frequently have you felt that you could accomplish more given complete freedom of action?
- How frequently have you received some type of recognition for your accomplishments?
- How often does your job give you opportunities for personal recognition?
- How do you feel about your present post as a job where you can continually shine?
- How do you feel about your organization as providing opportunities to learn?
- Outside of regular measurements of your job, how often do you feel you have achieved something really worthwhile?
- To what extent is it possible to discover whether you are doing well or poorly in your job?
- To what extent is it possible for you to introduce new (untried) ideas to your job?
- How often have you found your work interesting?
- Based on past experience in your present job, how often have you thought that you would like to resign or change jobs?
- To what extent do you consider your present post helpful for a person who wants to get ahead?

Note: This type of questionnaire is intended for personal use – to focus a person's thinking ahead of a training session, appraisal or some such event. It asks questions which many would not want to share directly. Care must always be taken with the use of instruments such as this since the aim is to help develop individuals and teams – never to damage them.

Note that instruments such as these need to be selected and used with care. They exist to provide a focus, or to allow an individual or group to express indirectly something they would not wish to tackle head on. They come from the same general source as motivational research (clinical psychology), and the best results come from trained and experienced facilitators, just as trained and experienced researchers are needed for motivational research.

Develop the habit of observing behaviour taking place around you. At the bus stop observe and analyse the behaviour of individuals as they join others waiting for the bus. Monitor an individual as they shop, and then get into their car and drive away. Watch groups and how they interact in a social setting such as a cafe or bar. Notice the unique behaviour exhibited at a cash point. Pay particular attention to the non-verbal language, for it is this that carries the main messages.

Filling gaps in the team

In Unit 2 we saw how the process of management development is facilitated by specific documentation. We can now, as promised, examine the process of recruitment and selection in more detail.

Remembering that we are dealing with individuals, we have to consider that the process can only be on-going. We have to provide for recruitment of people to posts in the expectation that they will outgrow their initial jobs and want to move on. We shall lose staff whatever we do. Staff turnover can be reduced by positive policies, but we can never complete the recruitment and selection process.

The role of human resource management (HRM)

All large organizations have developed HRM (personnel) departments and their managers can rely upon the existence of clear personnel policies, and back-up through every aspect of concern to personnel management.

For the majority of managers, however, there is likely to be little formal support and it is for them to recruit, select, train and manage. Even for managers with HRM support there is a need to understand fully the systems and procedures so that they have sufficient understanding to be able to exert control as needed. In this the relationship with HRM is exactly the same as with any other specialist function – you don't have to be able to do it, but it is far better if you know what should be done, what could be done, and what you want to have done.

Recruitment and selection

The full process involves clearly defined stages (Figure 5.5). Whether or not you have a natural talent for selection, the use of a systematic and proven approach will at least ensure that you don't overlook anything important and it will greatly reduce the area of subjective judgement where hunch and flair are said to operate.

- *Task analysis*   Determines the gaps in the team (see Unit 2, and The Training Plans, below).
- *Job description*   Also called a 'job definition', the job description is the focus of any employee's relationship with the employer. In establishing what the job is the manager provides the foundation for all the stages of recruitment, selection, training and appraisal that follow. In providing the basis of what should be done the job description is also the foundation of the contract of employment and the basis for disciplinary procedures should they prove necessary. It is, above all, the key document on which the whole process depends.

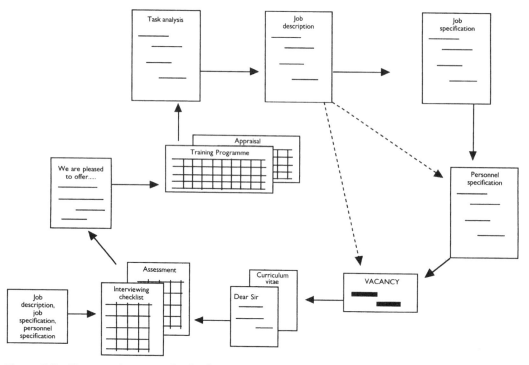

Figure 5.5   The recruitment and selection process

What's in a job description?
Take the job descriptions which you have collected, and the one from Unit 2. Spend 20 minutes comparing them and compile a list of the factors which should be included in a job description.

(**See** Debriefing at the end of this unit.)

• *Job specification*   The next step is to analyse the job to determine what attitude, skills and knowledge are needed in the job holder.

The job specification records the ASK factors needed to do the job – not necessarily the factors that the successful applicant will possess. The appointee should have at least some of the factors needed – the others will be acquired after the applicant has been engaged through activities such as induction training and planned experience. It is not usually good policy to appoint a fully qualified person – they are already almost ready to move on.

The job specification is particularly useful in determining the factors that a successful applicant must *not* have. The contra-indicative factors.

Contra-indicative factors.
If you were recruiting for each of these posts, what could be contra-indicative factors that would exclude any applicant?

Post	*Contra-indicative factors*
• Steeplejack	
• Delivery driver	
• Submariner	
• Team member	
• Manager	

(**See** Debriefing at the end of this unit.)

The contra-indicative factors allow rapid sorting of applicants since, by definition any with one or more of the factors must be excluded, however good they may be in other areas. Given this clarity of purpose, it is important to determine these factors with the greatest care.

Note: Overqualification should exclude even more so than underqualification. The overqualified gets to grips with the job and then becomes bored. Either they then try to change the job, or they become demotivated. They are also 'fish out of water' in comparison with others doing the same job, and can unwittingly become the centre of controversy.

Myros Inc., of Miami, lamented the fact that they could not keep their newly appointed management trainees. They recruited only those with Master's Degrees in Business and offered a very well paid job. But the staff turnover was horrendous.

On investigation it became obvious why. Each newly qualified MBA was put on a training programme that lasted 12 months and commenced with 10 weeks making up orders in a small cubicle in the warehouse. The working space was some 20 feet square, and each cubicle specialized in only one form of product. There was no air-conditioning. For those few who survived the low-grade work, awful conditions and boredom, there were equally mind-numbing jobs lined up.

> Management's view was that their managers had to know the job from the bottom up. 'These graduates don't know nothing about the real world'. Unfortunately, the management didn't know much about people management!

- *Personnel specification*   With the job description and specification in place you can now think about the person needed to do the job satisfactorily. You know what ASK factors are needed, you would like to recruit someone who has many or most of them, but you accept that you will be better to provide some after recruitment. You have to determine:

  (a) What are the essential qualities and/or qualifications?
  (b) What are the desirable qualities and/or qualifications?

  (You have already determined the contra-indicative factors.)

  Note: You have to think very carefully about what is really essential and, if necessary, review it from time to time to match the standards of the applicants available on the market. A marked downturn in the quality of applicants may force a review of the job itself rather than simply the terms and conditions of employment.

The job specification can be developed around either a five-fold grading or a seven-point plan – both of which provide headings under which ASK factors can be identified. The five-fold grading uses the headings: physical, attainments, abilities, disposition, and circumstances. We, however, recommend the seven-point plan because of the additional analysis that it makes possible.

The seven-point plan

This is most usefully constructed as a matrix so that key points can be entered to focus the recruitment and selection process (Figure 5.6).

Job title: _____

Attributes	Essential	Desirable	Contraindications
1 Physical make-up			
2 Attainments			
3 General intelligence			
4 Special aptitudes			
5 Interests			
6 Disposition			
7 Circumstances			

Figure 5.6   Personnel specification

1 *Physical make-up* What does the job demand in the way of general health, physical strength, stamina, eyesight, hearing, speech, appearance, etc.? This is an area which has come under increasing scrutiny. Legislation to prevent discrimination has stopped most of the specifications for 'attractive', 'young' etc. The increasing number of disabled people in the workforce has encouraged many managers to re-evaluate just what physical attributes are necessary for a post. However, where work involves long periods of driving, keyboard work, lifting, and so on, it is important that these requirements are identified and specified. Managers have to accept responsibility for health and safety factors, which include the levels of stress under which they place their teams. Putting the wrong people into jobs is a recipe for such problems.

2 *Attainments* What general education, technical knowledge, specialized training and relevant experience are required? To avoid becoming dazzled by qualifications and diplomas it is more useful to list specific knowledge areas, e.g. a marketing research job holder needs a proven knowledge of statistical sampling techniques. Conversely, there is sometimes an unwillingness amongst employers to recognize the real value of qualifications. CIM is working hard to encourage organizations to require evidence of some formal marketing training when appointing marketing professionals. Specific questions need to be asked to establish the job candidate's experience. Experience indicates not only knowledge or skill, but also the occasions when these have been used together. Much of personal development comes from experience. A key concept behind on-the-job training and apprenticeship schemes is that the best way to learn is through doing the job under guidance.

3 *General intelligence* What level of reasoning and learning ability is required? How alert and active, how creative should the job-holder be? This can be a difficult area to evaluate since it is extremely subjective in nature. For some jobs the need is for people who thrive on routine and who prefer to have clearly structured rules and procedures to follow. This *does not* mean that they have to be dull, or that an intelligent person cannot be fulfilled by such work. It is a mistake to equate intelligence with ambition. Intelligence refers to a quickness of mind, not to academic achievement.

4 *Special aptitudes* Aptitudes and abilities are difficult to quantify, but they can be specified as the ability to be creative in generating solutions, to work under pressure, to think strategically, to negotiate contracts, to sell ideas, etc. Once specified it is possible to devise ways for assessment and evaluation.

Note: Unless the vital areas are specified and assessed or evaluated they can only be tested in discussion, and by evidence of past achievement. A direct assessment is, of course, by far the more productive, even if more demanding and expensive short-term.

This section can easily become filled with meaningless jargon. Wherever possible be specific and always quantify when you can – the ability to speak conversational French, to have a keyboard speed of 60 words per minute, or use particular equipment or programs.

5 *Interests* Are any general interests likely to be relevant to job success? Perhaps tangible interests such as in the making or repairing of things, an active interest in outdoor pursuits, or membership of a chess team. All add depth, width and flavour to a particular candidate. Shared interests can help to build team spirit, certainly one cannot work for Body Shop without an interest in environmental issues! Conversely, a person who has interests totally at variance with the team is unlikely to be able to find a place within it since he or she will be excluded from a large part of the group dynamic.

6 *Disposition* What requirements are there to get on with people, to use initiative, to work alone, to accept responsibility, to work under pressure, to be persistent, to influence others? This is increasingly being recognized as important when individuals are going to be working as part of a team. Some effort can be made to assess the team roles an individual would take, and to consider how they might fit in and what contribution they might make. Characteristics such as loyalty and reliability may be more suited to the role of a product manager than to a sales person who needs to be out-going and independent, self-motivated and confident.

7 *Circumstances* Often overlooked is the importance of the individual's circumstances. What domestic circumstances are relevant, e.g. daily travel from home to work, time spent away from home on business, partner's willingness and ability to support – perhaps to move home. Are children of school age, and what implications has this on flexibility? Is working overtime possible, if needed? On occasion a candidate will be so anxious to get the job that the hard facts of his or her circumstances may be ignored, or at least minimized. It is important to spend time to evaluate this key area.

EXTENDING ACTIVITY 5.1

Select a job, perhaps your own, or choose one that you are familiar with – perhaps the steward of your sports club or the coordinator of a local charity. Draw up a job description, job specification and personnel specification for the post. For your own job you should have a job description (or it should be easy to write), but you should not have seen either of the other documents. If your job description is out of date take this opportunity to rewrite it.

Compare your documents with the ones produced by your manager, if possible, or discuss them with a colleague to test if your perceptions and judgements the same? If not, how and why do they differ?

When next you have the opportunity to help select a person for a post ensure that you follow through the full procedure. It requires practice to develop the necessary skills.

Preparing for the interviews – I

This is the time to begin preparation for the interviews you will be having with those who you short-list.

- Produce an interview assessment from the personnel specification to provide a commonality to the evaluations of yourself and any others who are involved. An example of an generalized interview assessment for a junior post (Figure 5.7) shows the principle.
- Book times for the selection procedure (see below) in the diaries of all concerned.
- Reserve special accommodation, equipment, etc., as needed.

Note: We shall proceed on the basis of the first, long-list interview only. The same administrative and management procedures are followed for interviews with short-listed candidates.

Advertising and the use of agencies

We are not going to spend very much time on this aspect of the recruitment procedure since advertising is, after all, a major marketing activity; and marketers use agencies regularly. Suffice it to say that the concepts of positioning, segmentation and targeting apply just as much to recruitment as to any other form of advertising. The management of a recruitment agency is much the same as the management of an advertising agency. Their job is to translate your needs into short-listed candidates, and the better agencies are very good. Whether their cost is justified by your savings in resources, including time, is a management decision.

Advertising is one area where problems can arise with HRM. Many organizations have a recruitment budget which is administered by HRM. Therefore they control the advertising spend and, not being marketers, may not use it in the same way that you would. You can perhaps help by working with them to ensure that your recruitment does not suffer from adverts that are badly conceived, wrongly placed, or contain poor copy. The only solution is through internal marketing – remember that HRM are very experienced and their views should be sought and carefully evaluated.

Name: _____ **Position applied for:** _____ **Date:** _____

Factor		A	B	C +	C	D	E	Comments
PHYSICAL	Appearance							
	Speech							
	Health							
ATTAINMENTS	Education							
	Training							
	Experience							
	Motivation							
	General intelligence							
SPECIAL APTITUDES	Words							
	Figures							
	Mechanical							
	Creative							
	Other							
PERSONALITY	Friendly							
	Shy							
	Self-confident							
	Nervous							
	Relaxed							
	Enthusiastic							
	Interested							
OUTSIDE INTERESTS	Intellectual							
	Practical							
	Social							
	Physical							
CIRCUMSTANCES	Domestic ties							
	Mobility							
OVERALL IMPRESSION								

RECOMMENDATION: _____

Signed: _____

Figure 5.7 Interview assessment form

Applications

If your preliminary analysis has been carefully thought through your advertisement should have excluded most of those with contra-indicative features. If you are misguided enough to advertise 'Sales Representative wanted by major international company' you must live with the 5000 or so applications that flood your postal system and lock up a team of four for a fortnight! (Don't laugh – we know of one huge company who did just that!)

Assuming that you have either called for a detailed CV, or sent out a formal application form in answer to enquiries, you will have live applications on hand. You need to process these quickly – and that is where your work on the personnel specification begins to prove its worth. With detailed knowledge of your requirements the preliminary screening can be carried through by a junior to produce a long-list of possibles. From the long-list you, perhaps with the assistance of colleagues, can compile a short-list. Again relying on your detailed personnel specification.

It is good manners to respond to all applicants, but in these days of recession it is a luxury that many organizations feel they cannot afford. Before making a decision on purely economic grounds remember that the applicants are all individual consumers in the market place. Is the opportunity of creating a favourable impression to be lost?

Note the following key points:

1 *Security* These applicants hope to join your organization. As soon as one or more does they will be colleagues, and their personal details will be treated as confidential. It follows that applications are also confidential documents – but some managers allow them to be scattered around their office. Do not do this! As soon as applications are finished with they should be shredded, or at least thoroughly torn up and disposed of.

2 *Subjective exclusion* Beware the assistant who excludes on subjective grounds. Applicants have been thrown out for writing on coloured note paper, for using embossed paper, for misaddressing their letter, or for not using black ink! Make a random check through the rejected pile before accepting the long-list.

Inviting applicants for interview

Your letter to long-listed candidates will set the tone for their entire potential future with your organization. It must be written with care. Ensure that it contains more than the minimum information that the interviewee will need – this is your first real opportunity to establish an image for your organization and yourself.

Preparing for the interviews – 2

- *Administrative* With a specific number of applicants attending on given days it is necessary to confirm the administrative arrangements – Security has to be advised, and perhaps the staff restaurant. Accommodation for interviews and perhaps for a group session must be reserved. Make a note to confirm the arrangements the day before! Make up a folder for each person involved in the selection process. This should contain copies of:

  (a) The job description, the job specification and the personnel specification.
  (b) The interview assessment.
  (c) Each application and supporting paperwork.
  (d) The programme for the day.

- *Management* Make personal contact with the others who will be involved – perhaps a colleague and your line manager. Ensure they know the part they are to play, e.g. perhaps the boss is not needed until after lunch whilst you and your colleague will be closely involved throughout? Thorough briefing is the key to success. Determine which area(s) each person will concentrate on to ensure that each of the seven points are covered in depth and without repetition. Encourage each colleague to produce an interview checklist of the key areas to cover. This should include actual questions (word for word) in areas where specific response needs to be checked.

  Arrange to meet your colleagues 30 minutes ahead of the first applicant. Revise the procedure for the day and, in particular, show how the assessment form is to be used. Focus on exploring contra-indicative areas early. Have a clear understanding (a coded signal) which allows the interview to be brought to a polite but earlier conclusion than would otherwise have been the case.

- *The interview assessment* When a succession of candidates are seen over a period it is essential to record accurate views on each immediately after each part of the process. Never allow interviewers to rely on memory. The interview assessment allows each of your defined categories to be rated and a justification noted. This greatly facilitates the discussions that must take place at the end of the session as the short-list is constructed or the successful applicant is identified. Do not allow any sharing of views about candidates until after individual assessments have been recorded in writing.

  Note: On occasion you may have to see an individual candidate several days before or after the main group. Unless you have an interview assessment in writing it becomes impossible to cross-compare fairly.
- *Debriefing* Arrange a de-briefing to:

  (a) Short-list or reject candidates.
  (b) Make improvements to the recruitment and selection procedures.

Research has shown that interviewers are uncomfortable with a numerical six-point rating. They are also uncomfortable with a rating that runs from A to F. This is because the letter F has become associated with 'fail', and most people are reluctant to fail a keen applicant. A six-point rating is desirable – because there is no midpoint interviewers are forced to rate either positive or negative. Therefore a solution is to use A, B, C + , C, D and E as the rating points. (C- is also rejected by interviewers because of the negative implied by the minus sign.)

The job offer

A job offer should quickly follow the final interview, but it is often best not to send out letters of regret to the other candidates until the selected applicant has accepted. (It is then possible to make an offer to an alternative candidate, if that is judged appropriate.) The job offer must cover all the aspects of the employment, but will not be the formal contract. It is important to indicate when the formal document will be available because this provides much needed security to the about-to-be employee. As with the invitation to attend for interview, the job offer should be fully detailed and helpful.

Training programme

The training programme is a break down of the ASK factors required of a person if the job is to be done effectively. This is easiest to illustrate for a junior post, where there are fewer tasks and a need for a relatively unsophisticated level of understanding. However, exactly the same principles apply to all jobs, no matter how senior.

Source documents are the job description and the job specification, with the personnel specification providing guidance.

It is convenient to show the training programme, as an outline of need, alongside an abbreviated job description. A training programme for a Junior Sales Assistant is shown in Figure 5.8. You will notice that the headings in the training programme are quite broad. The intention is *not* to specify actual training sessions, rather it is to indicate the training areas as a guide to whoever is responsible for training.

Note: This is yet another case of a manager indicating need, but leaving it to a specialist to identify and carry through the necessary activities.

Job Definition	Training programme		
	Knowledge	**Skills**	**Attitudes**
SALES AND SERVICE Approach prospective customer Show range of goods Advise on size, colour, etc. Make sale and wrap or bag goods	Methods of address Stock Merchandise	Social, conversation Handling Selling, wrapping	Correct, friendly, helpful
MAINTAINING CORRECT STOCK LEVELS Return/order goods to/from stockroom Maintain correctly balanced stock levels Assist at stocktaking	Basic stock control Making out orders Reason – stock taking	 Arithmetic	Commitment to the need for stock control and accuracy
MONETARY AND CREDIT TRANSACTIONS Obtain and check till float Take cash and record on cash register Give change Handle credit cards Cash up – verify balance Arrange and record credit sales	Where obtainable Make-up method System System/authority	 Use of cash register Cash handling Accurate addition Arithmetic	Commitment Need for cash register security Source of responsibility
CONDITION AND DISPLAY OF MERCHANDISE Arrange displays Ensure correct ticketing Fixture merchandise neatly for best exhibition Return damaged/faulty stock to stockroom Repackage items for return to fixtures	Display techniques Fixture filling Basic stock control	Display Accuracy Wrapping	Commitment Need for care Tidiness
EQUIPMENT Clean fixtures, counters, etc. Report broken equipment to maintenance department	Care of equipment Procedure		Willingness
AUTHORITY Exchange goods up to value of £5	Limits of authority		

Figure 5.8   Training programme for a junior sales assistant

The training plan

The training plan (Figure 5.9) is a summary of training carried out, and needed. The sources of information for training plans are:

- Training programmes and job specifications
- Appraisals and informal evaluations (see Unit 6).
- Job applications and selection interviews.

The most effective training plans are simple matrices, which can extend to wall-chart size if necessary.

Hint: It is best to work with small teams, or sections, within a department and then to consolidate, if necessary, into a departmental summary. The prime purpose is to produce a working document of relevance to individuals, not an overall summary – although that is very useful for budgetary and control purposes.

A training plan is completed in five stages (Figure 5.10):

1 Enter the names of those in the section in the vertical column to the left.
2 Extract the tasks which comprise the jobs in the section from the job specifications of those in the section and enter them along the top of the matrix.
3 Indicate how many of the team are needed to carry out each task. Only in some cases will everybody need to be able to do everything!

Section: _____

Department: _____

Names of personnel																Notes
Actual capacity																
Ideal capacity																
Variance																

Figure 5.9 Training plan

Section: Small Electrical

Department: Kitchen

Names of personnel	Induction	Approach customer	Show range	Advise customer	Make sale	Wrap goods			Cash up	Authorize credit cards	Authorize exchanges			etc.		Notes
Tina Brown	×	×	×	×	×	×			×	×	×					
Rashid Khan	×	×	×	×	×	×										
Monica Jackson	×	×	/	/	/	×			×	×	/					
Nasser Houssain	×	×	×	×	/	×										
Jackie King	×	×	×	×	×	×										
Brenda Long	×	×	/	/	/	/										
Actual capacity	6	6	4	4	3	5			2	2	1					
Ideal capacity	6	6	6	6	6	6			1	2	2					
Variance	0	0	−2	−2	−3	−1			+ 1	0	−1					

Figure 5.10 A completed training plan

4 Indicate with a tick which individuals should be able to carry out which tasks. Any shortfall against the needed number indicates a priority for either training or recruitment.

5 Cross through the ticks against each individual for the tasks where they are competent. Total the crosses and the training priorities are identified. Also, on occasion, an over-trained situation is revealed.

The training plan is an on-going action document. Once the basic programme has been completed (as above) it should be developed and refined:

- Instead of using ticks and crosses an evaluation of competence can be inserted on a scale of A (excellent) to E (basic).
- Using a slightly larger matrix the planned dates for training can be entered.
- Provision can be made for forecast staff shortages, i.e. if a member of staff is known to be leaving the shortfall will be obvious and training can be put in hand ahead of need.

When an effectively organized system of training is in place it encourages management to think forward and to introduce contingency planning to the personnel area. It also allows individuals to question when next they are to be trained, and to understand what longer term plans management has for them.

The introduction of training and appraisal is a long-term commitment by management. It is far more effective if training plans are open documents. When posted on the notice board individual staff members are able to check progress – and this public commitment forces management to continue training and to update the records regularly. It is therefore a serious long-term decision of investment in staff development.

Note: BACIE produce a master schedule for a full training budget which is based on this simple principle, but extended to allow a training budget to be managed.

Note: A development plan is an extended version of a training plan, but is broader in its vision of how development may be facilitated. Normally it is a separate document since the training plan provides for all the basic needs, which are usually completed first.

Induction training

Everybody needs some form of introduction to the organization and the job. The fastest way is through an induction package which covers all the basic knowledge required. Often this is supplemented with a Staff Handbook which amplifies and extends the material covered in the course.

A well-planned system of induction provides regular training sessions – if the organization is big enough. Large department stores, for example, have a continuing programme of induction with a new course starting every Monday – and special provision for part-time workers. Given that the basics are covered, professionally, it leaves individual managers in the comfortable position of receiving partly familiarized staff who are ready to receive training that is specific to their job.

Be sure to determine the impression you want to make on the examiner. Then practise the skills of answering so that you actually do convey a credibility in all your marketing exams. Use your examination answer book as a vehicle to demonstrate your attitude, knowledge, skills – and your credibility.

These are typical of approaches taken by failing candidates:

Characteristic	*Impression given to the examiner*
• Untidy presentation, difficult to read.	Careless, unprepared, unconcerned with the examiner's feelings.
• Scribbled and/or many liquid paper corrections.	Grossly unprepared. No planning, and no consideration of the effect on the reader. Absolutely no credibility.
• Last question unfinished.	Poor time manager. i.e. poor manager.
• Inappropriate tone or style for the specified role.	Inability to tailor approach (to market) to meet needs of identified audience.
• Lack of examples and/or absence of illustrations.	Careless – did not read the question and/or no practical experience outside study materials
• Unstructured, ad hoc.	Careless – did not plan and/or no understanding of the question and/or no ability to answer.
• No underpinning theory or knowledge.	Did not read the question and/or did no serious study.
• No decisions or recommendations when called for.	Did not read the question and/or avoids making decisions (which equates to a lack of credibility).

Take 10 minutes to complete this list:

The impression I want to give   *How to give it*

_____   _____

_____   _____

_____   _____

_____   _____

_____   _____

Invitation to interview

Draft a letter inviting a successful applicant to attend for an interview on a given date. Ensure that you give the applicant all the information he or she will need to succeed.

(**See** Debriefing at the end of this unit.)

John Adair: the UK's first professor in Leadership Studies

John Adair has devoted his life to a study of leadership and was largely responsible for the functional leadership approach adopted by the Royal Military Academy at Sandhurst. He is also, virtually single-handedly, responsible for today's understanding that management and administration are support functions. That the abilities of the manager-leader are required if an organization is to achieve its full potential.

His first book, *Training for Leadership*, was mainly about the leadership training at Sandhurst. His second, *Action Centred Leadership* was written, with contributors, to show how the Sandhurst training had been adapted for use in industry. His third, *Developing Leaders*, primarily addresses those involved in the education and training of managers and young people.

He worked with ICI from 1981 to help them develop 'manager-leaders'. In 1986 they became the first British company to make a billion pounds profit. The ICI experience has allowed Adair to refine his principles and present them to a wider audience.

One of Adair's central themes is that developing leaders is a line management responsibility, and that each chief executive should give a lead – by word and example. As Adair says 'No strategy, however right, will be implemented by an organization that lacks leadership at the top'.

He stresses that the paths of management and leadership development will run parallel for most of a career journey, especially in the middle stages. But he argues that the concept of leadership development has to be retained because it is wider and deeper than the concept of management development – and is not dull and boring. Leadership development, he says, 'is not free from jargon, but the language is so straightforward that any chief executive or line manager can grasp the principles and relate them to the strategic future of the enterprise'. Adair quotes one Chief Executive as saying 'Developing leaders is far too important to be left to the personnel department'.

Adair's views on the importance of leadership can be summed up in his phrase 'A business short on capital can borrow money, but a business short on leadership has little chance of survival'.

Key publications:
Effective Leadership, 1983
Developing Leaders, 1988

SUMMARY

In this Unit we have seen that:

- An 'instrument' has to be used with care as a management tool to achieve a specific purpose.
- An effective team has cohesion.
- Subgroups can exist, with their own priorities.
- The extended team is of key importance.
- Individuals are vitally important.
- A team is composed of individuals, each motivated to contribute.
- Teams form, norm, storm and then perform.
- Today's need is for manager–leaders.
- Group dynamics are of constant concern to the manager.
- Managers need to become people watchers.
- Recruitment and selection follow a clearly defined process.
- Recruitment adverts can be specific enough that they effectively short-list applicants.
- The personnel specification provides the key to effective selection.
- Preparation for interviews is of key importance.
- It is necessary to assess each candidate immediately after their interview(s).
- Training programmes allow structured and planned training of individuals.
- Development plans are extensions of training plans.

Debriefing

Activity 5.1

The key interests may be:

County players:
- Require use of the best courts for matches with other clubs.
- Require entertainment facilities in the pavilion for visiting teams.
- Do not want to lower their standards by playing with social members of the club.
- Think that beginners should not be admitted to the club.

Social members:
- Believe that all members should be obligated to play with all others.
- Want to improve by playing with better opponents.
- Want specific times set aside for social play.
- Want court priority given to club tournaments and specific playing times when the courts are free for use by all.

Beginners:
- Want equality as members.
- Need to improve by playing with and against better players who will be helpful.
- Need to feel welcome.

Tennis as a whole want:
- Funds priority given to court improvement.
- Courts (i.e. tennis players) protected from hard hit cricket balls.
- Cricketers and their opponents to move into the large meeting room and away from the bar for their social activities after matches.

It is immediately obvious – even from these superficial points – that the main groups within the overall group that is the club have different priorities. There will be much internal politicking, and the Club Officers and the General Committee will have major problems in attempting to reconcile the differing priorities. The club will, of course, immediately unite in a common cause such as obtaining planning permission to extend the pavilion or to secure a right-of-way.

Activity 5.2

Firstly, ask if there is still a purpose for the group? Should it be closed whilst on top of its success? Too often groups form, become established, and then fit snugly into a routine. Their purpose diminishes, they are like a product at the end of the PLC maturity stage – heading for decline.

If the group has a role to play then there are many things which management can do.

Problem	*Actions*
• Motivation of the challenge to succeed is diminished	Challenge is a powerful motivator – and is often a major influence in the forming and storming phases. The need is to acknowledge success (motivational) and to introduce fresh challenges – extend the project, amend the terms of reference.
• Complacency develops.	Too late once it is firmly embedded! The need is to shake up the group by indirect means, if possible. A comparative table of achievements of all groups may show the top group that they are slipping. Convening a meeting of team leaders to share views can be useful in itself, and can also stimulate individuals.
• Routine sets in	The need is to break the pattern. Possibly this factor has much to do with the familiarity/friendship issue.

- Familiarity/friendship deters challenges

Members of a fully active group want views to be justified. As friendship grows so may an aura of mutual self-protection – 'I won't challenge you if you don't challenge me'. There is need to change the composition of the team. Perhaps even to reconstruct it around new terms of reference that may be virtually identical. This reconstruction would allow old members to withdraw with high status. It would be excellent for morale since the new team would be in place and the old members would cheerfully accept redeployment.

Self-check 5.1

1 Attitude, skills and knowledge interlink. Without an appropriate attitude there is no motivation to learn and therefore, at best, limited knowledge and skills. Alternatively a highly knowledgeable and skilled person can withhold quality and/or quantity.

2 *For sub-groups*
- Support each other.
- Are loose, open, friendly.
- Develop individuals.
- Prioritize on group objectives.

Against sub-groups
- Pull against each other.
- Are closed, restrictive, secretive.
- Force conformity.
- Prioritize on subgroup objectives.

Subgroups unite against a common foe – but do not change their basic character and revert to normal when the danger has passed.

3 Security, guidance, clarity, confidence, protection, leadership.

4 Forming, norming, storming, performing – Managers have to use their people skills to help groups pass through these stages as expeditiously as is appropriate. Groups tend to vary in their need to spend a length of time at (or in) each stage.

5 Your three circle diagrams should be quite different. Perhaps one shows a disregard for the individual, with a total focus on the task? You may have drawn the circles at different sizes to indicate importance as well as relationship. If so, excellent. This is an open-ended, creative model. Use it dynamically to focus your thinking.

Now: Run the same exercise on yourself and, when you have the confidence, ask others who know you well to assess your leadership style. It is the only way to improve!

Activity 5.3

Your observation form should identify the key issues, and then provide for some form of grading and comment. The following is a typical observer's form – in this case for the evaluation of a speaker. (See illustration on page 123).

Activity 5.4

Job descriptions vary in style – which is not important. The contents are vital, however, and should include as a minimum:

- The title of the job.
- The main purpose of the job.
- Name of the department or team of which the post is a part.
- For whom the job-holder works – to whom he or she is responsible.
- What, exactly, the job holder has to do.
- Responsibilities – titles of other people or details of equipment the post holder is responsible for.
- Limits of authority – e.g. budget limits, negotiating freedom.
- Levels of contact – particularly important when working with external clients or subsidiaries, etc.

Job descriptions can extend to include how performance will be measured. Candidates, the person appointed, the responsible manager and HRM will certainly need this information. Better to deal with it as the job description is drafted than try to develop it later around an existing job description.

	Grading						Comment
	1	2	3	4	5	6	(1, Poor – 6, Excellent)
Appearance							
Movement							
Posture							
Voice Clarity/volume							
Voice Tone/stress							
Gestures							
Habits Vocal							
Habits Body							
Overall impression							

Overall comments: _____

_____

_____

Activity 5.5

These are generalized, almost cliché factors as examples. Using your job descriptions determine which factors would definitely exclude any applicant for each of the jobs.

Post	*Contra-indicative factors*
• Steeplejack.	Fear of heights.
• Delivery driver.	'Dirty' driving licence.
• Submariner.	Claustrophobia.
• Team member.	An introvert, a loner.
• Manager.	Indecisiveness.

Unit activity – Invitation to interview

Your letter should be written with a warmth appropriate to the success of getting on to the long-list. It should contain:

- An invitation to attend at a specific place at a specific time.
- A request for confirmation by telephone or in writing to a named person.
- A programme covering the selection process.
  - The form of first contact – interview, discussion, series of interviews, etc.
  - Any special expectations – bring evidence of qualifications, be prepared to make a presentation on a specific subject, operate a specified computer, etc.
  - The time they can expect to leave.
  - What short-listing is expected, and when the interviews are likely to happen.
  - When they can expect to hear how successful they have been.
- Information on what expenses they can claim, and when they will be paid.
- An offer to book hotel accommodation if needed.
- A named contact they should liaise with if in need of further information.

Techniques and tools for team building

In this unit you will:

- Examine the role of the manager–leader.
- Investigate the importance of motivation to individuals and teams.
- Be aware of the differences between motivation and incentive.
- Examine methods of monitoring and managing team performance.
- Understand the importance of appraisal.
- Be aware of the concepts of job enlargement and job enrichment.

By the end of this unit you will be able to:

- Operate as a manager, a leader and a team member.
- Determine appropriate ways to motivate and provide incentives.
- Recommend methods of monitoring team performance.
- Prepare for a formal appraisal by your manager.
- Carry through a formal appraisal with a member of your team.
- Plan and manage increased job satisfaction for members of your team.

Managers achieve results through people, and happy people work more effectively, more efficiently, and have less time off through illness. A happy team has a low staff turnover and often a waiting list of those wanting to join. We have mentioned Star Trek before, but it is a salutary lesson to note how concerned John-Luc Picard, as captain, is for his people – how much time and effort he devotes to their welfare and how little to the day-to-day operations of the ship. There is a waiting list of Star Fleet personnel who want to work for the best captain in the fleet. This situation is fictional, but exactly parallels what happens in the real world.

The teams which succeed best are those where the managers are leaders. A manager exists to achieve results through people. This means a concern (as Adair has shown) with three aspects: the individuals who make up the team, the team itself, and the task to be achieved. The managers who achieve the most – and have the most fun doing so – are those who realize that sometimes they are better employed fetching tea and coffee whilst their people get on with the job.

Your examiners will be looking for evidence that you understand that management is not about the three Ds of dominance, dictatorship and directives. You need to show through practical examples that you not only appreciate the theory of manager–leadership, but have actually put it into practice. This is not difficult for anyone to do because we are all involved with some form of team even if it is not a formalized working group.

As we have said before – and doubtless will emphasize again – a good manager (a good marketer) must be a people watcher. There is a need to automatically monitor *and learn from* actions and responses that take place in the wider environment as well as within the narrower workplace. There is need to monitor one's own reactions to others, especially the reactions to those who have any form of power over our actions and/or desires.

STUDY TIPS

You are embarked on a journey which is leading you to an important management qualification. Doubtless it will be hard going at times. What will keep you going will be determination – but isn't it easier to be determined when there is a short-term purpose, and especially when there are short-term rewards?

It will help your study if you plan short-term rewards for yourself. These can be as simple as allowing an ice cream after dinner *only if* you complete an assignment in time to catch the post. Or by awarding yourself an extra 15 minutes in bed *only if* your assignment comes back from your tutor with a pass grade. Do you think that it would be as effective if you planned to punish yourself by getting up 15 minutes earlier if the assignment doesn't make the grade?

These short-term incentives are nowhere near as important as the long-term motivation of achieving your Advanced Certificate in Marketing. And is this more or less motivational than the Diploma which will still be a year away?

Are you pleased when someone – anyone! – comments on your work? If so, do you set up opportunities to receive praise? Do you involve your family, your friends, your work colleagues? Do you show them what you are doing? Do you stand there a little embarrassed, but secretly pleased, when someone extols your virtues? Are you letting modesty get in the way of the praise that you are due? Or are you secretly frightened that your work may not be good enough – that somebody might be critical or, worse, laugh?

All of these emotions are typically shared by the vast majority of the human race. Come to terms with them as soon as you can because until you do they will hold you back from achieving your full potential.

Examiners also need to be motivated – they have to pick up answer book after book after book. It can become extremely boring! If your answer book helps the examiner to break free from the routine of marking routine answers it must be an advantage. Remember that marketers are expected to have USPs and to present their material effectively.

Explanations and definitions

1 *Aggressive* Implying hostility, aggressive behaviour is often interpreted as a personal attack. It can be hurtful, even though no hurt is intended. Its opposite is defensive behaviour, where individuals feel compelled to protect themselves even where there is no need.

2 *Appraisal* The formalized evaluation of an individual within an organization in terms of his or her performance, personal needs and career development. The overall benefit of an appraisal scheme to an organization is improved morale, lower staff turnover and higher performance.

3 *Assertive* This is recognized as a desirable alternative to aggressive behaviour. It is the confidence to say what one feels and to communicate personal views clearly to others. In interpersonal relations it may be difficult to be assertive without seeming aggressive and many people benefit from specific training to help them develop the needed skills.

4 *Assessment* A judgement of performance against a set of criteria.

5 *Incentive* An incentive is a motive for acting in a certain way. An incentive adds a further motive, usually extrinsic, to a motive already operating (*Dictionary of Psychology*).

6 *Interview* An interview is best thought of as a conversation with an objective.

7 *Job enlargement* Widening a job to take in more elements. Very similar to *Horizontal job enrichment* (see below). Has been said by Herzberg to 'merely add to the meaninglessness of a job'.

8 *Job enrichment* Vertical job enrichment increases an individual's involvement in an organization and/or a job by giving him or her greater opportunities for achievement and recognition. Often an element of 'job closure' is involved whereby an individual can see a task through to conclusion.

9 *Horizontal job enrichment* See *Job enlargement*.

10 *Job satisfaction* This is a 'portmanteau' phrase that actually is meaningless in itself. Job satisfaction, like 'improved communications' can only be achieved by a combination of factors that – together – amount to satisfaction for those engaged in the job i.e. job satisfaction is perceived to exist by those who are employed in the work, it is a behavioural response to a range of circumstances.

11 *Leadership* To guide, show the way, to hold a group together.

12 *Motive* A motive is a reason to move. More correctly defined as: 'An affective–conative factor which operates in determining the direction of an individual's behaviour towards an end or goal, consciously apprehended, or unconscious' (*Dictionary of Psychology*).

13 *Status* This is a perceived state that is understood by members of the grouping within which the status is recognized. It may be as definite and institutionalized as in the caste system of India, or as amorphous and transitory as some top performers in the pop scene.

Leadership or management?

A common view seems to be that leaders are born, but managers can be trained. This view is typified by the comment in a manager's appraisal – *Smith is not yet a born leader.*

Leadership, in this instinctive sense, does appear stronger in some rather than in others, but the same can be said of every other 'God given talent'. The brilliant concert violinist has abilities above those of professional orchestra players, members of amateur orchestras, and those who play for their own enjoyment. But nobody would claim that all violinists are born and not made. Nobody would claim that a violinist's skills cannot be improved with training and practice. So it is with leadership. Deep down we all have at least a flicker of leadership talent, in some it is more developed, and for some it is a more desirable quality to foster. But it is nonsense to say that being born with the skill is the only way to acquire it.

Leadership/Management – which is the subset of the other?

Two qualities tend to identify the leader:

- Enabling the group to fulfil its mission.
- Holding the group together as a working entity.

Leaders normally have to show the qualities required (or expected) by the working groups. A medical leader, for example, would show clinical and caring qualities, a builder must not be frightened to climb a ladder. But a leader does not need to be able to do every job in the team. He or she must know what needs to be done, and have a clear idea of possible techniques and solutions – but his or her skills are in the process of leading, not in the process of direct task achievement.

British army officers of 1914 went into battle armed only with walking sticks. Their job was not to fight, it was to lead – to motivate and provide incentives. The same principle holds today – but, by 1916, officers were dressed and equipped as their men because they were otherwise singled out as priority targets.

Derivations

- 'Lead' comes from the old North European *laed*. It means a road, a path, the course of a ship at sea, a journey. A leader accompanies people on a journey, holding them together whilst leading them in the right direction.

- 'Manager' entered the English language in the sixteenth century. The root is *manus*, a hand, which led to the Italian verb for handling, or 'managing', a war horse.

The British military adopted the terms 'manager' and 'management' to describe the handling of armies in the field, it extended to cover the handling of swords and of ships. In other words, 'management' was adopted in areas where a strict hierarchy and a rigid code of discipline were needed.

Merchants in the eighteenth and nineteenth centuries borrowed the term from the military and used 'manager' and 'under-manager' to describe those who had day-to-day responsibility for the efficient operation of their concerns. Strategic control, and therefore leadership and direction, was held by the owners – as Directors of the enterprise. It follows that the current understanding of management is shaped by misconceptions that have developed over some 200 years.

Managers, in the nineteenth century, were focused upon objectives to be achieved rather than upon *processes*.

Scientific management

Given the implicit understanding that managers 'handle' people within a disciplinary context it is not surprising that much time and effort were put into the development of 'scientific management' theories. Scientific management required systems of cost-keeping, time studies, functional foremanship and efficiency systems. (All centred upon achieving objectives; not upon processes.)

Scientific management was developed with two major objectives:

- To increase the output of the average worker.
- To improve the efficiency of management.

Those working to develop scientific management took as premises that managers manage, that workers work, that there is a divide; that efficiency is all; and that mass production techniques require manpower to be subservient to machines.

Frederick Winslow Taylor, in 1912, eliminated many of the by then accepted theories. His view was that a 'complete mental revolution' was necessary in both the workers' minds as well as the mind of management. Taylor believed that workers restricted output through a fear of displacement. He believed they should be educated to see that their economic salvation lay in producing more at lower cost – as a proof of his contention he believed that workers should be placed on piecework.

Taylor's principles of scientific management
- Management must gather, analyse and codify all existing rule-of-thumb data pertaining to the business in order to develop a science.
- Workers must be carefully selected and thoroughly studied so that each one may be developed to maximum capabilities.
- Workers must be inspired or trained to use the scientific methods developed as a result of analysing and codifying rule-of-thumb data.
- Management must organize in such a manner that it can properly manage and carry out its duties.

Taylor and his contemporaries were concerned with organization, efficiency and objectives. People were seen as necessary, but controllable; motivated by fear of loss of work, subservient to the machines that made mass production possible.

The view today is very different . . .

Business is about leadership; it requires understanding, courage, single mindedness, drive and an ability to persuade and lead others. To manage change one often needs to change managers – particularly managers who fail to involve their people and to secure their full commitment.
(Sir Michael Edwardes)

Leadership is getting extraordinary performance out of ordinary people (Sir John Harvey-Jones)

Your position never gives you the right to command. It only imposes on you the duty of so living your life that others may receive your orders without being humiliated. (Dag Hammarsksjold)

Human aspects of management

Robert Owen, found that mechanical equipment in his textile mill more than repaid the costs of maintenance, through increases in productivity and a longer working life. He reasoned that if this were true for 'inanimate machines' it should also be true for 'vital machines'. He applied his thinking to the personnel in his mills and claimed a more than 50% return on the money spent.

George Mayo and his team of Harvard researchers, worked in the 1920s to solve industrial problems in the USA. He is most famous for the *Hawthorne study*. Working with a group of manual workers he made significant changes to their working conditions and on each change achieved an increase in productivity. There was even an increase when conditions were changed back to exactly what they were at the beginning of the experiment. Importantly, there were also improvements within the control group where no changes were introduced.

Mayo's work points to the fact that people respond to attention being paid to them. Even the control group responded because they were singled out for attention – although this was passive attention. This was the beginning of our understanding that people respond to the social and psychological aspects of a situation. This has become known as the *Hawthorne effect*.

Mayo's work is a key to our understanding of human relations because the importance of attitudes to work, to management, and to the work group is now recognized as significant.

Leadership

> *But of a good leader, who talks little,*
> *When his work is done, his aim fulfilled,*
> *They will all say, 'We did this ourselves'.*
> (Lao-Tzu, sixth century BC)

Authority or rank confers leadership as of right – but it may be ineffective leadership unless the incumbent is capable of offering the leadership skills necessary to achieve the task and maintain group integrity.

Personality is of key importance. Leaders must have the necessary personal skills to influence and carry a group. Without the ability to motivate, a leader is forced to give management orders.

The situational theory of leadership emphasizes the authority of knowledge. A situation will bring out the leader best suited to handle it. Thus leadership can move within a group as circumstances change. This does not mean that overall command of a group shifts. It simply (and importantly) means that the one best suited to the current task should provide task-centred leadership. (For example, it would be foolish for a foreman with no first aid training to attempt to assist an injured colleague when there is a qualified first-aider in the team.)

Action centred leadership

We briefly met Professor John Adair's work in Unit 5. He has studied and written upon the subject for over 30 years and his Action Centred Leadership model has been widely adopted as a basis for modern day management/leadership training. The three circles of the model are conceptual in nature, but very easy to work with because individuals empathize with it without difficulty. A poor leader may have three separate circles that do not touch at all; a good one will have a considerable overlap.

As a consultancy instrument the Adair model can be extremely effective in analysing group dynamics. Individuals grasp the principle of the model very quickly and can then use it to express their view of the effectiveness of the group. The validity of the concept in use is proven by the similarity of models which are drawn independently by members of the group.

Once their views are committed to paper in a simple-to-draw diagram individuals find it easier to express their reasoning: 'I drew this circle large, and out here, because the manager has got no interest in us as a group. I mean to say, only yesterday he . . .'.

Functions and effectiveness

Adair sees a need to concentrate upon leadership functions and relate them to the factors that make up leadership effectiveness (Table 6.1). As you can see the functions could almost be applied to any manager. What distinguishes a manager–leader is the ability to be *effective* in the functional areas and this requires a sensitivity to and concern for people.

Table 6.1 Leadership functions and effectiveness

Functions	*Functional effectiveness*
Planning Seeking all available information. Defining group task, purpose, goal. Making a workable plan (in right decision-making framework)	*Defining task* Correctly specifies what needs to be accomplished and breaks this down into its discrete parts
Initiating Briefing group on the aims and the plan. Explaining why the plan is necessary. Allocating tasks to group members. Setting group standards	*Planning* Formulates an effective method for achieving the task(s), i.e. organizes people, materials, time and resources in such a way that the objective(s) can be met
Controlling Maintaining group standards. Influencing tempo. Ensuring all actions are taken towards objectives. Prodding group to take action	*Briefing* Allocates tasks and resources to subordinates in such a way that each person: (a) knows what is expected of him or her, and (b) understands the importance of their contribution
Supporting Expressing acceptance of persons and their contribution. Encouraging group/individuals. Disciplining group/individuals. Creating team spirit. Reconciling disagreements or getting others to explore them	*Controlling* Keeps things running to plan. Is sensitive to problems and delays and is quick to respond to them. Coordinates the work of the team
Informing Clarifying task and plan. Giving new information to the group, i.e. keeping them 'in the picture'. Receiving information from the group. Summarizing suggestions and ideas coherently	*Evaluating* Makes accurate and insightful judgements about proposals, past performance and people *Motivating* Creates and maintains the team's commitment to, and interest in, the task *Organizing* Creates a structure and hierarchy appropriate to the task
Evaluating Checking feasibility of an idea. Testing the consequences of a proposed solution. Evaluating group performance. Helping the group to evaluate its own performance.	*Setting an example* Exemplifies the value and behaviour he or she wishes to see in others *Supporting* Encourages group/individuals; builds and maintains good team spirit

Adair suggests that we should learn from the behaviour of successful leaders from history. On examining the total character it should be possible to deduce the key elements that made them successful. Other writers have followed this lead and have identified the key abilities of successful leadership:

ACTIVITY 6.1

Successful leadership

Take 20 minutes to consider leaders that you know personally, or who you have read about. Identify the key abilities that most seem to have in common.

(**See** Debriefing at the end of this unit.)

Manager or leader – does it matter ?

Leadership and management are both conceptual in nature. Each individual will lead and/ or manage in their own style. To an extent it does not matter what title a person has, many 'managers' through the ages have been extremely effective leaders. Many designated 'leaders' have been useless at both leadership and management.

It does seem, however, that leadership is a concept that has more value in today's business world than management, especially management in an administrative, organizational sense. Given that management is deciding what should be done, and then getting other people to do it there is a definite need for all managers to develop leadership skills.

Philip Sadler classifies managers along a continuum (Figure 6.1) leading from 'telling' to 'joining'. There are four main styles on the continuum, but individuals can place themselves where they feel most comfortable. There is no requirement to be defined as having one set style, although it is normal for managers to fit themselves in between the two which most closely resemble how they think they operate. It can be very instructive to ask members of a group to evaluate their manager–leader on the same continuum. This is instructive, but possibly dangerous to the ego of the manager, so always be very careful with subjective instruments of this type.

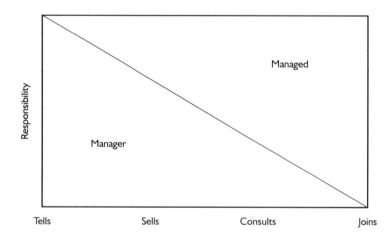

Figure 6.1 Sadler's continuum

Styles	Actions
Tells	The manager makes the decisions, announces them, and then directs staff to carry them out.
Sells	After making the decisions the manager will try to persuade staff of their rightness shortly before implementation or even as they are being implemented.
Consults	Problem is presented to staff, advice listened to, suggestions considered. Then the manager decides and implements the decision.
Joins	Also known as 'abdication' because the manager joins with the team to make the decision and abides by the consensus view.

Sadler's research shows that the 'consults' style is preferred by most employees. 'Tells' and 'sells' are too authoritarian, and 'joins' abdicates responsibility.

Consider which management style is likely to be of most value to a marketer. Surely it has to be 'consults', because marketers should have developed advanced listening and summarizing skills to help them communicate effectively with customers.

The continuum approach to management style has been found to hold value by many researchers. A typical example of a development to Sadler's work is in identifying the relationship between leadership activity and group response (Figure 6.2).

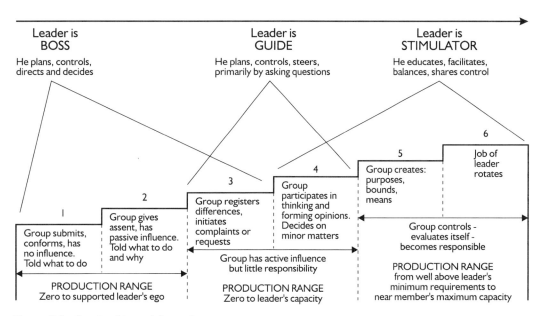

Figure 6.2 Leadership activity and group response

The leadership activity

In a 1980s study of British manager–leadership, *Deloitte, Haskins and Sells* developed a model which underpins the importance attached to the interpersonal, communicative role of the leader (Figure 6.3).

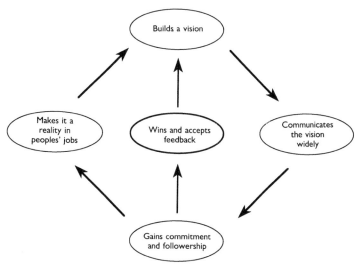

Figure 6.3 The activities of a leader

The use of terms such as 'vision' is deliberate because their view is that a leader needs in some degree to be charismatic – to hold a firm belief in the value of what has to be done, and to communicate his or her commitment to the team.

The actual manager–leader style matters less than the fact that a person is aware of the style that he or she is perceived to have. Two things become possible once that awareness is achieved:

- Matters can be put in hand to effect change, if this is desired.
- The manager–leader knows the reaction to expect from his team, and will act accordingly.

The most confused managers are those who have not come to grips with how they are perceived to act as compared to how they believe they act. Thus they tend to constantly receive responses that are at variance with what they expect.

Blake and Moulton developed their managerial grid to assist in the classification of managers on two important dimensions: their concern for people, and for production (Figure 6.4). Having worked through the supporting questionnaire it is possible for managers to self-classify themselves. **Note**: This, in itself, is of little value. As with the majority of management instruments the value lies in the results they stimulate. Classification on the grid is the first step of six:

- Classify self on grid.
- Evaluate the significance of the indicated position.
- Determine the grid position which would be more appropriate (desirable) to your personal needs.
- Set clear objectives for the needed behaviour change. Probably with sub-objectives so you can move in stages over time.
- Locate and arrange the necessary training, education and experience using the ASK headings.
- Evaluate achievement against need and intention until end objective is reached.

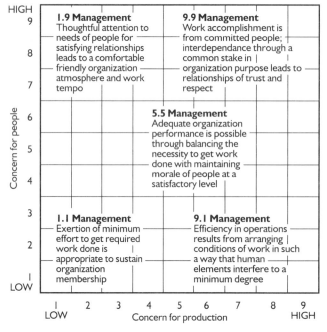

Figure 6.4 Managerial grid (from Robert R. Blake and Jane S. Moulton, Grid Organisation Management, *Personnel Administration*)

Note: Throughout this workbook, and especially from here onwards, we use the term 'manager' in place of the cumbersome 'manager–leader'. You should automatically think of the importance of the leadership dimension whenever management is mentioned, not only within this book, but in your everyday life.

Team membership

Being the leader of a team is one thing – achieving success as a team member is another. As a manager in today's increasingly team-focused organizations, the need is to be able to adopt a variety of roles that are applicable to each of the teams within which an individual will work.

The characteristics of successful teams are:

- Goal centred commitment.
- Results are recognized and appreciated.
- Standards are high.
- Skills base is competent and meets team needs.
- Leadership is fair.
- Leader has integrity.

Evenden and Anderson say that their work with teams has shown the following as the behavioural characteristics most important to members of a successful team:

- *Goal directed* – behaves and influences in a purposive way.
- *Enthusiastic* – shows interest and commitment.
- *Assertive* – pursues own needs, but not aggressively at the expense of others.
- *Competent* – has technical and social skills.
- *Open* – expresses feelings and conflict, so they can be dealt with.
- *Flexible* – demonstrates capacity to change and experiment.
- *Supportive* – displays helpful and friendly behaviour.
- *Constructive* – looks to build rather than destroy.
- *Leadership* – leads and accepts leadership with high standards and consensus decisions.

Team membership
Consider what the requirements of a good team member are within an organization that you know well. Write a brief description (about 70 words) that sums up how an experienced leader should modify his or her behaviour so as to become an effective team member.

(**See** Debriefing at the end of this unit.)

Motivation

A motive is a reason to move. More correctly a motive is defined as:

> An affective–conative factor which operates in determining the direction of an individual's behaviour towards an end or goal, consciously apprehended, or unconscious. (*Dictionary of Psychology*)

Thus motivation comes into play after the general (cognitive) area of knowledge has sifted the data (see below).

Incentives are defined as 'a motive for acting in a certain way' and can be linked to existing motives in order to strengthen them. Marketers will understand that sales promotion techniques are a way of adding incentive at point of sale. They work best when they link with customer's intrinsic, often unconscious needs. The same principle applies in management.

What does this mean to a manager?

Humans are goal driven, and act to reduce tension. It follows that:

- Tension(s) need to be identified.
- Tension reducing solutions should be created in the form of incentives.

Managers should appreciate the need to link incentives with the motivations of individuals within their team. Many tensions are associated with self-image, which is of considerable importance to human behaviour.

Self-image

In fulfilling our need to fit within society we are driven by five self-images (Figure 6.5).

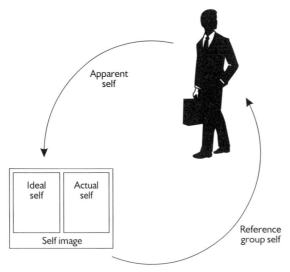

Figure 6.5   The five images of self

- *Apparent self*   As we appear to others. It is a composite of the other images, which we hold confidential to ourselves.
- *Reference group self*   The self we would like to emulate. Based on our perception of correct behaviour within the social groups and/or positions with which we wish to associate, or join. We may modify our behaviour in order to amend our apparent self.
- *Internal self-image*   A balance of two elements:
  - (a) Ideal Self – The best possible representation of our personality and desires.
  - (b) Real Self – our very private and most distressing self, comprising our most pessimistic view of ourselves.

Self-image has a major effect on individual achievement. It is a factor on which sports coaches work hard when helping their athletes to develop a certainty in their ability to win. – 'Show me a good loser and I'll show you a loser!'

It is very difficult to achieve a balanced self-image given the complexity of human nature and the number, nature and variety of our interrelationships. Meeting new successes and failures every day, it is no surprise to discover that we respond to kindness and, in particular, to praise. With an internal complexity in constant flux it follows that tension reduction is a major motivator.

Praise

The receipt of praise has a major motivational effect and is an incentive that need cost nothing except a little time. Yet it is a peculiar fact that many find it hard to give praise although they welcome it personally. Managers are in the privileged position of being able to give or withhold praise, to recommend a person for promotion – or to block them. Which they choose to do will have major repercussions on the effectiveness of their teams.

There is also the question of how to deliver praise. Many give it grudgingly – and ruin everything they are trying to achieve. We all know the kick-in-the-stomach feeling that comes when after praise we hear the dreaded word 'but'. As in 'That was very good, but if you had . . .' Other destroyers masquerading as motivators are:

- 'Well done – but did you think about so-and-so as well?'
- 'I liked that *very* much, except for . . .'.
- 'That's good, shame about the . . .'.

When developing a person it is a major effort, but one well worth making, to deny yourself any form of criticism. Yes! It can be done!

If you confine yourself to looking for and only commenting on the good points you will find it difficult at first. There are always plenty of errors that are easy to single out – but it is all too easy to destroy. Any fool can find fault. It takes a sensitive and interested manager to search out the issues of quality.

The reward comes when the trainee says: '. . . but you are being too generous, I really made an error when I did . . .'. You can respond: 'Perhaps . . . How do you feel we should overcome that problem?' Then, and only then, are you working from strength to build strength.

As Gerald Manley Hopkins said:

There is a point with me in matters of any size when I must absolutely have encouragement as much as crops rain: afterwards I am independent.

Tension reduction

Humans process incoming data through three mental stages:

- *Cognitive* The various modes of knowing – perceiving, remembering, judging, etc.
- *Affective* Our feelings, attitudes, emotional reactions.
- *Conative* The action state, with activity an ultimate type of experience.

Thus cognitive factors have to be dealt with first, only then can affective factors come into play and they, in turn, lead to the conative, action state. We do not use these terms in everyday management, of course – but good managers are aware that they need to package their communications so that the three stages are progressed in sequence. If this is not done the result can be a confused team who react badly to a decision which is baldly announced because they do not understand the reasoning behind it. Even an action caused by a blatantly unfair situation can become motivational if presented correctly: 'We've got no choice, folks, the customer demands a replacement – so let's roll our sleeves up and get it done – then he'll be out of our hair for another three months – OK?'

Tensions are recognized cognitively, but are dealt with affective–conatively, hence the need for mangers to focus on the psychological rather than physiological aspects of behaviour. The work of Herzberg is crucial to motivational understanding. (see Unit 1).

Reward

Humans are goal driven, as has been shown. It is natural then to expect some reward for goal achievement. Rewards are of two types:

- *Intrinsic/motivational* – feelings of challenge, achievement, success, etc.
- *Extrinsic/incentives* – pay, promotion, praise, etc.

Satisfaction should come from the receipt of both intrinsic and extrinsic rewards as the consequence of performance; but the satisfaction level will depend on how near the rewards are to the value the person puts on the performance. There must be a balance of intrinsic and extrinsic rewards, but for most an element of extrinsic reward is necessary to continued motivation.

Rewards can cause attitude change

A member of staff who receives praise is more likely to repeat the behaviour so that further reward can be earned. Even so small a matter as noticing (or not) a change in appearance – a new suit, or a change in hair style – can have major repercussions in terms of group cohesion and overall morale. Praise for specific work achievement needs to be generous, fair, and delivered often.

Response follows action, and inaction is taken as a deliberate decision to take no action! Thus the performance of a careless person put into a work group where safety standards are high may either improve, or the standards of the group may fall. Management holds the key – if the individual is 'rewarded' by non-critical acceptance of standards, the slack performance will be reinforced and individuals in the group will be more inclined to reduce their standards.

In any behavioural decision, however small, the individual is always weighing up three overriding factors:

- How will this impact on my self-image?
- What is the element of risk?
- What are my aspirations – what would I like to do?

Not many will act if they feel their self-image will be adversely affected. Very few will act if the perceived risk is too high – and nobody will act if they don't want to.

Self-image and risk

- Nobody wants to be picked up as in error. Many will continue to deny that an error has been made even when faced with incontrovertible evidence.
- Risk can only be evaluated from the perception of the individual who is to take the risk. It may not appear to be a situation that contains risk, but if the individual considers that risk exists then it must be accepted that, for him or her, there is a problem. He or she needs help – not bullying.
- Risk and self-image are often closely connected. Status from success is balanced against the potential damage that follows failure. These elements are usually subjective in nature and so the affective element – the feeling – will rule.

Note that individuals also take into account what they believe (fear) others will think of their actions. Thus potential peer pressure may prevent acceptance of an offer, or reluctance to accept an instruction.

The mental processing of risk versus image can become quite complex:

- That copier is needed and it is at the right price.
- But my manager works closely with the Director and I don't think the Director likes the make. It might cause a row because my manager will stand up for me.
- I don't want to cause problems so perhaps its best to play safe and delay a decision.
- The special deal ends today, but I have to let it go.

Human differences are a prime focus for the manager – just as they are for a marketer. In this sense a marketer comes to management with major advantages over contemporaries from other functions. In management it is necessary to achieve an understanding of underlying causes of human actions and reactions, and to have an empathy with each individual if success is to be maximized.

The principles of scientific management established that individual behaviour should be modified to meet the needs of the organization, and managers turned to the behavioural sciences of psychology and sociology for assistance. Their intention was to *manipulate* the workers whom they regarded as mere extensions to the equipment that they operated.

Today's management still relies heavily on the social sciences, but uses them to *motivate* through positive reinforcement.

Positive reinforcement

Positive feedback on success is far more effective than negative feedback on failure. Two types of positive reinforcement can be used:

- *Extrinsic* – the 'external' influences and rewards such as money, time off, or a company car.
- *Intrinsic* – the 'internal' rewards such as satisfaction with the work itself, status, praise, or recognition.

The most powerful results are achieved when an incentive is locked onto a motivator.

For example, you have a performance bonus of £100 to offer, and all in the team can qualify. You might make a simple offer: £100 if you achieve X by Y. How much more powerful to target the incentive on to each individual's personal needs, wants and desires:

Mary – Achieve target and you'll be able to afford that new CD player you have been talking about.

John – How would you like a new fishing rod? All we have to do is achieve X.

These approaches are, of course, highly dominant and controlling in style. How about:

Martina – We can all earn £100 this week. What will you do with yours?

Does this also smack of a manipulative approach? We shall return to this issue a little later.

Behaviour modification, in the sense in which it was originally used, is strongly centred on the need to change workers to suit organizations. For it to be effective, it had to take account of the need to:

- Define and explain the desired behaviour so that employees know what is expected of them.
- Define and explain the rewards and punishments.
- Decide on the use of incentive or motivation, or in what combination.
- Monitor behaviour to see if the reinforcements are having the desired effect.

Looking back from our current understanding we are not surprised that the approach is not very effective. The fact that it is still used by some managers today does not detract from the manipulative nature of the approach. But the work did initiate an interest in understanding more about people at work. It became apparent that there were greater depths to penetrate, and that the social sciences could be called on for aid.

Richie Sounds is a private company, famous because its London Bridge retail outlet is in the record books for having the highest turnover per square foot of any retailer. Led by a charismatic owner, Julian Richie, staff incentive schemes are both creative and effective.

The company Rolls Royce is competed for monthly by the retail outlet and head office teams who are judged by performance against specified targets. The resulting publicity when the car is delivered for use by the winning team makes it an incentive enjoyed by the staff, but which pays for itself.

Customer care questionnaires are attached to each till receipt – every 'excellent' score earns the staff member a £5 cash bonus.

The points that come from the attempts at behaviour modification are valid today:

- Human behaviour arises from attitudes – how people see the situation. An intended 'reward' may be regarded as a 'bribe' and have a negative instead of positive effect.
- Positive reinforcers tend to work well but a negative 'punishing' approach tends to make workers both hostile and resentful. Resentment, it has been found, can linger long after the event, with workers appearing to be satisfied whilst holding back on full commitment.
- A non-existent homogeneity was assumed as a basis for the standardization of rewards.

Problems of the individual at work
Two major problem areas can be identified and classified as:

- *Alienation* The feeling of being estranged from one's situation at work. A feeling that one is surrounded by obstacles that prevent fulfilment, and/or progress. A person may become alienated from his or her true self, as when a sales person is forced to sell goods in which he or she has little belief or confidence.
- *Anomie* A state of mind due to the confusion that often arises in large organizations. The individual may feel faced with pressures and problems not of their making and over which they have no control, even though they feel seriously affected. Anomie can be brought into the workplace from home, because it is a response to pressures and problems generally – not necessarily exclusively work-based ones.

ACTIVITY 6.3

Objective conditions – subjective responses
Alienation and anomie result in certain attitudes. Take 20 minutes to:

- Think through the responses you would expect to each of the specified conditions.
- Broadly set out the actions management should take.

Objective condition at work	*Resulting subjective attitude*
A lack of power and influence over the work situation	
Not understanding the purpose of the work required	
Situations which separate people from each other, e.g. noise, desk spacing	
Inhibition on use of the whole range of personal talents and abilities	
No integration into a social or work group	
Norms which govern behaviour are unclear, breaking down, or contradictory	
There are confusions over values and beliefs	

(**See** Debriefing at the end of this unit.)

This area is another where the marketer has an in-built advantage, as it is so dependent upon qualitative research. Attitude monitoring is equally as necessary with team members as with customers. Usually there is formal customer research. Formal research into worker attitudes is far less common – except that the good manager is constantly monitoring attitudes through the everyday interchanges that take place.

The formal systems of appraisal (below) coupled with on-going development in addition to the daily interchanges provide the alert and interested manager with considerable evidence of attitude, morale within individuals and the group as a whole.

Types of human need

Much work has been done in this area. Typical research results are:

- *Maslow* suggests that there are five levels of need priority (Figure 6.6), and that each succeeding level must be satisfied before it is possible to move to the next. Thus survival needs are paramount, closely followed by safety and security, with self-actualization and fulfilment only possible when all else has been achieved.
- *Argyle* identified seven roots of social motivation – to which an eighth has since been added. The original seven drives are:

  (a) *Non-social* Including biological needs for food and water, the need for money, various kinds of behaviour which can produce social interaction.
  (b) *Dependency* Acceptance, interaction, help, protection and guidance especially from people in positions of power and authority.
  (c) *Affiliation* Physical proximity, eye contact, warm and friendly responses, acceptance by peers and groups of peers.
  (d) *Dominance* Acceptance by others and groups of others as a task leader, being allowed to talk most of the time, be deferred to.
  (e) *Sex* Physical proximity, bodily contact, etc., eye contact, friendly and intimate social interaction.
  (f) *Aggression* To harm others physically, verbally or in other ways.
  (g) *Self esteem and ego identity* For other people to make approving responses and to accept the self-image as valid.

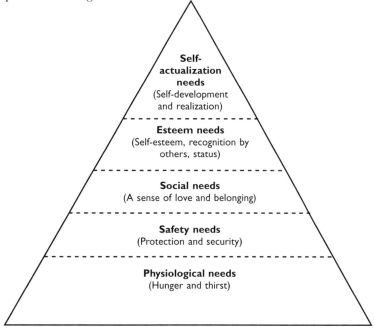

Figure 6.6 Maslow's hierarchy of needs

The eighth drive may be seen to derive from:

(h) *Culture*   The need to support cultural values and to behave in such a manner as to reinforce the importance of one's cultural heritage.

- *D.C. McClelland* suggests that there are three basic types of need:

  (a) *Affiliation*   People need meaningful relationships. Very few people are genuine loners. 'Who you work with' is an important contributor to the need for affiliation.
  (b) *Power*   Some are driven by a desire to make an impact, to shape events. If denied the opportunity in one area they will seek out another, e.g. note how many 'junior' staff hold senior positions in organizations away from work.
  (c) *Achievement*   The sense of 'getting on', progressing, being promoted, is very important to many people.

McClelland's work (Figure 6.7) is especially interesting because he associates different types of need with people at different levels in an organization. This, perhaps simplistic, view is nevertheless valuable as a general guide to the types of incentive and motivational factors that will have the greatest relevance to individuals.

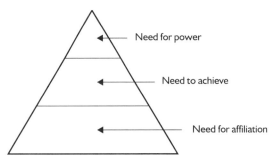

Figure 6.7   McClelland's three types of need

McClelland also argues that people become frustrated when they are not satisfied with their work lives. They may then seek satisfaction, become antagonistic, or become apathetic. They will often, of course, not be conscious of what is driving them.

He suggests that individuals have key personality features, and that job success depends on combining these into a satisfying pattern. He classifies these factors as:

- *Cooperation*   The desire to be helpful and carry out the wishes of those in authority.
- *Approval*   The need to be liked, to be accepted. Usually warm, friendly individuals who seek approval from others.
- *Power, prestige, money*   The money earned, power and prestige achieved are more important that the actual work. Status will outweigh unpleasantness in a job.
- *Curiosity*   Present in the majority of humans, it has considerable power when harnessed and directed. Note: this is not necessarily harnessed by management – individuals can and will explore and develop their own latent talents if given the opportunity and encouragement.
- *Achievement*   Some people's thoughts are constantly on meeting challenges and succeeding. This can be a powerful force in Western countries, and certainly is in the USA. It may not, however, be as dominant outside the USA as McClelland suggests.

Applying McClelland's model

The simple approach is to match incentives to an individual's personality needs as evidenced by his or her level in an organization. This, of course, is a crude generalization, and one that has proved to be only reasonably effective. It is necessary to identify the actual personality needs of each individual and only then to tailor incentives to suit.

McClelland's work is highly relevant because today's flatter hierarchies will lead to fewer promotional opportunities for management staff. Work satisfaction and challenges need to be redefined, and 'sideways' moves into new teams to open new opportunities must be seen as rewards. Too often, in the past, they have been seen as a way to shift the deadwood out of line and this perception may have to be actively countered by management.

Status

Social status refers to the amount of respect paid to an individual. Work roles can confer prestige on a person; status may also be perceived through the possession of symbols such as job title, size of office, even the colour of desk.

Nestlé in Switzerland used to indicate status through office space and the size and colour of desks. In an open office a junior had a small, brown topped desk. With promotion the top was removed, and replaced with green. At the next promotion the desk was replaced with a larger one, and the top was brown again. Next came a green top, and then a move into a cubicle. Finally, into an office with a door. The move into the office indicated that the person had passed into the ranks of senior management.

Status symbols can be used as positive reinforcers. They can also be divisive. Management dining rooms and reserved car parking can cause resentment in the many, even if they boost the few. Attempts to remove status by such tactics as having a single dining room are often negated by the staff who may delineate areas within the one common room. This is because there is never any doubt who is senior to whom, and many like to keep the distinction clear. Superficial actions are therefore counter-productive. A coat of paint can give an appearance of quality, but not when one stands up close.

Motivation or incentive – a need to match

All the work done on behaviour at work indicates that if an incentive can link to a motive it will have far more power than if it is simply used without consideration of its effects. Money, in itself, is not a great motivator. This is partly because money can mean so many different things depending upon context and need, but also because many individuals are motivated by *what money will bring* rather than by money itself.

Not all are motivated in the same way. As we saw, above, an incentive of £100 may be used by one person to buy a CD player, by another to fund a new fishing rod. We also saw that if handled badly the manager can appear manipulative rather than motivational. One needs to realize that the motivation is not confined to the use to which the incentive is put – it is also in the anticipation of success, the looking forward to the achievement, to the purchase of the item.

Managers need to know, to find out, what an individual would do with a bonus, and then devise an incentive that it is tailored to meet that need. In the majority of cases money need never come directly into the matter. An incentive of a weekend break, for two, or a furniture voucher to spend at a local store will often be more effective than a straight money incentive.

Good managers know that the incentive/motivation link is most effective when the achievement is within reach. Ask too much, and the individual(s) are not likely to believe in the possibility of success – and so not even bother to try. The result can easily be a decline in morale instead of the boost that was intended.

It follows that good leaders know and care about individuals in their teams. That they take trouble to work on the process of achievement, as well as on establishing objectives and control systems.

There is, of course, a negative incentive. People can be frightened. Fear is a powerful emotion. The good manager knows that when there is fault there is need to correct – but to correct in a positive way. Criticism is negative and destructive.

Peter Drucker, in his book *Management*, makes the point that there are 'big fears' and 'little fears'. Little fears, he says, cause resentment rather than conformity. Big fears, however, can still bring about action. He cites as an example that 'everybody knows' an alcoholic cannot stop drinking until he or she is down and out – and perhaps not even then. Yet 'a good many employers' are finding that alcoholics stop drinking – permanently – if told flatly that they will otherwise be fired and that potential new employers will be told of their problem.

Appraisal

Throughout the whole of every day the manager (manager–leader, remember) must be aware of how the role that he or she is taking is perceived. It is very important that when the manager moves from role to role – changes hats – very clear signals are given so that the individuals in the team know which hat the manager is wearing. Body language must support oral statements – we are judged on what we are seen to be doing rather than on what we may say we are doing.

Managerial 'hats'

The roles that every manager must take from time to time are:

- Decider
- Initiator
- Appraiser — Always within the context of good leadership. i.e. With every action designed to motivate and to strengthen both individuals and team
- Assessor
- Disciplinarian

Decisions, as we know, are the prime responsibility of management. Initiating action requires a combination of organizational skills and delegation. These are areas that have been covered earlier in the workbook.

The roles of appraiser and assessor must be clearly delineated, since in appraisal the manager is concentrating on the development of the individual. As an assessor a manager is reviewing the effectiveness of specific performances. It is always difficult to separate these two activities since there must be some element of assessment to underpin an effective appraisal. The key to success is to understand that the processes are different, and to approach them as discrete activities.

The two roles can be summarized as:

- Assessor   = Judge
- Appraiser = Helper

The term 'appraisal' is used (and misused) by organizations to achieve a variety of purposes:

- Improve current performance.
- Provide feedback.
- Increase motivation.
- Identify training needs.
- Identify potential.
- Inform individuals of expectation.
- Focus on career development.
- Award salary increases.
- Provide human resource management with information.
- Set job objectives.
- Assess the effectiveness of selection procedures.
- Reward or punish.

Appraise or assess?
Look carefully at the above list of purposes for which 'appraisal' is used. Add any others that you consider important.

- Remembering that the most effective use of appraisal is in the development of the individual, rate each of the purposes for their effectiveness. Use a scale of 1 (beneficial) to 5 (damaging).
- Then re-order your list in line with your ratings.
- Finally, make an overall comment on the value of and need to distinguish the two activities.

(**See** Debriefing at the end of this unit.)

Appraisal – the rationale
The logic is best set out in bullet points:

- All managers are continuously evaluating (appraising) their staff.
- This is automatic, routine, necessary.
- The prime focus is to 'get the job done'.
- There is little time to take individuals on one side and update them on performance.
- Consequently, individuals receive more criticism – when things go wrong – than praise, because most things go well most of the time.
- A manager's opinion of individuals remains confidential until salary review time or a promotion opportunity is created.
- The actions taken by a manager will be interpreted within the perceptual bias of each individual – nobody will really know the reasons for decisions, but there will be much speculation.

A system of formal appraisal tackles each of these points head on:

- Manager's evaluations are formally recorded, and notified to individuals.
- The focus changes to task achievement through people.
- Time has to be created for individual meetings with staff.
- Praise and criticism are put in perspective.
- Individuals can put their views on record.
- Management action will become clear – reasons why particular decisions are made can be questioned.

Once a formal system of appraisal is in place it has an effect on the day-to-day actions of management. Knowing that they have to go through an appraisal process, and that their actions can and will have to be explained, they are motivated to communicate more effectively at the time actions are taken.

The benefits
The three parties to appraisal – individuals, their managers, the organization – can all secure important benefits from an effective appraisal system. From the viewpoint of each party identify a minimum of three important benefits that can be derived.

(**See** Debriefing at the end of this unit.)

Why a 'formal system'?
Regrettably, although effective appraisal systems are beneficial to individuals, teams, management and organizations they tend to be resisted:

Managers
- Genuinely cannot find the time to go through the process.
- Feel that they do not have the time.
- Prevaricate, the external needs of the business are rated more important.
- Are not equipped to handle the interviews.
- Are concerned that their managers will criticize them.

Individuals generally are more prepared to welcome and support an appraisal system. Their concerns come from:

- Fear of criticism.
- Unwillingness to tell the truth in case it damages long-term prospects.
- Inability to handle the interview.
- Belief that it is just a paper exercise. That nothing will happen.

It follows that, to be effective, an appraisal system has to be:

- Initiated and supported by top management as a personnel policy.
- Carefully designed.
- Internally marketed to ensure acceptance.
- Supported with training of both managers and individuals so that the process is both efficient and effective.
- Processed by a designated manager within HRM (or with HRM responsibility).
- Followed through to ensure that actions result.

Managers, in particular, must have the appraisal requirement added to their job descriptions – and time must be found for the activity. Managers' commitment to appraisal must become a factor on which they are evaluated by their seniors.

A formal system inevitably requires forms to be filled in and time targets to meet. A balance has to be struck between minimum information/minimum organization and maximum information/maximum control At either extreme the system will fail. It will either be so loose that it is effectively ignored, or so tight that it is actively resisted. Good design and effective internal marketing are needed so that all can see the benefits to themselves.

Management commitment
The better appraisal schemes work on the parent and grandparent principle. The 'parent' is the immediate boss, the 'grandparent' is the next boss up the line – the manager's manager.

With each appraisal passed to the grandparent for counter-signature, individuals can be certain that they are brought to the attention of a senior manager – perhaps one that is seen only rarely within the team or department.

The use of the parent and grandparent analogy is standard practice in explaining appraisal – it does *not* and must *not* be taken to imply that management is a paternalistic activity. The days of a manager acting as a 'parent figure' are long gone.

This commitment – to appraise and to pass appraisal results up the line – helps ensure fairness and, importantly, formally opens a route for individuals to bypass their immediate manager. Thus if they feel that there is discrimination, for whatever reason, they can express it in appraisal and have it reviewed by a senior manager.

Inevitably, therefore, each manager's performance is put into perspective by the comments that individuals put in their appraisals. It becomes far harder for managers to bluff their seniors as – regrettably – human nature may encourage some to do.

Appraisal – the process
See Figure 6.8.

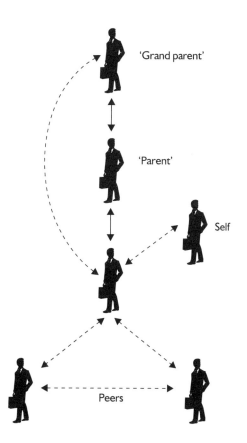

Figure 6.8   Who appraises?

- *Peers*   Appraisal can be by one's peers, i.e. by those with whom one works. This can, of course, be within the whole or part of the team. With the manager present, or excluded. Reports on such appraisal can feed into the system, and be of considerable value in staff and organizational development. The process is not formalized, however, and so cannot be used for HRM purposes.

- *Self* Self-appraisal is crucial to the success of the whole system. Individuals must be prepared for their appraisal interviews because these should be two-way processes. The relationship during appraisal interviews is more one of equality than a superior/junior interface. Appraisal interviews are not the place for a manager to itemize and evaluate performance factors . . . that is assessment.
- *Parent* The manager and the individual discuss various aspects of interest and concern – following a predetermined format, but with considerable flexibility so that individual needs can be taken into account. Matters discussed are recorded and at the end of the session both manager and individual sign the appraisal form. The individual should have a comments section in which any issues can be entered. In particular, this should be used to indicate any areas of disagreement – perhaps with a manager's perception of a particular incident or situation.
- *Grandparent* The manager's manager reads through the appraisal, takes note of action plans agreed and any comments made. The form is then counter-signed and copies circulated for action to:
  - (a) The individual – as a record, and to confirm the commitments made.
  - (b) The manager – as a record, and to act as a reminder to ensure that commitments are honoured.
  - (c) To HRM – For action regarding commitments and for addition to the individual's records.

Notes:

1 An appraisal record is a confidential document. Whilst HRM will use appraisals as source material for management development and for specific training plans, the training manager will not see the original documents. All the training manager needs to know is that there is a requirement to train a certain number of people to achieve specific objectives. It is for them to devise ways to make this happen.

2 Unfortunately, the appraisal system can never be unblemished by harsh commercial reality. The individual obviously regards a favourable appraisal as a vote of confidence, and a record of successful appraisals provides a considerable degree of job security.

It is impossible arbitrarily to dismiss a person who has consistently been given excellent appraisals. Conversely a bad appraisal can be used as evidence of poor performance and a succession of such appraisals can be a powerful weapon should a dismissal become necessary and should an individual take the matter to a union and/or to a tribunal.

Obviously, a good management will not be in the business of summary or arbitrary dismissal (except for cause, e.g. theft). Equally obviously, a bad management will not institute a fair system of appraisal. Perhaps it follows that only good employers have systems of appraisal? Perhaps.

The Mars Group has become famous for their personnel policies. Requiring only high-quality staff they pay above market rate, and add substantial bonuses that are linked by contract to company performance. They are extremely concerned with on-going personnel welfare.

Each employee is appraised each year on the nearest working day to the anniversary of their appointment. If this means that a manager has to travel from London to Bath on Monday, to Oxford on Tuesday and back to Bath on Wednesday – that is what happens. Perhaps a little over-zealous, but it does clearly indicate how important individuals are to the organization – and this is a major purpose for their insistence on anniversary interviews.

There is concern to keep good employees and the importance of management style and team behaviour is recognized. Thus every endeavour, including paying for redeployment of sales personnel, is made to retain good employees whose only problem is that they don't get along with a particular manager.

Designing an appraisal system

Appraisal is part of a performance management system (Figure 6.9).

Figure 6.9   Performance management system

- The role of the individual is established within the job description, which must be a dynamic document that changes, with agreement, as an individual's job develops.
- Individual objectives and action plans are based on the twin needs of self-improvement for long-term career development and better job performance.
- Reviews by self and superior are on-going against action plans and results in the job. Immediately before a formal appraisal session the individual should review the whole period since the last appraisal in order to be prepared for the next.
- Appraisal monitors progress, boosts motivation and sets new action plans to which all concerned are committed.
- Individuals perform better, have better prospects, and the group and the organization benefits.

Set objectives

As always in management, there is need to clarify the objectives. What does the organization want to get from appraisal? What benefits will it bring to all those concerned with it? Appraisal schemes can serve a number of objectives, so clarification is needed.

Typically, the attitudes of employees to the idea of appraisal tend to be welcoming, given that:

- Objectives primarily focus on employee job performance.
- Training and development needs are identified so that individual's career prospects can be improved.
- Involvement should be active – the scheme should open a conduit to management.

There are usually mixed views about whether appraisal should be linked to pay and conditions and/or potential for promotion. Inevitably there is an implicit understanding that the whole process of assessment and appraisal are closely related – the issue then becomes 'Can and should the use of appraisal be confined to personal development?' If so, how can management design and monitor the scheme so that this aim is fulfilled and *seen to be fulfilled?*

A survey reported by Evenden and Anderson is typical. Asked for their views on the importance of appraisal objectives, seven directors responded as shown in Table 6.2. Thus the three key items in order of importance were seen to be:

- Improve future performance.
- Review past performance.
- Identify employees' training and development needs.

Table 6.2 Directors' views on the importance of appriasal objectives (adapted from Evenden and Anderson)

Appriasal objective	Rank of importance							Weighted
	1	2	3	4	5	6	7	
Review past performance	–	3	2	2	–	–	–	2.86
Make decisions on pay	2	–	1	1	–	1	2	4.14
Improve future performance	4	2	1	–	–	–	–	2.14
Strengthen communication	–	–	1	2	3	1	–	4.57
Identify employee potential	–	–	1	1	1	2	2	5.43
Identify employee's training and development needs	1	2	1	1	1	1	–	3.0
To help succession planning	–	–	–	–	2	2	3	6.14

Employees naturally approach appraisal from a different viewpoint to management. The process can be fear-ridden and demotivational if handled badly, or it can be welcomed and highly motivational if handled well. Linking motivations to objectives is always good policy (see Table 6.3).

Table 6.3 Linking motivations for and objectives of appraisal (adapted from Evenden and Anderson)

Motivation from appraisal	How objectives and targets can help motivate
Purpose?	Discuss priorities and where job fits in
What is expected from me?	A chance to find out
How am I doing?	You will know
Challenge	Targets should be realistic
Achievement	Continuous, especially if targets are progressive
Job satisfaction	Can add interest
Recognition	Chance for self-esteem and praise
Responsibility	Increased
Advancement	Increased opportunities linked to known performance requirements

ACTIVITY 6.6

Appraisal objectives
Given that there is a wide range of objectives that may underlie an effective appraisal scheme, consider what primary and secondary management objectives would be most suitable for an organization that had a strong commitment to maintaining a low staff turnover.

Note: Don't forget the time element!

(**See** Debriefing at the end of this unit.)

Procedure and documentation

Appraisal interviews are a specialized activity with which nobody – managers or employees – are familiar. It is therefore necessary to create a procedure that is as straightforward and foolproof as possible, and to train everybody in its use. Well-designed documentation is essential so that everybody works from the same basis, and is guided through the process.

ACME INSURANCE LIMITED
STAFF APPRAISAL
NOTES FOR EMPLOYEES

You will be making an appointment to see your manager shortly. These notes are to help you collect your thoughts and to help you think about what you want to achieve during the next year. A copy of your last appraisal is also enclosed.

Your manager is concerned to understand your point of view regarding your job and your personal development – it will therefore be helpful if you make brief notes under each of the following headings and take them with you to the interview.

- **Targets**

  What job and personal targets were you working to achieve? How successful were you?
  What were the main reasons for your success, and/or what major problems did you encounter?

- **Control**

  What factors were within your control that you could use to help achieve your targets?
  What factors were outside your control and hindered you?

- **The Team**

  How effective is the team within which you work?
  What contribution(s) do you make to it, with what results?

- **Personal**

  What are the three most significant contributions you have made in the period?
  What are the three biggest disappointments?

- **The Future**

  What changes are needed to your job? Why?
  Where do you see your personal future?
  How do you want your career to develop?
  What suggestions do you have for improvements to the performance of the team/department/company?

As you know, the appraisal scheme is designed to help us all to make Acme Insurance a better place to work and a more effective power in the marketplace. The interview you are shortly to have is of major importance to your future career, and therefore of major importance to the company. Please relax, and take the opportunity to make your contribution to our overall success.

Figure 6.10   Pre-appraisal documentation

A typical scheme will have:

- *Guidance notes and instructions* These will be standardized, public, contain the agreed objectives and be issued to all.
- *Pre-appraisal documents* To allow both manager and individual to consider the areas that are subject to appraisal, and to come to the interview well prepared.
- *Appraisal documents* A standardized form for completion as the interview progresses. This needs either to be on multi-part stationery or designed for simple copying.

Typical pre-appraisal documentation will follow the pattern shown in Figure 6.10.

The appraisal form used in organizations with a developed scheme and experienced personnel can, essentially, be a simple list of questions with blank spaces for descriptive answers. When starting out, however, experience has proved that individuals need a more structured framework. Although it perhaps smacks of performance review, a section which allows a form of grading has been shown to get people into the interview smoothly. It provides a basis for a discussion as in:

Manager: 'Well, John, let's quickly see if we agree on your overall performance. How do you rate yourself on Customer Contact?'
John: 'I reckon a C +.'
Manager: 'Fine, I agree, you have done pretty well there since last we met. What about product knowledge?'
John: 'B? I've worked hard to get to grips with that because it's crucial to customer trust.'
Manager: 'Agree absolutely. Well done.'
John: 'On telephone manner I think I ought to have a B as well, perhaps an A.'
Manager: 'Oh dear – there we have to disagree – I would rate you around C or C +. Why do you think it should be higher?'

Once the minimum number of categories has been run through, and areas for discussion identified, the interview can open out to wider issues (see Figure 6.11).

ACME INSURANCE LIMITED
STAFF APPRAISAL

Name: _____

Job title: _____   Department: _____

Manager: _____   Date: _____

1. Describe the main purpose of the job:

2. For each of these headings evaluate the degree of success and make any necessary note.

Area	A	B	C +	C	D	E	Comments
Customer contact							
Product knowledge							
Telephone manner							
etc.							

Figure 6.11 Appraisal form

3. Amplify notes made in (2) as necessary.

4. Indicate the level of achievement under each of these headings. Say why each comment is made.

    4.1 Volume of work:

    4.2 Quality of work:

    4.3 Team participation:

    4.4 Time-keeping:

    4.5 Dependability:

    4.6 Initiative:

5. **Overall performance.**
   Summarize in a few words the overall performance and contribution made during the period.

6. **Action planning.**
   Itemize the key aspects of actions that are planned, with a time-scale for completion of each.

7. **Individual comments:**
   The individual to add any comments, and then sign and date the form.

Signed: Individual: _____   Date: _____

          Manager: _____   Date: _____

Review Manager's comments:

Signed: Individual: _____   Date: _____

Figure 6.11   Continued

Appraisal interviewing

The appraisal interview is possibly the most difficult of all personnel interviews that a line manager will have to undertake. This is because:

- Individuals come to the interview with the confidence and security of their job and job performance. They are not supplicants for work, nor for promotion. They are not to be disciplined. The manager's power, implicit in the other interviews, is diminished considerably. With this diminishment can also go a degree of self-confidence.

- Considerable interpersonal skills are needed to maintain a steady pace, whilst keeping reasonably to time and encouraging a majority contribution from the individual. At the same time identifying and dealing with possibly contentious issues.
- The process can be open-ended – especially with individuals who have major areas of disagreement with the appraiser's view. This can force an interview to be extended, and even on occasion only partly completed and resumed at another time. (Note: This should not happen more than once with an individual, it is a factor which is encountered when introducing appraisal to an organization where individuals have previously had no opportunities to express themselves.)
- Skills are learned mainly on-the-job. Simulated interviews are helpful, but can never have the full impact of the real thing, and using video or having an observer present negates the confidential and personal nature of the process.

As a rough guide, an interview can be expected to run for about 90 minutes, and this emphasizes the need for careful preparation.

Preparation
- Review performance against job description, other objectives and/or targets and know why you feel as you do. Hard evidence is needed – not generalizations.
- Consider whether the targets, etc., were too difficult, or too easy.
- Evaluate what the individual actually did to facilitate or prevent achievement.
- Note the effect of external factors on performance.
- Summarize in overall terms how you feel the individual has done, where you see him or her going, what actions you are going to recommend.
- Be prepared to modify your views in the light of evidence brought to the interview by the individual. (You cannot know everything that has happened, or how the individual reacts to situations.)

Involvement
Appraisal is an involving process. For success it needs commitment from both parties (Figure 6.12). With an individual who is prepared it is far easier to achieve a joint approach, which is the target of all appraisal interviews. As a rule of thumb, the balance of conversation should be weighted around 70:30 appraisee, appraiser.

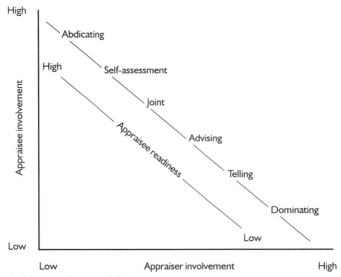

Figure 6.12   Appraisal interaction model

Interviewing guidelines
Appraisal interviews have to be more relaxed than other forms of interview, yet there is need to relax around the declared purpose and framework. As a general rule, the following approach has been found to be effective:

- Block off absolutely from normal duties. There must be no interruptions.
- Begin with a clear statement of purpose. Establish the timeframe and check that the individual has the necessary papers and is ready.
- Work hard to put the individual at ease, and to build a rapport.
- Encourage the individual to take responsibility for the interview.
- Share the documentation – it is a joint process to complete it and it belongs as much to the individual as to the manager.
- Aim for a 70:30 split of conversation – develop the skill of using open questions.
- Encourage the individual to expand, especially about areas where they have done well – to give you opportunities to praise – and areas where they are frustrated – so you can help.
- Do not generalize.
- Maintain a positive, forward-thinking, motivational approach.
- Close with a review of the conversation and a summary of the agreements made.

Note: Above all, avoid the management clichés such as 'My door is always open'. (If it is they will know. If it isn't why pretend to yourself?)

Follow-through

Appraisal as a paper-based exercise is not only useless – it is distinctly demotivational! Follow-through is essential. The objectives and targets that have been agreed must be monitored. Training promised must happen. Results must be seen to come from the process. It will take up to 3 years for a new system to become trusted, so full commitment to the whole process is particularly important in the early days.

Work motivators

It is one thing to understand how motivation works – another to translate the principles into effective work motivators. There is need to distinguish the core factors within a job, identify the psychological states that lock on to them and relate these to personal and work outcomes that satisfy and fulfil the individual.

Remembering the key motivational factors, we can provide a generalized range of options that are available to the manager:

- Variety.
- Responsibility.
- Interaction.
- Goals and feedback.
- Autonomy.
- Challenge.
- Task significance.

Job design

Job design uses motivational theories to construct a balanced job that will meet the psychological needs of those best suited to fill it. Note: Different jobs require different skills and different personalities. A sales order clerk is motivated differently than a R&D Lab. Technician.

Job rotation

Possibly the most popular form of adding variety and interest – perhaps because it is the simplest to organize? It requires a range of tasks that are similar in nature and can have the added benefit of authorizing individuals to arrange the rotation, provided that every job is properly covered at all times.

Job enlargement

Usually involving the widening of a job from a central task, job enlargement can empower an individual and free him or her from dependence on others for work performance, e.g. if in a chain of tasks an individual has to work at the pace of those before him.

Critics of job enlargement argue that it is merely extending the original task(s). Herzberg describes it as merely adding to the meaninglessness of the job.

Job enrichment

Horizontal enrichment is very much like job enlargement – it is from vertical job enrichment that the major benefits are gained. Vertical job enrichment increases an individual's involvement in the organization and/or the job. There is some element of 'task closure' – where an individual can see a job through to a conclusion and is not simply a cog in an overall activity. (The task may, of course, be a part of an overall activity, but it is complete in itself.)

Job enrichment can be applied to blue collar, white collar and management jobs. For managers it will link into organization design and structure, for others the issues involved are more targeted on the jobs themselves.

In 1968, Herzberg was commissioned to redesign clerical jobs in a very large corporation. Performance and attitudes were poor. He redesigned the jobs to add responsibility and give a sense of personal achievement and recognition (see Table 6.4). Monitoring against a control group, Herzberg found that performance fell at first, but that after 3 months it picked up, and within 6 months the job enriched group were performing significantly higher. Attitudes were considerably more positive in the job enriched group than in the control group.

Table 6.4 Enrichment principles and motivators (adapted from Herzberg, 1968)

Tasks	Job enrichment principles	Motivators involved
Experts appointed to answer queries without need to go to Supervisor	Individuals assigned specialized tasks, enabling them to become experts	Responsibility, growth, advancement
Individuals empowered to sign their own letters	Increased accountability	Responsibility and recognition
Checking of letters reduced from 100% to 10%. Check process moved from Supervisor's desk	Controls removed, accountability retained	Responsibility and personal achievement
Discussion of amount of work expected reduced and then abandoned	Additional authority granted to the individuals	Responsibility, achievement and recognition
Outgoing mail sent directly to mail room, not via Supervisor	Controls removed with accountability retained	Responsibility and personal achievement
Individuals encouraged to be more personal in their letters	Allowing individuals to associate with their work	Responsibility, achievement and recognition
Individuals held personally responsible for the quality and accuracy of their letters	Routing reports, etc., directly to individuals rather than through the Supervisor Increasing accountability	Internal recognition Responsibility and recognition

Significance to marketing management

Marketing managers, above all others, should be aware of the human dimension – and of the benefits to be gained by all from taking the time to link offerings to human needs. Taking the view that one is selling a job to an individual is a very positive way of ensuring that the job is tailored to the individual's needs.

Regarding a job as a product to be sold forces a marketer to go back to first principles:

- What are the needs, wants and desires of the target customer?
- Who are the target customers?
- What are their needs, wants and desires?
- How can we produce a product (job) that fulfils those needs, wants and desires?
- How do we package and promote it?

- What after-sales service is required?
- What on-going research is needed to monitor continuing success and indicate when modifications are needed?

HRM people come to this understanding from the social sciences. Marketers have a far wider base of technical skills and education – they should, therefore, surely, make far better manager–leaders than people from any other discipline. If not – why not!

EXAM HINTS

The contents of this unit are ideal for in-class assessment, and those who are able to take this course by continuous assessment will be able to take part in role-playing exercises that will allow you to practise your interpersonal skills. You will be able to take the part of the appraiser and the appraisee, and will find that both roles can be very stressful. They need not be, and they will not be with experience. It is a little like presentations. Everybody is nervous at first, but confidence comes with practice.

The manager, naturally, gets more practice and so should take responsibility for settling the interview into an interchange that both are comfortable with. That does not mean a heavy handed directional control – a balance must be struck which allows the appraisee to feel entirely comfortable and at ease.

Those who are taking the examination must do more than learn the process from the workbook. Interpersonal skills are developed only with practice. It is essential, therefore, to devise ways to experiment with motivation and incentive using those with whom you are regularly in contact.

If you are at work, try to secure a real appraisal interview. Ask others how they felt before the interview – and after. Discover what happened to cause the feelings you have identified. You need to be able to show the examiner that you have a degree of empathy – it is a very necessary trait for managers and especially managers, of marketing.

UNIT ACTIVITY

It is necessary to develop the skills required to answer exam-length questions in the time allowed in the exam room. This activity, therefore, comprises two typical questions which you should answer in 90 minutes. Set up, so far as possible, examination conditions. Be strict – clear 90 minutes and answer these questions sight unseen.

Read on only when you are ready.

Q1 (*Take no more than 45 minutes*)
You have recently been appointed as Marketing Manager of an industrial print products manufacturer. The team you have inherited is some 20 strong and includes eight field sales representatives.

Staff turnover is low – but morale and motivation are also low. You appear to have a number of individuals rather than any form of group or team.
Set out a timed plan to rectify the situation.

Q2 (*Take no more than 45 minutes*)
As part of an organization-wide cost-cutting exercise you have learnt that the management training budget is to be cut by 50%.
(a) Draft a memo to the Managing Director justifying your view that this decision should be reconsidered.
(b) Identify more cost-effective management development options which could allow the current budget to be cut by, say, 20%.

Elton Mayo: management thinker and writer, born in Australia

After an active, but mixed, career as a medical student, writer, academic, printer and teacher which extended from Australia to the UK and included Africa, Mayo emigrated to America in 1929. He was a professor at the University of Pennsylvania for 3 years before joining Harvard as associate professor of industrial research in 1926. Between 1929 and 1947 Mayo worked as a full professor at Harvard.

His work owes much to the foundations established in Australia where he lectured for the Worker's Education Association and studied the nature of nervous breakdowns during the First World War. In association with others he pioneered the psychoanalytical treatment of shell shock (what we call 'battle fatigue' today). His first book, *Democracy and Freedom*, applied his work on wartime nervous problems to industrial strife. He argued that the social aspects of work were important and that they related strongly to morale and to mental health issues. He called for sociological awareness from management.

Mayo's major importance lies in his research into the importance of non-economic satisfaction in employee productivity. Previously it had been thought that scientific redesign and piece work would increase productivity. Mayo was instrumental in showing that people responded to interest being taken in them, and that such interest should be personally and not economically based. In other words, people were not extensions of machines to be manipulated as inorganic controls.

Mayo's Hawthorne Studies extended over 10 years and covered around 20 000 people using between seventy-five and a hundred investigators – they were not the short-term activity that some training films have made them appear. He used scientific investigative methods to prove that taking worker's attitudes into account paid off in commercial terms. He was concerned with the individuals, and paid little attention to the work itself – a radical change in approach and a turning point in the study of motivation and incentive.

There is no doubt that Mayo opened an area of vital importance which later academics, notably Argyris, Herzberg and Maslow, were to explore more fully.

Key publications:
Democracy and Freedom, 1919
The Social Problems of an Industrial Civilisation, 1933

In this unit you have seen that:

- Leadership is a guiding and developmental force whereas management is an administrative, controlling, activity.
- Today's manager–leader is concerned with motivation – with achieving results through people. They are aware of the need to recognize, and interact with the people with through whom their results are achieved. Task achievement depends upon both group and individual motivation.
- Management style can be self-classified so that the results can be predicted and prepared for. Only from a self-awareness and classification can actions be initiated to achieve change or to reinforce and strengthen a satisfactory style.
- A good team is made up of active leadership and active membership. Role is important since leaders in one group/time may be members in other groups and at other times. Overall leadership will often be supplemented by short-term task centred leadership.
- Motivation is an internally directed reason to move. Incentives can link with it, but never replace it. Praise is by far the greatest motivator – yet is often withheld in favour of criticism. Positive reinforcement on success is far more effective than negative feedback on failure.
- In today's flatter hierarchies people must be motivated by challenge and new opportunities rather than promotion. A sideways move must be seen as a reward.
- Managers have to signal the 'hat' they are wearing: decider, initiator, appraiser, assessor, or disciplinarian.
- Appraisal is a coming together of line manager and individual so that progress can be assessed and a personal action plan initiated. A 'grandfather' figure should review appraisal documentation to confirm that the appraisal is being taken seriously and to open a route past a line manager for an individual if needed.

- Job enlargement widens a job and can free an individual from dependence on others. Job enrichment – if vertical – increases an individual's involvement in the organization.
- Regarding a job as a product to be sold forces marketers to go back to first principles – what are the needs, wants and desires of the target customer – the person in the job (or who is expected to take it)? How can the job be designed and packaged to make it genuinely attractive to the target individual(s)?

Debriefing

Activity 6.1

The list can be very long, but most agree that the following abilities are essential in a good leader:

- *Self-confidence* – the effective leader will always be confident, or appear to be confident.
- *Initiative* – the ability to take action or to show enterprising ideas.
- *Objectivity* – when making judgements. Not prejudiced, or showing favouritism.
- *Empathy* – the ability to put oneself in the position of another, and judge how the situation appears to them.
- *Communication* – an ability to convey attitude, confidence, enthusiasm. Far more than a simple channel of information.
- *Flexibility* – the ability to adapt to changed circumstances.

Activity 6.2

You will have applied the principles of leadership and team membership within your own experience and to your own needs. Our experience is that the needs are:

- To use personal qualities, work and team based skills and experience to strengthen the team.
- To be fully supportive of the leadership, without withdrawing from honest disagreements on matters of importance.
- To accept that group goals are best achieved through commonality of purpose, and that equally good results can be achieved from a variety of leadership styles.
- To be open-minded and to learn from the leadership displayed by the designated leader.

Activity 6.3

Attitudes are extremely important and so, having identified the typical responses (see table on page 158), it is for management to put remedial measures into place. It is, of course, far better to recognize the likely response to certain actions ahead of their implementation!

Herzberg (Unit 1) identified the motivating and hygiene factors. Concentration should be first upon the routine, hygiene elements – but *in context* with building in the personal stimulation and rewards so needed by people in life, let alone in work.

For example, telephone operators are absolutely vital in their role as first contact. Why, then, have they traditionally been put into small closed rooms with no visual stimulation? Progressive organizations have recognized their importance and set about boosting their morale and sense of importance to self and the organization. They have located them where they can see and be seen. Sometimes their jobs have been enriched by adding reception duties. Management has taken special note of them and their contribution.

None of this is difficult or expensive. It just needs thinking of – and doing.

Activity 6.4

Our ranking is:

- Improve current performance   1
- Provide feedback   1

Objective condition at work	Resulting subjective attitude
A lack of power and influence over the work situation	Feelings of being powerless, loss of control over one's life
Not understanding the purpose of the work required	Feelings that working life is meaningless
Situations which separate people from each other, e.g. noise, desk spacing	Feelings of isolation, of being alone in a hostile environment
Inhibition on use of the whole range of personal talents and abilities	Feelings of self-estrangement, of not being one's true self. A need to 'put on an act'
No integration into a social or work group	Loneliness and a sense of isolation
Norms which govern behaviour are unclear, breaking down or contradictory	Confusion – and no clear idea of how to behave
There are confusions over values and beliefs	Difficulty in recognizing right from wrong

- Increase motivation   1
- Focus on career development   2
- Identify training needs   2
- Identify potential   3
- Inform individuals of expectation   3
- Set job objectives   4
- Award salary increases   4
- Provide human resource management with information   5
- Assess the effectiveness of selection procedures   5
- Reward or punish   5

Appraisal should be centred on the individual with a view to helping him or her to self-develop. An individual cannot focus on this kind of very personal issue if potentially faced with a threat of punishment or a need to argue about salary.

Activity 6.5
You should have identified a minimum of three factors under each heading – it is important that all benefit, or else the scheme will not succeed.

- *Individuals*:
    - (a) Feedback from management.
    - (b) Sound basis for agreeing improvement plans.
    - (c) Gain an appreciation of the manager's views, aims and priorities.
    - (d) Can communicate views about the job, with the manager taking time to listen.
    - (e) Can discuss career options.
    - (f) Can identify and agree on training needs.
    - (g) Can receive recognition for achievements.
- *Managers*:
    - (a) Learn about individual's hopes, fears, expectations, anxieties and concerns.
    - (b) Can clarify and reinforce important goals and priorities.
    - (c) Can focus on areas where individuals will benefit from making changes – and where they should consolidate on present strengths.
    - (d) Identify areas of overlap, or omission, so that job descriptions can be modified if necessary.
    - (e) Secure a basis for considering transfer, promotion, career moves in general.
    - (f) Gain a unique opportunity for motivation.
    - (g) Can agree individual developmental action plans.
- *The organization*:
    - (a) Is assisted with succession planning decisions.
    - (b) Identifies actual or potential areas of human resource strength and weakness.

(c) Ensures that individual, team, departmental, divisional and corporate objectives are mutually supportive.
(d) Fosters improved internal communications.
(e) Updates personnel records.
(f) Fosters improved relationships, specific training and development as a major contribution to improved overall performance.

Activity 6.6

Your appraisal objectives should read something like this:

- Each member of staff shall be formally appraised once a year. Appraisals shall be completed within the calendar month of September.
- Appraisal pro-formas shall be returned to each employee within the month of October.
- The primary objectives of the appraisal scheme are:
  (a) To improve the current and future performance of employees.
  (b) To identify and agree the training and development needs of each individual.
- The secondary objectives are:
  (a) To review performance since the last appraisal as a guide to the future.
  (b) To verify the effectiveness of the action plans agreed at the last appraisal.
  (c) To identify areas for improvement within the appraisal scheme.
  (d) To strengthen communication within the organization.

Note: Most organizations cannot manage a full appraisal more than once a year, and therefore select what for them is their quietest time.

It is also common practice for new employees to go through a form of appraisal 3 or 6 months after engagement – this should not prevent them slotting into the regular appraisal for the year, unless the two events coincide.

Unit activity

Q1 There can be no definitive answer to this question since much will depend on your perception of the situation. Before you can answer you have to clarify the position in your own mind:

- Is the 'team' actually 20 strong? If so, it is very large – too large?
- Given that you have 20 in the 'team', of whom eight are field sales representatives, it follows that you have at least two types of personnel: inside marketing staff and external sales staff.
- Splitting the task in this crude way gives you two potential teams, one of manageable size, one still too large.
- But the inside group is likely to easily split again – into product or brand management, marketing research/information, support/administration.
- It is possible, therefore, that you can regroup and delegate to team leaders. Two internal teams and one outside team.
- If you feel this is practical you can aim for:

Short term: 6 weeks

```
                        Marketing Manager
        ┌──────────────────────┼──────────────────┐
     Product                                       │
     Manager                                       │
   ┌─────┴──────┐                                  │
Assistant Product  Research   Support/Admin.   Field Sales Reps
   Manager
```

Medium term: 6 months

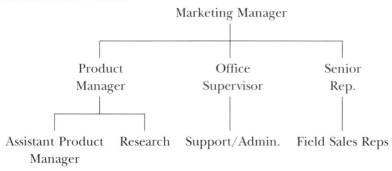

Note: No increase in staff is anticipated. New first-level managers are selected from existing teams.

- Given an overall appreciation of the situation, and a strategy to achieve, it becomes possible to establish a step-by-step, timed programme which picks up the tactical actions required.
- You must, of course, answer the actual question asked. To do so you have to demonstrate familiarity with group dynamics, motivations and incentives, leadership and delegation – as tactics within a strategic framework.

Q2 Your answer may vary in content depending on your perception of the situation. It should, however, be set out as shown and be similar to:

MEMO

To: Managing Director
From: Marketing Manager   DATE: XX XX 199X

Subject: <u>Training – a proposal</u>

1 It is appreciated that there is need to reduce our overall costs and, as you know, we are already showing substantial productivity improvements over last year's results.

2 These improvements owe much to the training budget which was approved as part of the overall cost-cutting exercise, and we are only partly through the programme. Thus we can confidently forecast further productivity improvements if we may continue with an effective training programme.

3 We can certainly modify our training programme to achieve additional savings, but I strongly feel that it would be extremely damaging to reduce by as much as 50%.
    My reasons are:

3.1 We committed ourselves to an agreed training and development package as part of the productivity programme.

3.2 This commitment was (and is) the keystone to our staff's willing acceptance of the structural and procedural changes that are actually showing the cost-saving benefits that we need.

3.3 We need the wholehearted and fully motivated support of our people if our programme is to proceed satisfactorily to the planned conclusion.

3.4 Our credibility as a management team has improved considerably since we began the programme and we are building a very strong sense of team identity by using the need to consolidate against the threats in our external environment.

3.5 A drastic change of policy can be interpreted as a withdrawal of support by management. Our credibility is fragile as yet, and I strongly recommend that we reconsider the size of the budget cut.

4 PROPOSAL

4.1 We should reduce our training budget by 20%, and achieve this by restructuring our programme.

4.2 We should not mention a budget reduction when re-structuring.

4.3 We should sell our revised plans as evidence of our overall achievements so far – we have done so well as a team that we can revisit and improve our original plans.

4.4 To effect the needed reduction I suggest that we should:

    4.4.1 Accelerate John Smith's Training Officer programme so that he can replace our Training Consultant within 3 instead of 6 months.

    4.4.2 Postpone 50% of the currently scheduled external courses so that they can be run, internally, by John Smith.

    4.4.3 Select our key staff for priority places on the courses in 4.4.2.

    4.4.4 Take advantage of software based training packages now that our new computer system is up and running earlier than we had expected. This will require an earlier investment than we had planned, but the pay-back already identified will come on line 9 months earlier than we had expected.

    4.4.5 Select two of our Supervisors for Instructor Training – a 3-day public course run by our Training Consultant.

    4.4.6 Use our newly trained Supervisors (4.4.5) for basic training – with the major spin-off of increased motivation.

5 SUMMARY

If you will agree to re-examine our training budget in the light of the above I am confident that we shall accelerate our motivational and productivity improvements. I am seriously concerned that a large cut will have very damaging effects in both the short- and long-term.

Signed: _____

Tools for maintaining and developing teams

In this unit you will:

- Examine the process of identifying problems in teams and with individuals.
- Understand the need to manage interpersonal relations within teams.
- Appreciate the problems of handling teams from different cultures and functions.
- Understand the importance of initiating and managing staff and team development programmes.
- Be aware of the process of counselling and disciplinary interviews.
- Examine strategies for improving the performance of marketing teams.

By the end of this unit you will be able to:

- Identify problems within teams and/or individuals.
- Manage a team of individuals from a variety of backgrounds.
- Initiate and manage staff and team development programmes.
- Plan and carry out counselling and disciplinary interviews.
- Improve the performance of marketing teams.

Marketing managers have often had to work with people, often customers, from a variety of backgrounds and cultures – but in many cases this has been possible only from a distance. With the increased emphasis on equality of opportunity, the radical changes in the ethnic and cultural make-up of society and the increased internationalism and globalization of business, this remoteness is no longer possible. It follows that the manager of today, and certainly of tomorrow, must be able to motivate a team made up of individuals each of whom comes from a unique heritage and thus brings with them all the advantages (as well as the disadvantages) of that culture and its approach to situations.

Allow 3 hours to work through this unit and bear in mind that managers must *actively* realize that all races, colours, religions and both sexes have their fair share of the competent and incompetent, intelligent and stupid, workers and idlers.

Before you begin to work on this unit take time to review the working groups and individuals that you know and of which you have personal experience. Evaluate each on their actual performance, and then give some thought to their background and think about how their unique background and experience influences their perceptions and performance.

If you are not disabled it can be a salutary experience to spend several hours in a wheelchair. Not 10 minutes, but a whole day! Your perspective on life will change as you come to terms with the problems faced routinely by the disabled. It is not easy to put oneself into another's shoes, but an effective manager will be alert to the problems which may be faced by individuals within the team. The older individual will have a cultural view markedly different from young colleagues; a new team member coming from another culture may feel as 'different' as a visitor from a foreign country.

You are heading towards not only an examination which will test your competence as a manager. You also head towards a career in which you will have to manage people from a variety of backgrounds and experiences. It is very important that you carry through a self-audit to identify any areas of prejudice and bias which may be clouding your judgement. Many of these prejudices and biases are unconscious, and not the fault of individuals – until they are identified.

It can be extremely difficult to give up long-standing biases, and review stereotyped imagery, but your examiner and your senior managers will not be able to feel that you are suited to management if you evidence prejudice. You need to be able to show, throughout your whole approach to the examination and in your working and social life, that you evaluate people on their achievements and for their potential. That you are suitable to be a manager – one who achieves results through people.

Explanations and definitions

1 *Bias* An attitude either for or against a particular theory, hypothesis or explanation, which unconsciously influences an individual's judgement; it may appear in experimental work as the so-called *error of bias*, the bias being due either to prepossession in favour of a particular theory, or previous judgements in the same experiment. (*Dictionary of Psychology*) It is most damaging in human-relations terms because of its unconscious and insidious nature. Thus people can display evidence of bias whilst protesting their neutral approach to situations and, especially, people.

2 *Prejudice* An attitude, usually with an emotional colouring, hostile to, or in favour of, actions or objects of a certain kind, certain persons, and certain doctrines. (*Dictionary of Psychology*) Usually used in reference to hostility as in 'That's a prejudiced person if I ever saw one'. Even when used positively it tends to carry undertones of criticism because it describes a fixed and unreasonable attitude that is likely to be deeply entrenched.

3 *Stereotype* 'Stereo'- is a prefix usually meaning 'solid'. 'Stereotyping' is the term given to the human tendency to make oversimplifications and generalizations about people or objects based on limited experience. Studies show that, although people have unique individualities, there is a wide belief that there are definitive characteristics associated with members of any national or ethnic group (e.g. Scots are mean, Americans are materialistic, Italians are passionate).

Developing a team

Sometimes teams come ready made. They are either in existence when a manager takes them over, or they are appointed by the same authority and at the same time as the manager. It is best practice (but not always possible) to appoint the manager first, and then either allow him or her to select and appoint the team members or, at least, grant the manager a place on the selection panel.

Once in post the manager will be held responsible for team performance and so it makes good sense to check the background details of those in a team which one is to lead. A manager must always get to know the team members before making decisions on their competencies and/or potential – however, if taking over a team which has had problems it can be very important to establish the authority to make necessary changes *before* taking up the post.

If you have prior knowledge and concerns about any particular individual this should be recorded before taking on the team management responsibility – even if it is not possible to change the team composition.

Team composition

Teams should be composed of enough individuals with sufficient skills and experience to get the job done. Unless they are it is difficult to see how they can succeed! The manager, therefore, needs to consider the:

- Task objectives.
- Skills and experience needed.
- Time that the team will function as a unit.

Obviously, long-term objectives requiring a multi-skilled team will necessitate closer interrelationships over a longer period and mutual compatibility becomes more of an issue. A short-term task can be achieved with a team who do not need to develop the same degree of close personal links.

Professionals, in theory, should be able to operate in a team, divorcing their professional from their social lives. But humans are social animals, and the chemistry between them is subtle and all-pervading. Within a short-term team the professional approach is undoubtedly possible, but over a period of time the presence of an incompatible person can greatly detract from team performance. Managers have enough to do without a constant drain from a incompatibility that is causing tensions which will lead to problems.

Complementary roles

In Unit 5 we examined how teams form, and the need for complementary roles within them. In Unit 6 we saw how it is necessary for leadership to revolve, depending on the situation, provided that the command function is not abrogated.

Team assessment

Results are the bottom-line test of team effectiveness. If a team is producing the results, on time, efficiently and effectively it must be considered successful. In such a case it may seem that issues such as management style are only relevant if a team is failing to perform. But is this so?

Consider:

The project team had been working together for 2 years. After a slow start that had fired up and begun to produce good work. Objectives set were met to time, and the team were generating new projects, and throwing up suggestions that were of value away from their area of speciality. The manager was enthusiastic and all the external signs were good. Three months later the team had collapsed. The Assistant Production Manager had left the company to become Head of NPD with a competitor. Investigation showed that the team had been driven by the one person, with the others either making up the numbers or working to his direction. The manager had been content to ride along on the success, with no concern for the longer term. The company were now faced with the prospect of having to build a replacement team from scratch – and a major lesson in the need to monitor team performance had been learned the hard way.

Team assessment is a necessary part of long-term team success, but it can be damaging rather than developmental if wrongly handled. A team will normally unite against a common foe and so an 'outsider' arriving with a questionnaire or some other form of instrument will

Figure 7.1   Team assessment schedule

often be rejected – or receive a bland response. It is far better to provide the team leader with the tools to do the job, and to take the time to show the team members the benefits that they will personally derive from the process.

A typical team assessment schedule uses a Likert-type scale with the focus areas carefully selected to meet the needs of the team and the organization (Figure 7.1). As always the instrument is a vehicle, a tool, which points to areas of strengths and weakness, to individuals who appear to have certain strengths to offer and weaknesses which they may be helped to overcome. It is the use that management make of this information which justifies the use of the instrument. In this it is identical to marketing research. Managers make decisions and take action on the basis of the research information. Research is never a substitute for decisive action.

Team Assessment

As the Training Manager of Acme Boating Company you have processed the results of the NPD team assessment (Figure 7.1). The results are shown below. You are to meet with the team leader in an hour. What action(s) might you recommend?

Questions	Weighted results
1 Team goals How clear are your team goals?	3.5
2 Acceptance How are they accepted by the team as a whole?	4.5
3 Teamwork How well does the whole team work together?	2.9
4 Unity How united is the team?	3.0
5 Standards What standards does the team set?	4.5
6 Achievement How often does the team meet its standards?	5.2
7 Membership Are the team happy with each other?	5.1
8 Professional standards Are the team members satisfied with the professional standards of all team members?	3.8
9 Development How many creative ideas are developed within the team?	2.3
10 Exchange How open is the team to the exchange of ideas?	2.9

(**See** Debriefing at the end of this unit.)

Equalizing opportunities

There are certain groups in every society who are discriminated against because of prejudices and preconceptions. Stereotyping ensures that individuals who appear to meet certain criteria are categorized and it is incredibly hard to break free from this pervasive and pernicious human peculiarity. The larger groups are easy to identify:

- Women.
- People from other racial backgrounds.
- Disabled people.
- Older people.

Within each of these lurk many subgroups: the BBC Radio Programme 'Does he Take Sugar?' demonstrates vividly the tendency of healthy people to treat any handicapped person as if they have lost the use of their minds. Women are automatically expected to pour the tea, to act as the secretary. Disabled are avoided, older people's views are disregarded.

Superficially, there may not appear to be too great a problem. The problem is acknowledged. Legislation exists to ban inequalities. Most individuals readily admit that everybody is equal. But the problem does not lend itself to a logical answer. At the logical level all is in hand – the problem is being faced – it will be solved – things are improving.

It is at the emotional level that managers have real problems. The very people who, approached logically, will agree that discrimination is evil will often reveal their underlying prejudice with a phrase such as 'They can do it every bit as well as we can'. There is also a certain lack of awareness of the cruelty that is inflicted by unthinking people who casually dismiss the very serious and real problems of the disadvantaged.

Legislation exists to ban discrimination, and there is recourse to a variety of statutory bodies for any who feel that discrimination is taking place. That is all very good and proper. Organizations have their declared equal-opportunity policies – but the fact remains that people from certain backgrounds have far less chance of equal opportunity in the real world than those who are 'more equal' by virtue of being able to fit within the accepted criteria.

What can a manager do?

Blindingly obvious is the need to identify and face up to one's own prejudices. This is not to say that they can be removed overnight, but at least the problem can be tackled, and progress made. The first step is to start to believe what is reported. It is far too easy to ignore what is unpalatable, even to say they are exaggerating. The safeguard phrase 'It can't happen here' has been proven wrong, with every country reporting mindless violence against minorities.

A useful technique is to quite seriously place yourself in the shoes of another person, as we suggested earlier. How would you feel in the circumstances you have read about? How would you react? How would you be affected if your job applications were not even read? If your job interviews terminated abruptly? If the promotions and special events always went to others who fitted some classical stereotype?

Why do managers really need to care? Not just because of the morality, legality or cultural policy on equal opportunities, but because such an approach is the only way you can have the choice of the variety of skills and experiences which could be available to your teams. A team of clones, all from the same age group, class, sex or ethnic background is unlikely to have the diversity of experiences, skills and attributes which could make a really great and creative team.

Working within diverse groups has apparently not yet been an issue which has permeated to standard human resources texts, but it is an issue which today's manager will need to recognize. Equality does not imply everyone must think and be the same.

Equal opportunities could make some managers think 'if everyone's the same, it doesn't matter who we choose!' This is naive and incorrect. Life experiences do influence the individual. We now recognize that women managers have people skills which add great value to the organization. Equal opportunities mean getting to know individuals and valuing them for their unique contribution – it is about giving everyone an equal chance to contribute on an equal footing.

Whilst there are the statutory frameworks for individuals to fall back on, the need for one of your team members to have to recourse to them should be seen as something of a failure – of the system, and of the manager. Managers should vigilantly search for evidence of discrimination and take positive action both to prevent it occurring and to remedy any instances where it has already done it's work. In this area the manager, in particular, must lead by example.

Is it important?

Not only is it an important dimension of ensuring harmonious working of individuals and groups, it is costly in terms of prestige and legal costs to get it wrong. In June 1994, an Irish worker won a case for unfair dismissal. He was sacked because 'he didn't fit in'. His failure was an unwillingness to laugh at 'Irish jokes', i.e. jokes made at the expense of the Irish people. The court ruled that this is racist behaviour and that management should be vigilant in their prevention of it.

One of the company's managers, interviewed after the verdict, complained that the ruling was unreasonable because management could do nothing to prevent joke telling at work. Yet as managers we are constantly influencing people's behaviour. We expect staff to be courteous to clients, to wear safety helmets on site, and so on. The fact that some will break the rules is not an excuse not to have rules, nor to allow them to be ignored. In this example the rules are, of course, empowered by statute!

What can the manager do?
There are a number of positive actions which can be taken by a manager:

- Be alert to the style and tone of the behaviour of team members to others – within and without the team. Informal channels of communication and social gatherings can be particularly informative, allowing the natural reactions to show through what may be a cultivated superficial behaviour pattern.
- Lead by example. Do not tell, or allow, 'ist jokes – racist, ageist, feminist – all the 'ists hurt somebody. Do not make remarks which could be construed as offensive – and remember the offence is judged from the viewpoint of the listener. If you are uncertain what is offensive – find out.
- Take strong action to set the tone. Offensive material such as some calendars must not be permitted. Incidents should be directly and immediately tackled. Staff must be clear about what is accepted behaviour, and what is not. They must also know that unacceptable behaviour will result in censure.

General Dwight D. Eisenhower was appointed Supreme Commander of the Allied Forces who were assembling to invade Occupied Europe in 1944. One of his first orders was to the effect that, whereas an officer might refer to another as a 'Stupid Bastard', he would not tolerate reference to a 'Stupid XXX Bastard'. (Where the XXX referred to that person's background of race, religion, sex or colour.) It is reported that a Major General disregarded this order and was immediately removed from command and shipped back home.

Eisenhower realized that to lead one of the largest multi-ethnic, multi-cultural and multi-linguistic teams ever assembled it was imperative that personalities and talents should be judged – never the background of the individuals.

Other types of cross-culture teams
As organizations break down the traditional functional 'chimneys', managers will increasingly find themselves working with teams drawn from other functional areas. Accountants and marketers, or operations and human resource specialists can experience similar cultural problems. The divide between their specialisms can, of itself, set up different cultures. Language is used differently, norms and expectations vary, the reference base tends to be specialism centred.

Similar differences are apparent when individuals from different organizations come together as a result of a merger, or within a joint venture. The IBM dress code, for example, is quite strict, and quite formal. Virgin Records staff have a dress code – which is to be unique within current pop fashion. If IBM and Virgin came together for a joint venture one can imagine the need for considerable emphasis on group dynamics – there would be a lot of ice to break!

Where potential cultural differences can be identified the team leader(s) should anticipate problems and make special efforts in the early stages of team formation to help individuals to come to understand and come to terms with each other.

Staff and team development

When a group is assembled to work together it is not a team. It is a gathering of individuals with the ability to form into a team. Thus the 'working materials' for the manager are individuals. This key factor must never be forgotten because at all times the team is composed of individuals who, for their own reasons, are lending their support and involvement to the team.

Thus the ultimate key to successful development – of individual staff members and the teams they belong to – is to understand that each individual has to be motivated to join the team, and then remotivated to remain with it.

Key factors which affect the way that individual groups form include the:

- Technical factors such as place within the hierarchy and physical location, i.e. the tangible indications of the group's perceived importance to the organization.
- Group dynamics.
- Personal characteristics of the members.
- Leadership.

Many authorities have observed that groups move through a number of stages before developing into an effective team. Team assessment criteria (above) can then indicate the level of team effectiveness – anything from highly productive and cohesive, to low performing and divided. It is obviously better to work harder in the beginning to achieve a high level of effectiveness – it is always much harder to make changes to a group which has stabilized and established its behaviour norms.

Individual factors

An individual can be ordered to join a group, and will doubtless turn up in the appointed place and at more or less the appointed time. The problem is: Will he or she bring their mind with them?

Team leaders don't need bodies! They must have fully committed individuals who are willing (eager?) to share their expertise, to pull their full weight. One person holding back from involvement is a dead weight with which the team has constantly to cope. This, of course, detracts from the effectiveness of the team as a whole. (Adair has stressed the importance of individuals as members of teams that achieve the task.)

It follows that:

- Recruitment is necessary.
- Selection is crucial.
- Motivations must be identified and provided for.
- Promises and commitments must be honoured.

Once again marketing's routine approach to situations provides the marketer with an in-built advantage. Examining the situation from the viewpoint of the audience or the customer is crucial to the package of benefits that is developed. Securing team members can be approached in exactly the same way.

ACTIVITY 7.2

Team recruitment
Assume that you have to recruit a team of five members to work together on a project for at least a year. Meetings will need to be at least weekly, supplemented by interactions between team members as an on-going process.

Identify:

1 A project with which you have familiarity – perhaps an extension to the pavilion of your sports club.
2 Your objectives.
3 The skills and experience needed in your team members.
4 Possible motivating factors you could use to develop your recruitment package.

(**See** Debriefing at the end of this unit.)

Selection

There will always be a range of people from whom one could, in theory, select. These will range from the useless that must be resisted to the extremely desirable – who will already be extremely busy with other projects. Some will be willing to serve, but not skilled. Others may be available, but unwilling to join the team. Skills can usually be bought in from consultants, but this may be inappropriate and, perhaps, too expensive.

At the end of the day one has to be pragmatic and take the best blend that one can secure. Given the inability to predict how a group will shake down, however, a manager with a blend of reasonable people is as likely to do well as another with a group of 'stars'.

It can be argued that 'stars' are not team workers, and may dominate and therefore detract from overall performance – but this is to assume that 'star' refers to idiosyncratic individuals. Some people are star team performers, but not very effective on their own. These are the stars that a manager wants to recruit because their skills are in such areas as team development, mutual support, and self-effacement, in addition to their functional, specialist abilities.

Promises and commitments

During the selection process there is often a period of negotiation as each individual weighs up the benefits of joining the team. It may be necessary to make special arrangements so that team membership is possible – workload may have to be adjusted, time away from the office may be needed.

If such commitments are to be entered into they must be honoured. Before full commitment is given line managers must be consulted, and agree to partial (or full) release of the staff member. Authority to travel must be secured. All the details needed must be tied down.

If this is not done you may find yourself in the embarrassing position of taking the team away and finding that half are entitled to Business Class travel, whilst the others have to go Tourist. That some can stay in four-star hotels, with the others limited to two-star establishments. Bureaucratic distinctions such as these must be identified and dealt with before they arise as problems – they are far more damaging to team spirit and morale than is any internal team dispute.

Membership and authority

The process of group dynamics starts long before the group forms. It begins with the first thoughts that a team may be necessary and develops throughout the recruitment and selection process. Individuals are bound to ask 'Who else is on the team?' and immediately begin the process of slotting the relationships together. This process has been described, by Schultz, as determining who is in or out; who is top or bottom; who is near or far. These stages relate to issues of membership, authority conflict and the development of team relationships.

In some cases individual members will know each other so well that the group dynamic process will be well advanced – for good or ill – long before the group has its first meeting. The experienced team leader knows this, and takes it fully into account in the planning stages. The inexperienced assumes that everybody starts equal on day one of the formal existence of the group – and suffers a rude awakening!

Team development

We have seen in Unit 5 that teams tend to pass through the stages of forming, norming, storming and performing. This can be expressed slightly differently as an aid to understanding the processes needed to develop the team – see Table 7.1.

There is no guarantee that any one group will develop through all the stages and become a fully functioning and effective group to which all are happy to belong. But it is unlikely that the fourth stage will be reached without awareness of the need to pass through the formative stages and a conscious effort to help the group to progress.

Table 7.1 Team development

Stage	Process	Need
Getting together	The members are selected and begin the process of identifying each other	Social interaction
Getting angry	Sorting out formal and informal leadership and authority issues. Exploring skills, experience and credibility of others in the group	Positive leadership that allows time and delays the introduction of important issues until the group is ready to handle them
Getting ready	Group identity begins to form and members develop a sense of belonging	Activities to bind the team. Success in small issues is a great binder
Getting going	Group feels independent and members are clear about mutual roles and the inter-relationships	Task achievement can be fully targeted. Leader's job becomes one of maintenance

Note: It is crucial that team building is done with the group. From inside it. Things done to the group are done by outsiders who, by definition, are alien and cannot share the group identity. It is crucial to recognize this sense of group identity, which can be extremely quick to form.

Some authorities liken the role of the leader to that of a midwife, aware of the stages that must be gone through and making each as smooth and painless as possible.

A new intake of 32 post-graduate students joined a University Business School for a familiarization day at the beginning of a 2-year part-time course. Nobody had met any of the other students. All were new to the university. In the school they were divided into two groups, of 20 and 12.

A week later the course started and the two groups met in separate rooms for their first lessons. At coffee break, after 90 minutes, the Course Director arrived – 'Sorry, we have a slight problem. The classes are not equal, we miscounted. What we need is for four of you to join the other group.'

It took a long time, with much to-ing and fro-ing between the groups before the course team accepted that neither group was willing either: (a) to lose members, or (b) to have new members thrust upon it. The result was that for the whole 2 years the course ran with groups of unbalanced size.

Developing the team

In just the same way that a marketer is aware that every communication is a marketing communication, and that every action or inaction has an effect, so must a team leader be aware that every action, interaction and non-action that is associated with the team has an effect on the team:

- 'That's Joshua in the paper – he's a part of my team at work!'
- 'Good for Mary, she deserved that promotion. Hope she can stay with the team'.
- 'Chris has screwed up again – just what I'd expect without the team to make sure his ideas are implemented'.

There are many behavioural exercises and instruments available to the team leader. These are readily available from any good book shop or, of course, from HRM and/or training.

Ford Motor Company in conjunction with The Industrial Society have taken the unusual step of publishing a loose-leaf binder *Opportunities for Change*, which contains sixty-two instruments for group development (in the context of change). The uses to which each can be put are identified and each is fully explained so that the trainer or manager can use them effectively.

To give one example of such an instrument we have selected the critical-incident analysis (Figure 7.2). This has been chosen because it is suitable for people from a wide range of backgrounds and experiences, and is adaptable to suit many group dynamic needs from self-introductions through to the beginnings of the binding process.

Note: Behavioural instruments can look either very silly, or great fun, depending on the perspective. They have been developed for a specific purpose and if they have survived it is only because they are effective *in the purpose for which they were designed*.

A critical incident is an important, abnormal occurrence. Critical incidents can encapsulate many positive and negative factors, for example, proper training, understanding of health and safety issues, good teamwork, or poor communication and working relationships, lack of training, safety problems, tiredness. It could be a positive incident like a technological breakthrough, or a crisis such as a salesperson losing a key account, but is more likely to be a crisis. It is a very flexible technique and is readily adaptable to a variety of situations.

Uses of critical incident analysis
Analysing an extreme example, a critical incident, is a means of illuminating the everyday situation.

Step-by-step through critical incident analysis
1 Ask each participant to spend a few minutes recalling a critical incident from his/her work experience – in a crisis or at a turning point
2 Ask one person, a volunteer, to describe their critical incident to the group
3 People can ask questions to clarify
4 Ask if anyone has experienced the same or a similar incident. If so, ask them to describe what happened
5 Move to open discussion to find out what the key factors and learning points were for the person, and whether the group can learn anything from this critical incident that they may use in the future

Benefits
• The importance and personal nature of such an incident can lead to insights.
• It sometimes helps the participant who described their critical incident to come to terms with it if it was a painful experience.
• Sharing the incident helps to build trust between group participants.
• Other participants can empathize.
• There are learning points for the whole group.

Limitation
• Take care if the incident was stressful.

Hints
• Don't rush. Better to have one incident take the whole session than to limit discussion.
• Do not use until people feel secure in the group.

Size of group
Up to 12 people.

Time
Allow 45 minutes to 2 hours.

Figure 7.2 Critical incident analysis

When considering the use of such an instrument remember:

• You have to believe in it totally. If you don't believe, then the group won't either.
• It has to be used for the correct purpose, at the correct time. Focus and timing are all. An experienced trainer may carry up to three similar instruments into a session and decide which to use only when there has been time to assess the make-up and mood of the group.

- It has to be understood. All the benefits that can be extracted from the instrument must be appreciated. In many cases there is a superficial use which is obvious, but of far more importance are the subtle points that can be illustrated by an experienced user.
- Always have a dry run with a new instrument. If possible, observe it in use – but always run it through, even if only with the family at home.

> Betterwear Brushes, the door-to-door sales company experimented with US motivational methods in the UK. To whip up enthusiasm they tried to get British sales people to stand on their chairs and whoop the company slogan at the tops of their voices. They tried fast response: Who are We? – We're the Best ... Who Are We? – We're The Best ... WHO ARE WE? – WE'RE THE BEST!!! They tried a company songbook – with Betterwear centred lyrics to be sung to such melodies as John Brown's body. All failed miserably. The British were far too embarrassed to take it seriously. The endeavour was quickly abandoned!

A final point: Team development is an on-going, never-ending process. Even if there are no new members to meld into the team there are psychological changes within the team members themselves as time passes and their skills, experience and seniority develop. Team leadership requires a constant monitoring of the group dynamics and actions with individuals to reinforce or modify attitudes and/or behaviour. Potential problems must be identified and dealt with early if they are not to develop into serious issues.

Counselling

Note that in HRM the term 'counselling' is reserved for issues of personal concern – the Samaritans, for example, are counsellors. Line managers are best advised not to attempt HRM counselling; instead they should be able to suggest a source of help to an individual. Many larger organizations have their own counsellors, and these are available to help with personal problems in conditions of total confidence.

On occasion, it is necessary to engage in counselling, in which case there is need to appreciate these key issues:

- The other person's needs are for counselling rather than advice.
- Advice is from your experience and tends to be prescriptive.
- Counselling helps them to think through a solution from their own experience.
- Often the need is to talk – the actual process of opening up to the problem can of itself be cathartic and show the way to a solution.
- Counselling issues are not normally immediately solvable – be prepared for a long-term counselling relationship if once you open the door.
- A counselling relationship can be intensely personal and restrict your courses of action as a line manager.

If embarking on a counselling relationship there is need to:

- Ensure privacy and ample time.
- Reassure the individual of total confidentiality.
- Show that you are genuinely interested in listening.
- Remain calm throughout.
- Never advise.
- Listen actively.
- Ask open questions.
- Restrict your input to the minimum.
- Make supportive comments and sounds.

- Allow silences to run on for a time.
- Show you are human by revealing things about yourself, almost in passing.
- Act as a sounding board.
- Never pass judgements.
- Don't take over the problem.
- Don't try to take decisions – or force a neat conclusion.
- Establish facts and identify choices.
- *Help the individual to find their own solution.*

Coaching and mentoring

Coaching and mentoring have to do with assisting individuals with job- and task-centred performance and are therefore a form of training. For simplicity, we shall use the term 'coaching' in this section.

One-to-one

The prime requirement is that contact be one-to-one. There is a need to build a personal rapport between manager and individual, and for the relationship to develop over time.

Formal training sessions can input very quickly – but the depth of attitude, skills and knowledge required to do the job effectively is only obtainable on the job. It is here that a coach or a mentor can be highly beneficial.

Coaching is systematically assisting another to acquire skills and knowledge, but it will also involve motivational and attitudinal issues. A coach works closely with another individual and the issue is one of skills and knowledge transfer. Rank does not come into the equation. Therefore a junior can coach a senior and equals can work together. Effective coaching is based on mutual desire – to impart and to learn.

A good coaching relationship has major benefits for both individuals:

- *The individual*:
  - (a) Learns under the watchful eye of an experienced coach in conditions of psychological safety, i.e. errors can be made without fear of criticism and in the knowledge that they will be picked up and corrected before they can do harm.
  - (b) Can develop at their own pace, gradually taking on more responsibility as experience and confidence develop.
  - (c) Have the reassurance of the coach as a fallback, usually not needed, but comforting to have available.
- *The coach*:
  - (a) Learns more about the job through having to break it down so that a beginner can understand it.
  - (b) Can see new/different ways that the job may be tackled.
  - (c) Develops interpersonal and communication skills.
  - (d) Takes a positive step along the manager–leader development path.

To be effective a coach needs a blend of skills, and probably will need to acquire the ability to maximize their use through a formal training period (see Table 7.2).

Learning progress

Learners move through four stages:

- Unconscious incompetence – where they don't know what they don't know.
- Conscious incompetence – where they are aware of their ignorance/inability.
- Conscious competence – where the job can be done with concentration.
- Unconscious competence – where the job is done routinely.

It is the task of the coach to identify where on this continuum a particular individual is located and then to devise learning strategies to help reach the level of unconscious competence.

Table 7.2 The role of the coach

Planner	Identifies and agrees what development is needed Sets objectives Evaluates achievement and modifies plans, as necessary
Partner	Creates opportunities Supports, services, resources Helps with problems – is available
Communicator	Sets communication tone Establishes the learning relationship Advises and suggests Is clear and informative Gives positive feedback
Motivator	Sets expectation level Encourages Gives recognition Challenges

Protector	Sets up conditions of psychological safety
	Prevents overload:
	    Controls the learning flow
	    Restricts additional responsibility until the individual is ready

Learning styles

Individuals have preferences in the way in which they learn, as we saw in Unit 2. One of the problems with group teaching is the inability to tailor the material to the needs of each learner. Attempts are sometimes made to identify learning styles and then to group students by style – but almost always the logistics make this impossible.

A coaching relationship is, by definition, one-to-one and so it is possible for materials to be presented in such as way as to maximize the individual's ability to learn. This, of course, requires a coach who has the ability to change his or her teaching style!

People have different strengths and skills. This means they will tend to enter the learning cycle (Figure 7.3), which we met in Unit 2, at different stages. A good coach will identify where it is most appropriate to pick up the learning, and which style to adopt.

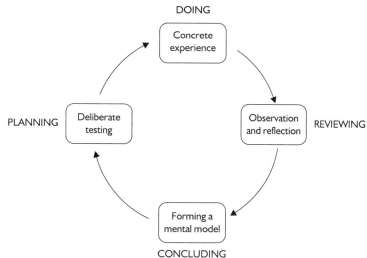

Figure 7.3 The learning cycle

Learning styles
In Unit 2 you identified four learning styles. Using these as the framework, think about the alternative ways you might go about coaching a new staff member in the use of a piece of equipment, or a computer program with which you are familiar.

There is an old trainers' aide-mémoire which does *not* describe coaching:

I do it normal,
I do it slow,
You do it with me,
Then off you go.

'Sitting alongside Nellie' – learning by observation – is *not* coaching. It is a form of training which has been in use for thousands of years. It works, but it is by no means the most effective.

Coaching types

Coaching requires a relationship between the coach and the individual. It is a two-way relationship with both contributing to the learning experience. There are many forms of coaching, the one(s) that are most applicable to need should be selected:

- *Experiential coaching* Where the coach is sharing, or observing at first hand as the individual works through an activity. The role is to encourage, reinforce good habits, and guide away from bad.
- *Reflective coaching* After an experience the coach takes the individual through the key areas so that the act of recalling reinforces the activity. This can be particularly effective in providing new insights and understandings.
- *Guideline coaching* The coach adopts a direct teaching role for a time.
- *Trial coaching* After both parties have evaluated the degree of risk, the individual tries out a new skill as a test for the real thing.
- *Preparatory coaching* If a formal training session is scheduled the coach can be of major benefit in maximizing the learning by talking through the upcoming experience and establishing motivational hooks to underpin and learning objectives to attain.
- *Reinforcing coaching* New learning needs to be reinforced, and put into use. The coach can plan to do this as part of a structured learning plan.

Coaching styles

Evenden and Anderson suggest that five coaching styles can be related to interpersonal roles (Table 7.3).

Table 7.3 Coaching styles and interpersonal roles (Evenden and Anderson)

Interpersonal role	Coaching style	
Judge	Tough	Pushes hard; challenges; makes demands; critical
Helper	Protective	Takes care not to hurt; kindly; reassuring
Thinker	Calculator	Calm; dispassionate; logical; questioning
Fun lover	Whoopee!	Everything is fun; creative; exciting
Defendant	Manipulative	'Winds you up'; provokes; teases; cajoles; humours

Learning styles
The four learning styles from Unit 2 are: activists, reflectors, theorists and pragmatists. Quite obviously, it is for you, the coach, to identify which is the preferred style – which will usually be a blend of two from the four. Then you must set up your teaching so that the materials are presented in a way that makes it as easy as possible for the learner.

> **Note**: There is every reason to use styles that the learner does not prefer – providing it is done deliberately and for a specific purpose. For example, a reflective learner will gain benefit from an activist approach *after* he or she is comfortable with the base material. Similarly, an activist will benefit from being encouraged to penetrate the material and come to grips with the key theories and concepts that make the activity possible.

Coaching styles
For each of the five styles, determine the positive and negative aspects which can impact on the individual and, therefore, on the learning experience.

(**See** Debriefing at the end of this unit.)

ACTIVITY 7.3

Preparing to coach

When preparing to take on a coaching role with an individual it is essential to first distinguish if coaching is really required, or if a short skills or knowledge input will suffice. If coaching is needed then it is necessary to:

- Discover details about the individual to be coached.
- Plan both long- and short-term objectives.
- Review the subject area carefully so that you are up to speed and in practice.
- Make a checklist of equipment, aids, etc., that you will and might need.
- Arrange to meet the individual when both of you can clear space in your days.
- Ensure you have all you need to hand.
- Concentrate at first on building the beginnings of a relationship.
- Agree the long- and short-term objectives. Secure commitment.
- Establish the ground rules:
  (a) When you are to meet.
  (b) How each should and may contact the other.
  (c) That the focus is on the individual, but that both will gain.
  (d) That this is not formal training, not school!
- Ensure that the individual's ability is improved, however slightly, at the first meeting.
- Review the first meeting whilst it is fresh in your mind.
- Make your plans for the second meeting – including the checklist of needed items.

Overall, the intention is to build an on-going and lasting relationship that will provide a foundation on which the individual can rely.

Discipline

Unfortunately, every manager has to discipline staff on occasion. Nobody likes doing it, but experience proves time and again that it is better to deal with an issue whilst it is fresh and relatively insignificant than to delay until it grows into a major problem.

The best way to exert discipline is by withholding praise. A manager who is on top of their role as a people watcher and motivator of individuals has many opportunities for praise, all of which should be taken. A praised team is a happy team. In such circumstances the simple withholding of praise is enough of a signal for an individual to check what is wrong. To want to restore the relationship, to cease feeling that they are letting the team, themselves and the manager down. Note carefully that this is a subtle matter. The manager who stresses the point is verging on bully tactics. Using a heavy club when the lightest of taps is sufficient.

If we assume, however, that matters have gone beyond the point where day-to-day checking is sufficient, we are forced into a formal situation.

Discipline must be formalized

Once it is decided that discipline is necessary it must, reluctantly, be assumed that it may be required again. Thus a disciplinary event must be recorded *at the time* so that it cannot be misremembered or misinterpreted on a future occasion.

This is *not* to say that a formal entry to a personnel record is necessary, but an entry in the manager's desk diary is a worthwhile investment of time. Such an entry keeps the matter 'in house' and can truly be forgotten as time passes and there are no repetitions.

Discipline can be formal or informal. The disciplinary checklist shown in Table 7.4 sets out the stages. The stages are clear and self-explanatory. It is crucial that *facts* are determined and that facts and facts alone are used in the subsequent interview. The individual will probably invoke emotional issues – it is very important to remain calm and to stay with the facts. Never get drawn into an emotional response and never allow personal feelings to cloud your judgement. (Far easier said than done – but absolutely essential.)

Table 7.4 Disciplinary checklist

	Formal discipline	Informal discipline
Don't pre-judge	1	1
Establish the facts	2	2
Listen to the individual(s) involved	3	3
Consult your own management supervision	4	4
Consult the personnel department	5	–
Convene a disciplinary hearing, informing the individual(s) and representative involved	6	–
Listen to mitigation	7	–
Consult further with personnel and your own management/supervision	8	–
Decide on action	9	5
Inform, warn and record	10	6

Disciplinary procedures

If matters reach a state where the situation merits a strict warning as to conduct, then the organization's personnel policy must be checked and followed religiously. Employment law is complex, and not the direct concern of line management. The only safe procedure is to check with HRM, the Company Secretary, or whoever has formal personnel responsibility, and follow the procedures established by them.

There can be only two conclusions to a disciplinary procedure. Either it is followed all the way through to dismissal, or the individual is reinstated. As dismissal is always a possibility, it follows that the provisions of the law, and of any agreements with trade unions and employee bodies must be followed. If they are not followed to the letter, and seen to be so followed, the result can be damaging legislation initiated by the individual against the organization and, in some circumstances, the individual manager. It is vital to check and then follow procedures!

Summary dismissal

In certain circumstance, notably theft, an employee can be summarily dismissed. In such circumstances it is still wise to involve the next layer of management before taking action. It is also extremely important to follow procedure, since summary dismissal can only be for very serious offences and an individual wrongly accused – or wrongly processed – will undoubtedly take legal action.

If tempted to dismiss an individual for theft it is vital to ensure that you have hard evidence. You must have seen the theft, you must know where the stolen items are, and you must not have taken your eyes from the suspect from the time of the theft until the Police arrive.

A manager of a retail records store locked up a shop thief until the Police arrived. This was in itself unlawful, but the situation was made far worse by the choice of the storeroom as the 'cell'. Several hundred records and tapes were in the storeroom and when the police arrived they couldn't identify which the manager had seen the suspect put into his pocket! The accusation – plus the unlawful arrest – could have cost the company dear, but the thief was only too happy to get away on that occasion!

Managers with a suspected thief in their team will do best to report it and then cooperate with experienced security and/or Police Officers who will set out to secure the needed evidence.

Discipline procedure

When you have exhausted the informal procedures and decide to proceed formally, the stages are:

- Review the facts and everything that has been produced as evidence for and against the individual.
- Consult your own manager to confirm that you are supported in the actions you propose.
- Check and confirm that you or your team have not contributed to the actions of the individual, and that your procedures have been followed correctly, i.e. make sure that your own house is in order.
- Consult HRM (and hope that they will take the matter over!).
- Convene a disciplinary hearing. You must inform the individual and his or her representatives, and convene the hearing at a reasonable time to allow them to prepare their case. This must, however, allow proceedings to go forward within any statutory period after the offence.
- The formal hearing should be held away from the individual's place of work.
- State the case, and present the facts.
- Listen to mitigation.
- Allow a recess for further consideration of the facts – and consult with your advisors.
- Decide on action and reconvene the hearing.
- Inform, warn and record. If a verbal warning is issued this is a formal warning and must be so recorded. A written warning will be issued to the individual, but also formally recorded.

Note: Any notes in your diary about previous incidents are not formal warnings and have not, therefore, been formally recorded. In formal terms they do not exist.

It is open for an individual to take out a *grievance procedure* or to take the matter to an *Industrial Tribunal*. In either event the matter should be dealt with by those in the organization with the necessary experience. The manager will normally be called as a witness and the formal records will certainly be entered as evidence. It follows, therefore, that they must be exemplary.

Problems in teams

The ideal team is pictured as a unit of harmony and helpfulness with all team members being valued and valuing others in their turn. But what if this ideal situation does not (yet) exist?

What, for example, should the manager do about conflict in the group? Does this always imply a poor selection of group members? Is conflict always a bad thing?

About conflict

Spend 10 minutes and produce a list of all the benefits and problems you think conflict within a group might create. Use your own experience of groups to help you.

(**See** Debriefing at the end of this unit.)

The team leader should monitor the level of conflict to ensure it has not and does not become destructive. Aggressive contributions, rather than more open assertive statements are a danger signal and managers need to be ready to intervene. If the conflict begins to escalate towards the destructive end of the continuum it takes considerable tact and experience to deal with the situation. The lesson is to monitor constantly, and to move early.

Improving the performance of marketing teams

In this unit we have been considering many of the issues and problems which might face any team leader. Now we shall turn our attention to the specific issues of the marketing team.

The marketing team

Take 10 minutes to identify:

- The special characteristics of a marketing team.
- The implications of these for a marketing manager.

(**See** Debriefing at the end of this unit.)

The marketing manager will be most directly concerned with improving the performance of the marketing team. There are a number of things which can be done.

- Ensure that others in the organization understand the role of marketing. Too many individuals still see marketing as the operational level function responsibility for promotion and publicity. The manager who takes responsibility for 'selling' marketing internally at the strategic level will be helping to win the organizational support and understanding essential to the successful performance of the team.
- Ensure that the team knows what is required of it. This means specific marketing plans with quantified objectives – and the criteria by which the team's performance will be judged should be clearly established and communicated to all involved. The planning framework needs to be understood, with each team member participating in the process and contributing to it. The marketing plan must be broken down so that each section and individual appreciates both the overall strategy and their contribution to its achievement.
- Marketing managers must convince and motivate the team so that the set objectives are seen as achievable. If they are felt to be impossible there is likely to be a reluctance to commit fully to their achievement. A self-fulfilling prophecy of failure! Managers must recognize the need not simply to present plans, but also to sell them to those who have to deliver.
- Teams need the resources to accomplish the tasks in hand. The marketing manager can help performance by proactively identifying resources and support needed and by seeking this out on behalf of the team.

- Teams need the skills to do the job. A manager who knows his or her team is in an excellent position to:
  (a) Evaluate the task in hand.
  (b) Identify any skills gaps.
  (c) Take action to fill those gaps.
  Either training or seconding a new team member for the duration of the project can be equally effective in filling a skills gap. The manager who thinks ahead will ensure that the team's performance is not hampered by a predictable bottleneck.
- Constructive feedback on performance is vital as a motivator and to keep open the channels of communication within the group. The manager who actively seeks feedback at all levels will be:
  (a) Better able to anticipate possible problems.
  (b) Able to take corrective action(s) sooner.
  (c) Able to cascade 'best practice' into the rest of the team.
  (d) In a position to improve performance levels through more effective planning.

A vigilant and involved marketing manager will identify potential problems early, and take appropriate action before an unfortunate situation develops.

The most effective marketing team will be a group of individuals who respect and value each other's skills and expertise, and share the same goals and objectives. They need to pull together, but must be able to accept the input of others and to work flexibly with other functions and agencies.

There is no magic formula which the manager can apply to ensure success. Dealing with people is challenging and complex, but empathy and awareness will help any manager to monitor and improve a team's activities.

EXTENDING ACTIVITY 7.2

Take some time to consider the team you work with. This could be a marketing or sales team, or a less formal grouping such as a syndicate group in college.

How much positive action can you identify which is taken to enhance team performance? Produce a checklist of five actions which could be taken to help improve the team's activities.

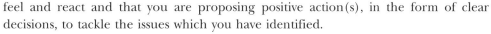

EXAM HINTS

In the Effective Management for Marketing paper you will often be faced with scenarios which require you to deal with problems – or, perhaps, will allow you to anticipate possible problems. The examiners will value highly evidence that you are thinking about how team members might feel and react and that you are proposing positive action(s), in the form of clear decisions, to tackle the issues which you have identified.

For example, a new staff member needs to be integrated quickly. Recommendations for introducing them, promoting their skills as of value to the group and ways to involve them effectively would be required. A member of staff who must be disciplined is likely to feel defensive and/or aggressive, and you need to show that you would take care in identifying the causes of the problem and in handling whatever you found to be the true situation.

Take a structured approach to questions which require some thought about the best strategy for handling the problem(s). Use the first section of your answer for a background or overview to specify how you think individuals may be feeling and how they might respond. This empathy is an important characteristic of an effective manager and you need to demonstrate that you have skills in that area before moving on to recommend solutions to the problem(s) identified.

Allow 20 minutes to think through the implications of the following scenario and then write your answer in no more than 25 minutes. (In your examination you will have only 45 minutes to answer a question of this nature.)

You have been offered an earlier than expected promotion – you know you have done well in the 6 months you have been with the organization, but to become a team leader so quickly . . . you feel very flattered. Then you meet a long-standing team leader at the coffee machine:

'Oh, they've given you the push then.'
'What on earth do you mean?' 'That team you're taking over – it's had three leaders in the last year alone. Nobody ever lasts. Good luck. You'll need it!'

You are committed to the new job, and start in 10 days. What actions do you plan to take to make a success of the appointment?

W. Edwards Deming: quality crusader

A key originator, together with J.M. Duran, of the concept of total quality management (TQM), Deming had to go to Japan from his native America in order to find recognition of his ideas. Japanese-manufactured goods were once proverbial for their shoddiness, but after the Second World War the Japanese realized that something drastic had to be done if their economy was to recover. Instead of trying to 'improve their image' or adopt any other essentially cosmetic solution, they went directly to the heart of the matter under the leadership of W. Edwards Deming.

So successful were his ideas, and so effectively were they instituted by Japanese management, that he became a national celebrity in Japan. Even today a Deming Prize is awarded each year in a nationwide quality-improvement contest. He was 'discovered' by the Japanese in 1950; it was not until the late 1980s that the Americans produced a National Commitment to Quality, and the European Union its own TQM commitment.

Ford has given Deming much of the credit for its turn around in the early 1970s – they estimate that 95% of their employees became aware that quality was their first priority. Deming claims that only 15% of production faults are the fault of employees; 85% are down to management. He has produced 14 points for top managers who want to promote quality – failure to adhere to any one of them, he warns, can be catastrophic. His key priorities have not changed since 1950, they are: precision, performance and attention to customers. His 14 points of management are:

1 Plan for the long-term future, not for next month or next year.
2 Never be complacent concerning the quality of your product.
3 Establish statistical control over your production processes and require your suppliers to do the same.
4 Deal with the fewest number of suppliers – the best ones, of course.
5 Find out whether your problems are confined to particular parts of the production process or stem from the overall process itself.
6 Train workers for the job you are asking them to perform.
7 Raise the quality of your line supervisors.
8 Drive out fear.
9 Encourage departments to work closely together rather than to concentrate on departmental or divisional distinction.
10 Do not be sucked into adopting strictly numerical goals, including the widely popular formula of 'zero defects'.
11 Require your workers to do quality work, not just to be at their stations from 9 to 5.
12 Train your employees to understand statistical methods.
13 Train your employees in new skills as the need arises.
14 Make top managers responsible for implementing these principles.

In this unit you have seen that:

- Any areas of prejudice and bias which may affect your judgement should be identified through self-auditing – and then corrected through appropriate actions.

- Teams should be formed around task objectives. The manager should help to select the team to ensure the necessary blend of skills and experience to do the job, plus the ability to quickly function as an effective team.

- Team assessment is necessary as a part of long-term success, but can be damaging rather than developmental if badly handled.

- It is very hard to break free from stereotyping, but this pervasive and pernicious human peculiarity must be resisted – quite apart from the legal necessity to do so.

- 'It can't happen here' has constantly been proven wrong, with every country reporting mindless violence against minorities. Unfortunately many sincere people believe they are not prejudiced, even in the face of clear evidence to the contrary.

- Placing yourself in the shoes of another person will reveal the actual degree of equal opportunity and displayed prejudice. Once identified it will require firm action, often over considerable time, to correct the actual as compared to the theoretical situation.

- Positive action is required to avoid damage in terms of prestige, legal costs and internal demotivation. Be alert to the behaviour of team members; lead by example; remember that offence is judged from the viewpoint of the listener; take strong action to set the tone.

- Cultural differences can be created by functional 'chimneys' but may only become apparent when individuals from different functions (cultures) come together. When organizations merge, or operate as a joint venture, the issue of culture must have priority to minimize misunderstandings – and to avoid giving offence.

- Constant monitoring, as routine, will allow conflict to be identified early. Identification allows appropriate actions to be taken and may prevent disciplinary or grievance procedures.

- Both discipline and grievance procedures must be entered into carefully, carried through with precision, and rigorously documented.

- Groups move through developmental stages as they form into effective teams. Each individual has to be motivated to join a team, and re-motivated to remain within it.

- Recruitment is necessary; selection is crucial; motivations must be identified and provided for; promises and commitments must be honoured.

- Star individuals may not make good team members; star team members may not be effective on their own. Individuals and tasks must therefore be matched, and each individual's skills valued. Team membership is an on-going, never ending process.

- Counsellors must appreciate that the other person needs help to think through a solution from their own experience . . . they do not need advice. A counselling relationship can become intensely personal and restrict a line manger's courses of action.

- Coaching is systematically assisting another, of whatever rank or status, to acquire skills or knowledge. Coaches need a blend of skills to develop learning strategies that help learners reach the stage of unconscious competence.

- Marketing team performance can be improved through ensuring that marketing is understood within the organization; the team knows what is required of it . . . and is convinced and motivated; the resources to accomplish the task are to hand; the team has the skills to do the job.
- Effective marketing teams are groups of individuals who respect and value each other's skills and expertise, share the same goals and objectives, and receive constructive feedback.
- The examiners value evidence that you are thinking about how team members might feel and react and that you are proposing positive action(s), in the form of clear decisions, to tackle the issues which you have identified.

Debriefing

Activity 7.1

As Training Manager, you may have some serious concern about the manager who is leading this team. Thus the prime need may be to help him or her to acquire the skills that are either absent or not being used. Discover which!

This is a NPD team, and so low scores on questions 9 and 10 (creativity and exchange) must lead to serious concern. Standards: questions 5 and 6 cannot be taken at face value given the answers to questions 7 and 8. This team seems happy to be together, but does not show up too well in terms of its own rating on the key issues. Thus there must be a question of whether their standards are too low?

Goal clarity is low rated, at 3.5, and acceptance is not surprisingly too low also. It is quite good to see these two figures quite close – it may indicate a reliability to all the figures.

The teamwork and unity scores of only 2.9 and 3.00 are what causes the concern over the manager. Perhaps the immediate needs are to develop leadership skills in the manager, and then to take the time to develop the team into a working entity. Forming has happened, but the norming stage still seems to be causing a problem. There is a way to go to get through storming and into performing. Let us take it one step at a time. The manager is the key priority. We have to win his or her confidence and develop from there.

Activity 7.2

Midland Sports Club – Pavilion extension.
Requirement: To have the new extension open and fully operational ahead of the 199X Club Day, i.e. within 15 months.

Objectives:

1 Within 4 weeks to recruit a team of five people with the necessary skills and experience to take the project through from concept to completion.
2 Within 8 weeks to have the team established and working as a unit.
3 To hold the team together through the life of the project so that the requirement is met.

Skills and experience needed:

1 Financial skills sufficient to negotiate budget with Club Committee and contractors.
2 Negotiating skills developed by experience.
3 Building and/or surveying and/or architectural skills.
4 Local Government experience, especially of Planning and/or Building Regulations.
5 Club experience and contacts.
6 Marketing skills.

Note: This blend is of skills – not of people. Between them the five recruited people must possess all these skills; they are not to be held exclusively by individuals.

Motivations that could be used include:

1 Status:
   (a) Within the Club as one of the team that made it possible.
   (b) Within the Community as part of the opening publicity.
2 Achievement:
   (a) Pride in the achievement.
   (b) Addition to CV as a factor to improve value as an employee.
   (c) PR potential for self-employed specialist, e.g. surveyor.
3 Responsibility – opportunity to take responsibility (to manage).
4 Authority – chance to act independently.
5 Curiosity – opportunity to explore, to develop new ideas and to expand skills base.
6 Gratitude – chance to repay the Club members for kindnesses, etc.
7 Club spirit – desire to enhance the Club.

Note: Probably a mixture of motivations that tapped into club spirit but provided opportunities for self-development and/or publicity would be the most effective combination. Providing that the mixture was blended for each individual.

Activity 7.3
You will probably have come up with the issues in the following table. It should be apparent that each style has a place, and that individuals will benefit from a coach who has the skills to select and use the appropriate style to suit the present need.

Positive	Style	Negative
Can push through difficulties when the going gets hard	Tough	Can produce rebellion. May lead to bad feelings
Can lift a person when they are low	Protective	Can stunt development by being over-protective
Can help the individual to find solutions and help them work them out	Calculator	Can be seen as impersonal and distant. All head and no heart.
Can motivate by energy and enthusiasm	Whoopee!	Can be seen as frivolous. May avoid tough issues
Can energize and influence	Manipulative	May produce anger and feelings of betrayal

Activity 7.4
These are our lists. Use them to extend your thinking.

Benefits	Problems
Stimulates different solutions	Breaks up trusted relationships
Encourages creativity and brainstorming	Divides the group into camps
Focuses on the opinions and contributions of individuals	Causes people to erect barriers and become defensive
Allows the letting off of steam – opens communication	Leads to win/lose negotiations
May challenge the accepted approach and/or the status-quo, thus encouraging thinking	Distracts the group from the main objective(s)

As can be seen, conflict is not always totally negative. Major benefits can come from managed conflict.

Activity 7.5
The key characteristics are:

- Diverse backgrounds and skills. The team may contain MkIS and MR specialists as well as account planners and creative people. The diversity of backgrounds can be the basis of 'cultural' problems.
- The team is directly involved with customers. At the sharp end they need support and additional motivation when things become difficult.
- Individuals may be physically distanced from each other. Sales people, especially, are remote from the team, and special efforts are needed to ensure that the team is united and motivated.
- External agency staff may be in the team, but not within the organization. Marketing teams frequently include PR, advertising and research agency staff who need to be integrated if optimum benefits are to be achieved.

Unit activity
This is one of several possible approaches to the situation. It is a credible approach which managers of a certain style could adopt with confidence. If your preferred approach differs it does not mean that you would fail! In the examination the need is to show the examiner that you have a style and that you are willing and able to make clear decisions based on reasonable assumptions.

Working on the assumption that there are some good people in the team you decide that they either have a major compatibility problem, or that one or more team members are particularly difficult. You decide that you:

- Are going to succeed where others have failed.
- Need hard evidence, not rumour.
- Want management support if you discover the root of the problem to be one person or a minority of individuals.
- May need to be a tough manager at first – you can always relax later.
- Will be honest and open with the team.

The grapevine probably identifies the key figures in the group, and adds a little colour, but you are aware that this is an external view which may be deliberately encouraged by the team. They may love their reputation as a hard bunch!

Armed, hopefully, with management support you keep the first meeting brief, crisp and to the point:

- We have a bad reputation.
- We need to look at that and see if it is how we want to be, how we want to behave.
- If we do want to be the bad guys, fine, but let's enjoy what we do. (Note: A tactical position, see below.)
- First thing is to get to know each other – you need a manager and I need a team.
- My job is to make it possible for you to enjoy what you do.
- Talk to me, tell me what needs doing. I can't promise results but I do promise effort.

Then meet each individual in as relaxed a situation as possible. Tease out the skein of interrelationships, discover why previous managers left. Is the group feeling abused? Why?

When there is sufficient information, and not before, convene a closed-doors staff meeting. No-holds-barred, get the facts out. If an individual is difficult grant him or her the right of the floor until (if) it is necessary to tackle the issue head on. Thus it is vital that this meeting not be held until you are confident you have the facts.

Carry through with individual meetings that examine the situation in depth from each individual's perspective.

Determine if there is anyone who is too disruptive to keep in the team. Ask management to exclude him or her. Fire them if necessary.

Build a future for the team, of which you must work to command respect and then membership. Determine what motivates them, and go out of your way to secure resources and praise for the team from management.

Make it clear that you are with the team, in the team, and staying there. Naturally, you will ensure that any negative, defensive grouping is dealt with – but overtime. At first you may even have to go along with a defensive role to secure group acceptance. So be it – providing your sights are clearly set on the long-term good of the individuals and of the team.

Managing change

In this unit you will:

- Examine the importance of change for today's managers.
- Review the processes for implementing change.
- Identify the elements of an internal marketing plan.

By the end of this unit you will:

- Appreciate the critical importance of a positive attitude to change.
- Understand the complexity and challenge of managing the process of change.
- Be aware of techniques to maintain motivation and facilitate change through people.
- Be able to produce and implement an internal marketing plan.

Change is seldom popular and most of us are less comfortable with the unknown than with the known. Marketers are themselves often at the leading edge of change activity involved in identifying new opportunities and directions for the organization. Marketing skills are increasingly being called upon to help to market change to the internal customers who must be informed, persuaded and committed if change is to be effective. It is therefore no surprise to find that this topic is an important one within the Effective Management for Marketing syllabus. It is one which you can expect to arise both directly and indirectly and will influence the way in which you tackle questions and present your recommendations within the scenarios you will be set.

It is important, for example, to recognize that when you make recommendations to reorganize, introduce quality initiatives or for further staff training that these may be met with concern, resentment or even hostility.

The examiners will be looking for evidence that you are able to 'market' your recommendations, and that you have presented relevant benefits to meet the needs of the audience(s) with whom you are communicating.

You should allow 2 hours to complete this unit and a further 2 hours for the activities.

It is not only within the organization that you will be faced with change. The Effective Management for Marketing syllabus is itself a change. It is a part of the revisions introduced by the CIM with Syllabus 94 and, like all papers, you can expect minor modifications and development over time. Although these workbooks will be updated regularly it is important that you ensure that you are up to date with any syllabus changes which the examiners might have recently introduced.

- Take time to check the syllabus against that which you will have been sent by the Institute on enrolment as a student for the course – this will probably be found in your Fact File.
- Keep up to date with any changes communicated to you through the student publication, *Marketing Success.*
- Ensure that you have copies of the latest examination papers. These are obtainable from the Education Department at the CIM, Moor Hall. Use these papers to help you identify the areas which the examiner is concentrating on and to identify any change in emphasis as time passes.

Explanations and definitions

1 *Change* Any alteration, positive or negative, to the status quo. The tendency is for change to be resisted - even a return to the original situation after a time working in a changed environment. 'Just as we got used to it they changed it back!'

2 *Internal marketing* Treating the internal audiences as customers, and applying the marketing concept to internal need.

'This is the way we do it round here . . .'

It is phrases like this which anchor an organization to its tried and trusted modus operandi – to the custom and practices of the past. These words can be used to quiet the voices and kill ideas for change. Explicitly spoken or implicit to behaviour they can be particularly effective in silencing the new staff member. In keeping them in 'place' until they have been indoctrinated into the old ways. But are these advocates of the tried and trusted correct?

Why is change needed, and if it is desirable why are we so resistant to it? Do we need change?

Change is inevitable, it is a fact of life. There is nothing new about change, only our awareness of the process and possibly the speed of change are unique to the 1990s. Organizationally, change is precipitated by the external environment. It is caused by changing legislation or technology, by the changing demands resulting from demographic or cultural shifts amongst our customers or the activities of our competitors.

To survive, organizations have to change, to evolve in line with environmental pressures. If they fail to move with them they will waste resources in the unproductive activity of resistance and in trying to shore up old and inappropriate structures and systems. Organizations have to be dynamic to survive in today's challenging business environment. In this context change can be seen as an inevitable, if undesirable activity, but it also has positive features.

Change can engender creativity, it can be refreshing. As individuals we relish the stimulation of spending 2 weeks in a different country, the new experiences and activities associated with our holiday. The new experiences help us to recharge our personal batteries. We talk about 'a change being as good as a rest'. Organizations can similarly benefit from change. Introduction of new methods, rearranging systems and reorganizing the people can increase productivity and freshen a maturing operation. It can reposition the organization in a way which increases its competitive advantage and gives it a greater opportunity for growth.

ACTIVITY 8.1

Why do we resist change?
If organizational change is inevitable and potentially beneficial, why do people in business resist change? Spend 15 minutes drawing up a list of the reasons why people oppose change. Draw on your own experience of change to help you.

(**See** Debriefing at the end of this unit.)

Once you appreciate why individuals are likely to resist change you are in a much stronger position to manage the process of change. Take away the barriers and offer incentives to those whose behaviour you want to influence and change will occur more smoothly.

Developing a culture for change

The attitude or culture of the operation is critical to the acceptance of change. Culture is strongly influenced by management and the successful manager of tomorrow will need not only to be flexible to change, but excited by it – actively seeking new methods of work. A management team which actively seeks out change will create a culture where change is the norm and therefore less frightening. An organization used to change will find further change easy. As in taking exercise, muscles which are painful at first become stronger and more flexible with use.

ACTIVITY 8.2

Test your own attitude to change
Look at the following pairs of statements and tick the one which best represents your view.

1 (a) I believe if something isn't broken don't try and fix it.
  (b) I believe there is nearly always a better way of doing something.
2 (a) Years of experience in an industry or role can generate advantages because the learning curve for new people is steep.
  (b) New people challenge old wisdom and bring with them new ideas and approaches which make the cost of learning new roles worthwhile.
3 (a) I enjoy going to new places and doing new things on holiday.
  (b) I prefer to go to places I know and do things I am sure I will like, holidays are too precious to risk!
4 (a) I enjoy the opportunity to work on new projects or with new customers.
  (b) I prefer to look after established activities.

Add your own questions to this list, they will help you discuss the attitude of others to change at work.

(**See** Debriefing at the end of this unit.)

What creates the right environment for change?

Having identified the factors which individuals do not like about change it is possible to produce a checklist of factors which would create an environment to stimulate and encourage a positive response to change.

Attitude

High on the list of critical factors is attitude. We saw in Unit 2 the importance of attitude and have identified that the attitude of senior management is central to the culture of the organization. Managers have to set the tone for change, be eager to look for new ideas and approaches and reward those staff with innovative ideas.

The organization has to establish a culture which is excited and positive about change. This means becoming a 'learning organization'. A learning organization is one where everyone in the organization is expected to constantly learn and develop new skills which equip them not for the job today – they are expected to be competent at that – but for the changed job they will have tomorrow. This process requires all managers constantly to audit the available skills and forecast future needs and develop contingency plans. Development is designed as an on-going process to fill the emerging gaps. All systems and processes are similarly reviewed and modified as part of the growing and learning process.

In organizations which recognize the inevitability and desirability of change managers can take a positive attitude to it. Pro-active not reactive responses means that the pace and direction of change can be managed, thus removing one of the worries about change.

Systems to encourage creativity and innovation

Feedback systems, suggestion schemes and creative sessions such as brainstorming can all be established to encourage staff to contribute ideas which will help improve the efficiency or effectiveness of the operation. The actual process of idea generation encourages people not to accept the status quo, but constantly to review, question and seek for change.

Ideas . . . Ideas . . . Ideas . . .
Imagine being asked to set up a staff suggestion scheme at your company or college. Spend 20 minutes and draw up a checklist of factors which would be important if such a scheme was to be successful.

(**See** Debriefing at the end of this unit.)

ACTIVITY 8.3

Rewards

To encourage change, rewards must be built in to help overcome individual's resistance and to compensate them for the 'pain' and 'risk' of change. Rewards need not be financial, they can take the form of improved skills, more interesting work, more responsibility, or enhanced personal or company prospects.

Flexibility

Forward-looking organizations recognize both the need for and frequency of possible changes and are increasingly looking for techniques which will help make the organization more flexible. Staff are employed on temporary contracts, organization structures favour flexible matrices and changing teams are supported by a small core of central services. Management writers such as Charles Handy predict the increased use of consultants and self-employed outworkers, who can be brought in as and when needed.

The Civil Service has a custom and practice of job moves on a regular basis. An Executive Officer working in traffic planning one year can find his or her next placing in education. This enforced frequent change encourages a certain flexibility amongst officers and avoids the more static specialization which has tended to dog the private sector. On the other hand, it can be argued that an individual without a long-term commitment will take short-term decisions. Thus there is a need for careful management control!

Involvement

No one likes changes which are imposed. If senior management simply 'informs' staff of change decisions they are more likely to be met with resentment. Change which involves all the people, from idea generation to implementation, is more likely to be greeted more with enthusiasm and less with suspicion. Effective internal marketing of change can help to achieve this. We will be examining how to develop internal marketing plans later in this unit.

The catalysts for change

The marketing manager may be involved in managing change on a large or small scale and the catalyst for that change may be found inside or outside the organization.

External catalysts

A change in legislation can force change on people, although this is often relatively small change. New rules involving the storage of fresh foods, for example, may require retailers to change their display equipment and marketers to review their merchandizing strategy. More significant changes like the relaxation of Sunday Trading Laws or the deregulation of the Financial Services Sector clearly generate more significant changes.

Organizations may actively lobby against changes, such as when the UK Brewers were faced with restrictions from the Monopolies and Mergers Commission, but if they fail to influence the politicians, then they have to adapt to the enforced changes. The marketing manager must then play his or her role in helping the changes be implemented.

Similarly, activity by customers, suppliers or middlemen can force change upon an organization. Retail supermarkets in the UK have increased pressure on the manufacturers to change their approach to branding and competitive activity. The retail customer has little to gain from brand wars which switch market shares, but fail to increase total spending.

Environmental interest from consumers has been a significant catalyst in encouraging reviews of product policies from development through testing to packaging and presentation. Consumer groups have forced changes in labelling and promotional activity.

Information systems which monitor developments that could lead to enforced change give organizations advance warning of possible change and so allow the maximum time to lobby and/or to plan for change. There is a need to either introduce an MIS with this capacity, or to modify the present information system so that it provides the needed information in time for it to be of value. An effective MIS is proactive.

Internal catalysts

The second source of change catalysts is from within and finds its source in the organization seeking to retain or gain competitive advantage. Change is likely to be needed when, for example, responding to newly identified markets, or taking up the cost-saving opportunities offered by new technologies. These changes are more proactive and resistance to them, at least from senior managers, is likely to be less. Often they are sponsored by a 'champion', perhaps a new Managing Director or Marketing Director. New senior appointments are less likely to be influenced or silenced by 'that's not how we do it around here' arguments. More junior appointees may find their enthusiasm blocked by line managers who have sufficient power to block initiative. They may need a senior manager to positively identify and deal with the problem. If there is a high level of staff turnover in one department it may well be for this very cause.

Work alone, or better still, find some colleagues and brainstorm the changes which your department and organization have implemented over the last few years. Use a college or social club if you don't yet have work experience.

Hint: Use a mind map, whether you are alone or with others. It will provide an excellent focus and stimulate creative and innovative thoughts.

- Identify whether each change was caused by internal or external factors.
- Which were the easiest and which the most difficult changes to make and why?
- Make a list of the ways in which your team or company could manage change more effectively.

Self-check 8.1

Take time to answer the following questions to help you assess your understanding of the material covered so far in this unit.

1 Why is change inevitable?
2 What would you say are the main costs of change?
3 Are there circumstances when change would be inappropriate?
4 Can you think of a single question most likely to promote a questioning and positive approach to change within an organization?
5 How can improved internal communication help the management of change?

(**See** Debriefing at the end of this unit.)

Managing the process of change

Change cannot simply be allowed to drift, it must be managed if it is to be implemented effectively. Note: Management always requires a control on activity. Management of change requires particular stress on the monitoring of the process – in detail. Management of change requires a specific plan and we can use the familiar planning framework as a checklist for reviewing the change process.

- *Background* Why do we need to change? An analysis of the current position, identification of the relevant forces catalysts driving us towards change and an audit of the factors resisting any proposed change.
- *Objectives* What do we intend to achieve through this change? Our objective(s) must encompass management's vision of change. Like all objectives they should be specific, measurable, achievable, relevant and timed.

An objective to change
Review this list of change objectives. Comment on the value of each.

   (a) To gain a quality award, e.g. BS 5750, for the company as soon as possible.
   (b) To reduce the number of customer complaints from 10 in 1000 to 2 in 1000 by the end of next year.
   (c) To introduce a new computerized customer records system within 6 months.
   (d) To implement a proactive equal opportunities policy over the next year.
   (e) To increase the proportion of disabled people employed by the company from 5 to 15 per cent over the next 3 years.
   (f) To attract an average of three suggestions per employee in the first 12 months of our new staff suggestion system.
   (g) To improve our customers' perception of the quality of our customer care from an average of 50 per cent to an above average 70 per cent, within 12 months.
   (h) To complete the integration of the sales and marketing teams within 4 weeks.

(**See** Debriefing at the end of this unit.)

Strategy

Once objectives for change have been established, management can go about the task of identifying an appropriate strategy for change. Choice criteria should enable the identification of options as well as of approaches which best suit the strengths and philosophy of the organization.

Major changes, such as changing the organization culture from a product to customer orientation are likely to require a combination of strategies employed over a considerable time. This might include reorganization of the operation, customer care training throughout the company and the achievement of a quality award such as BS 5750.

Tactics

Specific action plans need to be drawn up if change is going to be implemented effectively. These must identify what needs to be done, who needs to do it and by when. Major changes are often managed by an external consultant who is perceived to be more objective and specialized in organizational development or, what is currently a popular approach, 're-engineering'. At this tactical level the internal marketing of the change needs to be considered and an internal marketing plan developed.

Control

The control stage is essential and will incorporate the budget, a specific timetable and feedback systems to enable managers to monitor the implementation and impact of change.

For example, a bonus system implemented for retail managers and assistants may be monitored:

- Total bonuses paid per week.
- Changes in store turnover.
- Changes in staff turnover.
- Changes in absenteeism.
- Changes in customer complaints/compliments about service levels.

Marketing managers need to recognize that, although the scale of changes they are proposing may seem less significant than perhaps organizational level change, they can affect individuals, their security and perceived roles within the team much more dramatically. Plans to change the office around, to develop a new reporting system, or to introduce an appraisal system can meet with a great deal of resistance. All change should be taken seriously, planned and implemented with consideration and care.

EXTENDING KNOWLEDGE

Because change is seen as so fundamental to successful organizations, it has been the subject of many books on management. A number of these are not traditional textbooks, but written as books on 'How I did it', or as a series of observed cases. Make a point of choosing one or two of these and reading them before the end of your course. Most are widely available in libraries and high street book stores. The short list below is only a starting point, you will find many more examples and will certainly find more than one which is an enjoyable and entertaining read.

- *In Search of Excellence*, Tom Peters
- *The Change Masters* and *When Grants Learned to Dance*, Rosabeth Moss Kanter
- *Making It Happen*, John Harvey Jones
- *Up the Organization*, Robert Townsend.

The marketing of change

Only in the traditional command style hierarchies associated with scientific management could you expect change to simply be imposed. The only exception to this would perhaps be at a time of crisis, when there is no opportunity for internal marketing decisions or long-term planning.

As the increase in knowledge spreads, and the flattening of hierarchies leads to the general recognition that the more informal and responsive manager–leader style is generally more effective, so the need to involve staff in planned change and to 'market' change to them becomes increasingly important. In this context the skills of the marketer are being called upon to develop internal as well as external plans.

We refer to this as internal marketing, but this term along with 'internal customers' has also been picked up by those involved in quality initiatives. It is used to refer to the concepts and systems involved with ensuring quality service. Internal marketing encourages staff to recognize those whom they deal with within the organization as 'customers' and to strive to satisfy their needs.

Current research indicates that internal marketing is recognized and undertaken within firms, but in an informal and often uncoordinated way. It is seen as being an important device for evolutionary change within companies, promoting understanding between functional areas and stimulating improved communication within and between teams. At the end of the day individual managers are likely to recognize the value of taking time out to 'market' their plans internally,once they see for themselves the effectiveness of so doing.

An element in the shift towards flatter management structures is the need for teams to share the vision and culture of the organization, understand the objectives set, and believe in the agreed strategy. Achieving this requires effort, information, persuasion and reminding, but the resulting synergy from a team pulling not only towards the same goal, but along the same path is worth the internal marketing investment (Figure 8.1).

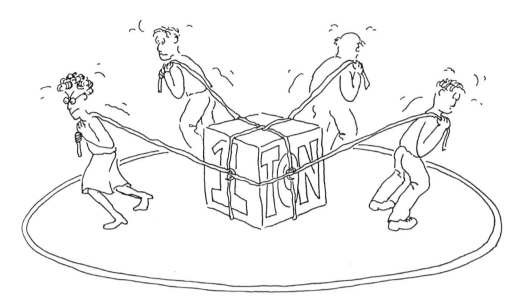

The goal is to get the box over the line

Better this way!

Figure 8.1

QUESTION 8.1

Think about a change which has recently been introduced in your organization. Would you say it was marketed effectively internally?

Use the space below to help you review this event.

What was the change? _____

_____

How important (on a scale of 1 to 10) was the change to the team/organization? _____

How important (1–10) did the staff involved perceive it to be? _____

How was the change presented and marketed internally? _____

_____

What was effective about this approach? _____

_____

How could this approach have been improved? _____

_____

Produce a short personal checklist to help you when faced with introducing change to your team.

Planning for internal marketing

As was indicated earlier, in practice the process of internal marketing is likely to be handled informally, probably not documented as an external marketing plan would be. However the framework of the marketing plan is equally valid for any type of marketing and certainly provides a focus for internal marketing. In the examination you may well be required to present your internal marketing proposals explicitly in the form of a marketing plan.

Internal marketing audit

Once you know what change you are trying to achieve you can undertake research to assess your current position. What is the behaviour or attitude today? How big a change is necessary? What is the likely cause and scale of resistance?

It is important that the manager identifies the target audience(s) directly and indirectly influenced by the change and establishes:

- The decision making unit. e.g. trade unions may act as advisers or influencers.
- Who are the key opinion formers?
- The channels of communication, both formal and informal – the grapevine can be critical when implementing change.

Establishing a strategy for change

How do you intend to introduce the change:

- After consultation with those involved?
- Quickly (revolutionary change)?
  Slowly (evolutionary change)?
- Is the change going to be tested, evaluated and rolled out – or applied universally?
- How do you plan to 'position' the change – as exciting/new/improving or as critical/ enforced/unwilling, e.g.

     'I'm sorry but Head Office has insisted we adopt the new sales call report systems.'

  or

     'This new sales call report system is a change we badly needed. It looks like it will save time and provide us with better sales data.'

The internal marketing mix

Product

What is the change you are planning to introduce? What will it do (functionally), and what is its likely image? A good marketer and manager will think through how best the change can be 'packaged'. That means recognizing the needs of the team and turning the features of the change into relevant benefits for them.

Introducing a customer-oriented culture is a change which many staff believe will make them more work. This is usually not the case.

The Personnel Department of a Local Authority were being threatened with decentralization. They called on marketing to help promote their cause, to communicate the benefits of their role to their internal customers.

The audit stage showed that, whilst the Personnel staff were generally perceived as friendly, helpful and approachable, they were not rated highly for efficiency or effectiveness. A central issue was the time taken to issue contracts of employment to new staff. Several weeks delay caused concern, anxiety and was a poor first impression of the service.

Resource cuts and staff shortages were blamed for the poor performance in this area, but it was felt impossible to deliver the group's product – the employment contracts – any faster. Marketing asked the Personnel team to consider the real needs of this target audience – new Local Authority employees.

Clearly it was not the 'contract' which staff wanted. Their need was for reassurance that they were on the staff, covered by the terms of their contract and going to get paid! A change in the procedures was recommended. A standard letter was introduced to be sent out as soon as the relevant paperwork reached the Personnel Office. It welcomed the new member of staff, explained the contract process and likely delay, and gave a named contact person.

Personnel staff's response to the proposed change was at first negative – more paperwork was felt to further delay the activities of the team and to add more work. Persuaded by the promised benefits of an improved image the new system was piloted.

The results were impressive. The letters reassured the new employees and improved the image of the sector. Phone calls demanding contracts declined sharply – freeing up staff to process the paperwork. As a result the lead time was nearly halved in only a few months! Fewer queries and fewer calls improved the working environment.

The change benefited all, but had to be packaged to convince the team to 'buy it'!

Price

Managers should not make the mistake of ignoring 'price' in their internal marketing mix. Price may not be obvious. It is not a list price, but almost every change proposed has a price for the individual, be it direct or indirect. For example, the price of reorganization is uncertainty, the effort to work with new people, the inconvenience of a new office location. A proposed training programme costs the individual time. If sent away from home it may have the added 'cost' of stress and of painful personal development.

Managers who want to implement change effectively need to put themselves in the shoes of their staff. They have to appreciate the 'price' tag attached to the proposals and ensure that the benefits they are offering outweigh the costs. It is very important to judge 'cost' from the viewpoint of the individuals – as we know, not everybody is motivated in the same way. Identification of need and setting up a mutually profitable exchange is as important here as in external marketing.

Establishing the price point
Look at the following proposed changes. What do you think the 'price' may be for those involved?

1 Relocation of our offices from Central London to a greenfield outer London site.
2 Introduction of 'home working' – with staff networked by fax-modem and coming into the office only for key meetings, etc.
3 Development of a new sales bonus scheme, increasing the commission element of the sales teams' remuneration package.
4 Closure of the separate managers' dining facilities to encourage improved inter company communication.
5 Appointment of a new marketing manager to your team.
6 Introduction of a formal staff appraisal scheme.
7 Launch of an 'employee of the month' scheme.
8 Expansion of the current 'opening hours' in a service sector such as retail, education or a GP's surgery.

(**See** Debriefing at the end of this unit.)

Place

In the marketing mix, place is about availability. In this context it can be used to consider when and where the change will be introduced and implemented. A new computer system introduced during the busiest season will be less effective than if planned for the quieter months. A new bonus scheme may be better introduced in small groups than announced at the National Conference.

Managers should think carefully about the timing of proposals. Is a Monday meeting likely to be better than a Friday? Also the length of time taken to implement the change can be critical. Too long and the change will lose momentum, too short and there can be disruption and anxiety with the possible result that staff have neither the skills nor the systems required to enable the change to work.

Promotion

Promotion is about communication. The options for communicating change should be clearly identified and evaluated.

Getting the message across
Produce a mind map indicating the range of communication options open to a firm wishing to introduce change to its employees.

(**See** Debriefing at the end of this unit.)

Two-way communication options enable staff to feel they have participated in change decisions. In time, policy will be agreed and established. It must then be clearly communicated to everyone. It is important that all those involved:

- Know about the change.
- Understand it.
- Have the skills and resources to implement it.

It is the manager's task to ensure all three of these elements are in place. Simply *telling* people is not sufficient.

Promote the benefits

Most important is to ensure that communication highlights the benefits of change to those expected to implement it. They are unlikely to be the same benefits as those for the organization. Saving money for the organization would help sell a plan to the Directors, but unless coupled with an incentive offers little to members of staff.

Offering 'value' for the price
Return to Activity 8.5. For each change, list the possible benefits you could present to the staff.

(**See** Debriefing at the end of this unit.)

Control

As in every plan, the manager must give consideration to the control elements of:

- Budget.
- Timing.
- Feedback.

The process of change can carry a high price and take time – far more time than many imagine or allow for. The budget will need to be justified in terms of the cost benefits of the change to the company.

Think about realistic timings. For an organization of 500 staff to attend a one-week Customer Care Training Programme would take a minimum of 20 weeks if 25 staff were on each course. It is not always possible to release large numbers of staff at a time if the operation is to be kept working, and the exercise may have to extend over, say, 25 weeks.

But then there is need to consider course numbers. Is 25 too many for effective learning? If 18 is the learning-effective number the time needed extends to 28 weeks.

To balance this we have to consider the problems caused by having staff trained over such a long period. Those going early will, in theory, be ahead of the others, but have to work with untrained staff. How effective will their behaviour change be?

Perhaps it would be far better to target training on individual departments, teams, units, and hit harder, tighter, over a shorter time frame?

Measuring and monitoring the resulting change in behaviour and attitudes is essential to allow plans to be modified and further actions developed as and where necessary.

Selling plans up the hierarchy

Faced with 'selling' an idea or proposal to senior managers the same process should be adopted, but the needs of the Management Team and the stakeholders need to be considered and benefits such as raised profitability quantified and communicated.

Change has long been suffered as a substitute for positive action This quotation comes from a Roman Legionary from the 1st century – just as the Roman Empire was going into decline.

We trained hard . . .

But it seemed that every time we were beginning to form up into teams we would be reorganized.

I was to learn later in life that we tend to meet any new situation by reorganizing; and a wonderful method it can be for creating the illusion of progress while producing confusion inefficiency and demoralization.

Caius Petronius AD 65

The examiner is your audience, and plays the role set up in the question. Think about his or her needs and present the appropriate benefits. Presenting proposals for a new sales territory design would be very different if asked to:

- Make a report to senior management.
- Prepare a presentation for the next sales meeting.

It is *always* important that you answer in the context of the question. Take care when reading it to establish:

- Who you are and what is your role?
- What are your objectives?
- Who is your audience and what are their needs?
- What format/approach has been specified?

These questions should be the starting point, the way into every exam question.

NOTE: Don't forget that, whilst he or she is playing a role, the examiner still has specific needs that you should always remember. The examiner wants an easy script to mark, so offer the benefits of clear presentation, structured layout and tidy writing if you want to effectively 'market' your script as worthy of a pass.

Identify a change you would like to make at work or in your social life. Take time to produce a marketing plan to help you implement this. Present it to those concerned. It may be to get the children to tidy their rooms weekly or to persuade your line manager to rearrange the office. Choose something large or small, it doesn't matter because it is the knowledge of the process and skills in practice that you need.

Don't forget objectives must be realistic! Your effectiveness will improve with time and practice.

In the Effective Management for Marketing paper you are likely to be asked to recommend actions which require a change of attitude or behaviour. You need to consider how this change can best be managed, and the examiners will be looking for evidence of your thinking in this area even when not specifically requested.

At Diploma level, in the Strategic Marketing Management – Analysis and Decision Case Study, as well as some of the mini-cases you are likely to be faced with organizations which are product/sales oriented and you will need to be prepared to make recommendations for managing the process of change to a customer/consumer orientation. In the International Marketing Management Strategy paper you are very likely to be asked for recommendations on how an organization should change from a domestic to an international orientation.

UNIT ACTIVITY

This House believes . . .

The local branch of the CIM is hosting a debate on: 'Change – The Bane Of The Modern World!' You have been asked to oppose the motion and have 10 minutes to convince the audience of the benefits of change.

Prepare an outline of your presentation indicating the key arguments you will use.

(**See** Debriefing at the end of this unit.)

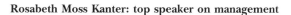

Rosabeth Moss Kanter: top speaker on management

As a consultant and a professor at the Harvard Business School, Rosabeth Moss Kanter was US Woman of the Year in 1985. Her consultancy skills are in high demand by the world's leading blue-chip companies and she is one of the world's most sought-after speakers on management. In 1986, at the Management Centre, Europe Conference she was introduced as 'If you think of Tom Peters as the right brain and Peter Drucker as the left brain, then Rosabeth Moss Kanter has to be the whole brain!' A 'fearless critic of management tradition' she has blended high level academic study with highly practical and effective top-level consultancy. Each has played back to the benefit of the other.

It was in 1983 that her book *The Change Masters* elevated her to star status. The *Harvard Business Review* commented: 'The depth of reach here is great, Kanter's deservedly popular book is concerned not merely with the detail, which is rich, but with the theory. . . . She integrates the opposites that bedevil business managers – the individual versus the group, personal motivation versus the environment, getting things done versus being nice.'

Kanter says that change masters are 'literally the right people in the right place at the right time. The right people are those with the ideas that move beyond the organization's established practice, ideas that can form into visions. The right places are the integrative environments that support innovation, encourage the building of coalitions and teams to support and implement visions. The right times are those moments in the flow of organizational history when it is possible to reconstruct reality on the basis of accumulated innovations to shape a more productive and successful future'.

Kanter challenges the attitudes of businesses to change: 'Change is always a threat when it's done to me or imposed on me whether I like it or not. But it's an opportunity if it's done by me. It is my chance to contribute and be recognised.' She also challenges the modern methods of rewards: 'What's capitalism about except the fact that people should be earning what they get, instead of having it automatically handed to them because they occupy a certain desk all the time?'

Her guidelines for building commitment to change are:

1 Allow room for participation in the planning of change.
2 Leave choices within the overall decision to change.
3 Provide a clear picture of the change, a vision with details about the new state.
4 Share information about planned changes to the fullest extent possible.
5 Divide a big change into more manageable and familiar steps; let people take a small step first.
6 Minimize surprises; give people advance warning about new requirements.
7 Allow for digestion of change requests – a chance to become accustomed to the idea of change before making a commitment.
8 Repeatedly demonstrate your own commitment to the change.
9 Make standards and requirements clear – tell exactly what is expected of people in the change.
10 Offer positive reinforcement for competence; let people know they can do it.
11 Look for and reward pioneers, innovators, and early successes to serve as models.
12 Help people find or feel compensated for the extra time and energy change requires.
13 Avoid creating obvious 'losers' from the change.
14 Allow expressions of nostalgia and grief for the past – then create excitement about the future.

Key publications:
The Change Masters, 1983
Creating the Future, 1988
When Giants Learn to Dance, 1990
The Challenge of Organisational Change, 1990

SUMMARY

In this unit we have seen that:

  • Change is a natural part of the environment, but is seldom popular and is usually resisted.
 • Environmental changes inevitably cause organizational change – either re- or pro-actively.
 • An organizational culture for change is needed – one that is prepared for and experienced in handling change.
 • A learning organization expects everybody to be preparing for the job they will have tomorrow.
 • Rewards, flexibility and involvement are the motivational keys to change.
 • Change, as a process, can and should be managed. It is as much subject to management planning and control as any other process.
 • All change should be taken seriously, and planned and implemented with care.
 • An outward looking, challenging view must be cultivated by managers and encouraged in staff.
 • Major changes that are typically faced by commercial organizations are the switch from a product/sales to a marketing/customer approach; and from a domestic to an international orientation.
 • Internal marketing is of crucial importance in efficiently securing change with the maximum of effectiveness.
 • Internal marketing exactly parallels external marketing, but is often not as rigorously documented.
 • The key, as always in marketing, is to evaluate change from the perspective of the identified audiences within the organization and then work to meet their needs.
 • Change always requires a price to be paid. Partly in resources, but most importantly in human terms.
 • Promotion of the benefits – once the package has been designed – must be as carefully conceived as for external marketing.
 • Selling plans up the hierarchy is necessary, and requires the different needs of senior management and stakeholders to be identified and taken into account.

Debriefing

Activity 8.1

1 Change involves risk, both to the organization and, more importantly to the individual. Change may weaken our performance rather than enhance it, reduce our market share not increase it. For the individual, change may result in a new role, less powerful or influential or, even more alarming, there may be no role for the individual in the new structure. Fear of the risk and of the unknown can collectively generate a considerable support for maintaining the status quo.

2 When change is imposed it can make people feel out of control. This is not a refreshing sensation but a highly stressful one. Not knowing where we are going and unable to control the pace or direction of change is a frightening experience that is likely to be resisted.

3 Change is a painful process. It takes an effort to change. Have you tried to change? Giving up smoking or getting into a new habit like clearing your desk every night? It takes time and effort to change. If the benefits are not obvious, if there are few incentives, the cost of change can easily out weigh them.

4 Both apathy and fear of the unknown can work against change. The sheer size of some organizations means reorganization is a major effort and so less likely to be considered. Large bureaucratic organizations tend to be most resistant to change.

Activity 8.2

Enjoy change	Resist change
1b	1a
2b	2a
3a	3b
4a	4b

If you have identified that you are not naturally excited by change think about ways you can increase the experiences of the changes to which you are exposed. Eat out in a different restaurant, try a new dish, look at different holiday destinations, ask for the chance to manage a new project at work. Develop, slowly and carefully, a more adventurous attitude to life.

Activity 8.3

1 The scheme needs to be planned properly if it is to be effective. That means quantified objectives – x ideas per employee in y time. Adequate resources to deal with ideas generated and to reward staff must be provided.

2 A system for screening ideas needs to be established, with criteria for selecting ideas for further investigations. Targets for reviewing each idea within a set time should be agreed.

3 Effective mechanisms for communication with the staff need to be set up. Staff should initially be briefed, and access to the system should be simplified.

4 Feedback must be prompt. All ideas submitted should be acknowledged (possibly rewarded) and the results of the screening passed on to the individual. Ideas successfully implemented should be widely promoted and the rewards publicized.

Self-check 8.1

1 Change is inevitable because the organization exists within an environment which is constantly changing and bringing new opportunities and threats which need to be responded to. The organization itself is constantly evolving. A growing operation may require a different organizational system than will a small cottage industry. A multinational company may require a different approach than will a regional supplier.

2 The main costs of change can be associated with the uncertainly and stress which poorly managed change causes employees within the organization. Depending on the nature of the change there may be direct costs including new building, moving expenses, training, development, and so on.

3 Yes, there are times when change would be inappropriate. Change for change's sake can bring only the benefit of novelty. Change should be planned and take the direction indicated by the organization's mission and strategic direction. Any proposed change where the costs outweigh the benefits would seem unwise!

4 There are a wide variety of questions from which you will have chosen. One of the most effective is 'Why do we do it like this?' If people are encouraged constantly to question behaviour and approaches, then the concept of evolutionary development and improvement will be embedded within the organization.

5 Improved internal communication helps to remove the barriers of fear, uncertainty and resentment. Without effective communication rumours are likely to be rife and the job of eventually implementing the change will be much more difficult because staff will have already made up their minds about possible hidden agendas. Encouraging internal communication complete with both information and feedback enables all staff to feel that they have participated in the organizing process.

Activity 8.4

(a) BS 5750 is a clear objective, but no time frame has been given and so no sense of priority for the achievement of the changes that would be necessary in order to gain the accreditation.

(b) Customer complaints have been identified as a problem area and here we have a specific objective quantified over time.

(c) We have a time frame of 6 months, but no indication of the effectiveness or efficiency of the new systems. Presumably having the system available, perhaps with terminals on individual's desks, might count as introduction but would not achieve the purpose since active use is not an objective.

(d) Rather woolly. No quantified objectives and only a broad time frame of a year, with no real indication of what this would imply.

(e) This is a much more clearly quantified target to be achieved, implying changes in both recruitment, selection and the attitude of managers and other staff within the organization. However, it could be met by no change in years 1 and 2 with everything left to achieve in year 3.

(f) Quantified over time and a realistic target for a new system.

(g) Quantified over time and so a reasonable objective which can be used as a basis for change implementation.

(h) A time frame exists but no indication of what is implied by the integration of the sales and marketing teams. This could simply be integration of office space rather than the achievement of a team working effectively together.

Activity 8.5

1 Costs of physically moving house or perhaps longer travelling time to work. Inconvenience of upheaval for the family – maybe new schools, loss of a partner's employment and the need to make new friends.

2 The loss of companionship and the 'social' aspects of working. Higher costs of heating, electricity etc. from being at home all day – the loss of space at home and the cost of work intruding on home life.

3 The risk of lower take-home pay, causing uncertainty and stress. Anxiety of more 'public' scrutiny of performance.

4 Loss of 'privacy' for both groups. Loss of status benefit for the managers.

5 Uncertainty and risk you won't fit it – reduced security. Possible resentment if you were overlooked for promotion, hassle of learning new approaches and style.

6 Stress, cost of criticism (it can be painful). Being more accountable may in itself be new and should be associated with the cost of being expected to improve performance.

7 Internal competition may cost the harmony of the team. The worry of public 'failure' to achieve and the need to change behaviour to meet the agreed criteria will cost effort.

8 Costs individuals the certainty of days off. May involve expectation of overtime working and the cost of disrupting home and social life. May force 'voluntary' acceptance, simply because there is no alternative employment.

Activity 8.6

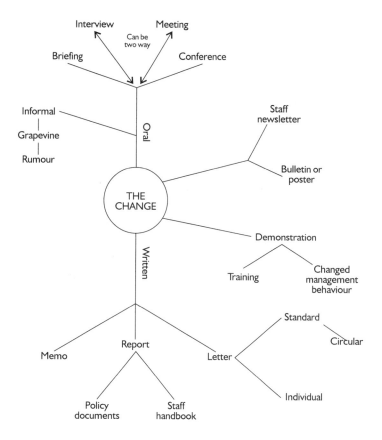

Activity 8.7

1   Pleasant working environment, more space, possibly less travelling time, more leisure and less travel costs.
2   *X* hours per day saving on travelling, less travel expenses. More flexible working, more control over personal time and work.
3   Increased potential earnings, greater rewards for greater effort – recognition of achievements.
4   Less internal company tension, more cooperation, improved communication opportunities.
5   Fresh ideas, new start, more objectivity, excitement, challenge!
6   Improved communications opportunities to give feedback and to determine personal development opportunities. Can increase individual confidence and security.
7   Adds interest, a challenge, the opportunity to win the prize, to achieve status and recognition.
8   More flexibility of working hours, opportunity for overtime earnings, expansion of the business leading to enhanced promotional opportunities.

Unit activity

Objectives:

- Plan to present four benefits of change.
- To win at least 57 per cent of votes for the opposition to the motion.

Introduction:

A change is as good as a rest! The rejuvenation aspects of change are clearly embedded in our language and culture.

Change, like anything worthwhile, has a cost – but brings with it considerable benefits.

Body:

Marketers exist because of change – promotion of marketing within the company culture depends on embedding change to a customer orientation.

More change equals more demand for marketing which is needed to help promote change internally as well as for the creativity and skills needed to help identify external opportunities for strategic change. Change (if managed correctly) adds interest and excitement to work, is an important aspect of motivation.

Organizations which are eager for change tend to be more proactive, flexible and dynamic. Are good to work within.

In a rapidly changing business environment only those who commit themselves to change will survive and thrive. The prospects for your organization and therefore your job depends on you supporting the concepts of change.

Conclusion

Organizations that recognize change as an integral dimension of the business and where managers have been helped to develop the skills to manage change are operations which effectively take away the barriers and problems associated with change. The problems described by opposers as a 'bane' of modern life.

A commitment to growth, not stagnation, to the new and exciting, not the old and tired, means more opportunities for ourselves as marketers and employees and greater success for our organizations.

To survive we must change so we might as well learn to enjoy it!

The building of a customer base

In this unit you will turn your attention to people outside the organization and you will:

- Examine the role and importance of relationship marketing.
- Identify the Marketing Manager's role in maintaining and building customer loyalty.

By the end of this unit you will be able to:

- Appreciate the needs of suppliers and the benefits of relationship marketing.
- Recommend techniques for monitoring customer loyalty and satisfaction.
- Plan an effective customer visit.
- Identify the elements of successful negotiation.
- Identify possible customer problems and recommend actions to improve client/company relations.

STUDY GUIDE

Whilst all managers have some responsibility for maintaining and developing the organization's client base, the real onus for this falls on the Marketing Manager. With a front-line responsibility for communication between the organization and its customers the marketer has to develop an empathy with customer needs and problems. It is not surprising, therefore, that the examiner expects candidates to demonstrate that they can accept trouble-shooting responsibilities and provide ideas for on-going improvements in this area.

We would expect this unit to take you about 3 hours to complete, with a further 2 hours for the activities.

It will help if you can collect samples of organizational communication with clients – brochures, letters, statements, and so on. If possible, try to get hold of a sample of client complaints and/or questions and copies of how these were handled by your organization.

STUDY TIPS

As you come towards the end of your work through this subject it is a good time to review your progress and to identify areas which need further attention.

Before starting on this unit we suggest you take 30 minutes to work through the following questions. They will help you identify a checklist for your further attention.

1 What state are your study notes in? Have you completed each section, added your own ideas and illustrations, and produced a checklist of key points to help with your revision?
2 Have you completed the various activities and extending exercises for each unit? Have you summarized your experiences with each of these?
3 When did you last add any material to your cuttings file? Make a point of reading the current issues of magazines such as *Management Today* and *Marketing Business*.
4 Have you reviewed your personal development progress against the specific objectives you set yourself earlier in the programme?

Explanations and definitions

1 *Complaints*   To express dissatisfaction (*Concise Oxford Dictionary*). When a customer expresses dissatisfaction it does not follow that there is anything technically wrong with the product offering. There is, however, something wrong with the customer's usage or perception of the product offering in use. It follows that it is crucial to identify the 'genuine' complaints where there is a fault in the offering so that urgent action can be taken. 'Routine' complaints, such as a misreading of the instructions, should be used to guide management in improvements to the way in which the offering is packed, promoted, etc.
2 *Relationship marketing*   A relationship-marketing-oriented organization brings together customer service, quality and marketing. **See:** *Relationship Marketing*, Martin Christopher, Adrian Payne and David Ballantyne (CIM/Butterworth-Heinneman).
3 *Quality*   Quality has been described as 'what attracts, delights and holds our loyalty.' It is a factor which can only be judged from the perception of the recipient, since quality is a combination of both tangible and intangible factors. Unfortunately for the marketer, different segments judge quality differently – it is necessary to create a quality offering for each identified target customer.
4 *The business and its external audiences*   The quality of the internal operations of the organization is judged only in terms of the quality of the products and services it generates, and the satisfactions these provide for its customers.

Quality

Quality should not be mistaken for 'best'. A Rolls Royce is no more a quality product in this context than is a Raleigh bike. Quality is measured in terms of customer expectation and the degree to which the offering satisfies their needs.

Marketing professionals have a fundamental and critical role in ensuring that customer needs are thoroughly investigated and understood, *before* the business uses its expertise in producing outputs designed to meet them (Figure 9.1).

The suppliers and intermediaries

Most organizations are not alone in working to satisfy the needs of customers. Directly and indirectly a number of other organizations are likely also to be involved.

Figure 9.1   The steps in ensuring customer-oriented outputs

- The local authority who has subcontracted refuse collection to a private company.
- The manufacturer who uses retailers to provide product information, delivery and after-sales services to the customers.
- The service company who uses an agent to provide advice and booking services.
- The producer dependent on a third party for the quality and supply of fabrication parts such as engines, transmissions and headlights.

The development of relationship marketing has been important in encouraging managers to recognize the shared interests which exist between organizations and has led to many organizations identifying the benefits and values of developing longer term partnerships (relationships) focused on jointly solving customers' problems and exploiting new opportunities. To do this effectively the needs of both parties must be identified and both should benefit from the new cooperative approach.

A producer seeking to lower stock holding and increase productive flexibility can negotiate long-term commitment to a supplier of parts in exchange for just-in-time availability. Delivering this benefit may require the supplier to relocate warehousing or even production to within easy access. In some instances the two may even occupy adjacent sites.

ACTIVITY 9.1

The supplier's role – partners or adversaries?
What do you see as the potential advantages and disadvantages of adopting this partnership approach to suppliers? Use the framework below as a guide to help you.

Supplier as a Partner to:	Advantages	Disadvantages
The supplier		
The buyer		
The end-user		

(**See** Debriefing at the end of this unit.)

As you probably identified, the concept of relationship marketing is a good one which, if developed and managed properly, should generate benefits for all those concerned.

Interestingly, marketing departments are possibly the most experienced at managing these kinds of long-term partnerships. Whilst the operations team have 'shopped around' for supplies and sought to negotiate better and better contracts, marketers have tended to build long-term relationships with those whose services they buy. From PR specialists and research consultants to advertising agencies, the tendency has been joint problem solving and long-term involvement. Arguably the nature of their contribution has facilitated this, but the detailed knowledge of the client and his or her strategy and market takes some time to acquire, and there is little advantage in getting close for only the duration of one project or campaign.

Similarly, the need for continuity in image and in approach to external markets makes frequent change a problem.

What is the relationship between your organization and its suppliers? Use the following questions as the basis for your own research in this area. If the business is complex choose just one product area to focus on. Talk to the buyers and the production people. It is a good opportunity to find out more about the activities of others in the organization.

Note: Service providers are always involved in tangible as well as intangible factors: cleaning contracts are needed; caterers require food, drink, dry goods, laundry, etc. in order that they can deliver their service. The value of their service depends very much upon the quality of the products and services supplied to them.

Find out about the cleaning contracts, raw material suppliers, etc., depended on by an organization that you know.

1 Who are the key suppliers of goods and services to this organization?
2 What proportion of total costs do they represent?
3 How are contracts with them agreed?
   (a) By whom?
   (b) How often?
   (c) How many others compete?
4 When was the supplier last changed?
5 What do those using and/or responsible for the suppliers think about:
   (a) Quality?
   (b) Reliability?
   (c) Availability?
   (d) Service they receive?
   (e) Price?
6 Has the company changed its view of relationships with suppliers since the increased general interest in quality and in relationship marketing?
7 Are clear criteria established to help management assess the supplier's performance?
8 How could a change in approach benefit the organization?

You may be able to use your findings as a basis for a report or presentation to senior management. If so, remember to stress the good points as well as encouraging a review of any weaknesses you have identified.

If you are working with others, compare experiences of different sectors. Try to identify examples of successful implementation of the principles of relationship marketing.

The suppliers and quality

We began considering relationship marketing because the suppliers are in essence an extension of the organization's internal customers and we considered in the last unit the importance of internal marketing to encourage motivation and promote change within the business. But why are these relationships important to the effective marketing manager? Why is this material included within the CIM syllabus?

We can see that, for the manager, the challenge is to make the most of the resources available – adding the maximum added value (as judged by the customer) to the inputs. As markets have matured and technology has advanced there is less and less functional difference between the product offerings. This has encouraged customers to increasingly judge by criteria such as customer care, after-sales service and availability. People, both within the organization and employed by suppliers, are critical to the perceived quality in these other areas.

Relationship marketing and internal marketing are techniques being actively employed by organizations seeking to find ways of maximizing the contribution of the people resource. Both seek to improve quality – thus helping to win and keep customers (Figure 9.2). It follows

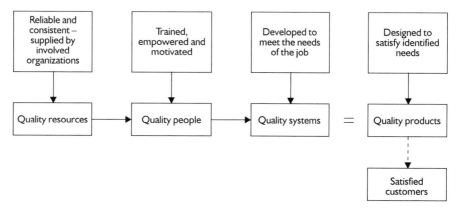

Figure 9.2 Maximizing effectiveness and efficiency

that the key management objectives are to satisfy more effectively and efficiently the needs of the customer base:

- *More effectively* means customers will prefer their offering over those of competitors and so help them win market share.
- *More efficiently* requires that they achieve their competitive advantage with less resources and so increase profitability, to the satisfaction of the stakeholders.

The organization can only continue to exist if both parties are satisfied. It is to this end of mutually profitable exchange that the marketing manager is constantly striving.

New customers or old?

The organization's customer base is often the result of years of investment and effort and is extremely valuable. Like anything of value it needs treating with respect and investment if it is to be retained and maintained or even increased in value. It is all too easy to take the familiar customer for granted until he or she is no longer there.

The value of these customer bases is notionally recognized in the valuing of 'goodwill' within a business, and in the debate about the valuing of brands within the balance sheet. In both examples the conservatism of the financial profession clearly reflects the fragility of the customer base. A problem can devalue a brand almost overnight, and goodwill is often found to be related to the people in the business and not to the business itself. Change the one and you can quickly lose the other. 'Under New Management' is not a sign which automatically attracts new customers, but it will almost inevitably alarm the old!

Relationship marketing also has a role to play here. This time the organization is in the role of supplier seeking to build long-term relationships with clients and customers. This model illustrates the relationship marketing aim of bringing quality, customer service and marketing together. Advocates of a relationship marketing orientation accuse traditional marketers of having been too keen on attracting 'new' customers and of paying inadequate attention to the critically important task of retaining the existing ones. Relationship marketing accepts the dual challenge of both winning and retaining customers (Figure 9.3).

Figure 9.3 Relationship marketing orientation, bringing together customer service, quality and marketing

Getting started

The marketing manager has a critical role to play in maintaining and building the customer base. Getting started is easy – as we have seen so often in this workbook the basis is an audit of the current position:

- Who are the current customers?
- What proportion of our business does each present?
- Who is the 'buyer'?
- Are their needs being satisfied?
- In what ways can we improve the service we offer them?

These are the types of question which form the basis of any business or market audit, and they should be very much in the forefront of the proactive marketing manager's thoughts.

ACTIVITY 9.2

The customer's value
Use the questions below to help you focus your thinking.

1 Are all customers of equal importance to the organization?
2 Should a low value small customer be given a lower priority than a larger value well-established client?
3 Is it easier to win sales from new or from existing clients?
4 Would you prefer to have a small number of large clients or a large number of small ones? What are the implications of your choice?
5 What would the Pareto principle probably demonstrate if applied to your customer base? How could this help you?

(**See** Debriefing at the end of this unit.)

EXTENDING ACTIVITY 9.2

Take time to find out about your own customer base:

- How much information exists and who controls it?
- Which are the key accounts?
- Does Pareto's Principle apply for you?
- Can you identify 5 per cent of your customers who are regular but light/medium users of your services who could be usefully targeted for additional sales?

The process of adding to the customer base cannot, however, simply be ignored, no matter how carefully the current base is maintained and developed.

- Growth of the business will normally require further market penetration or market development.
- Some existing customers will go – firms can go out of business, and end-users can leave the market for a variety of reasons. Both firms and end-users can switch to a competitor.
- The people involved in the decision-making process can change – often with little or no warning.

One of the responsibilities of the marketing manager at the customer interface is constantly to monitor the existing customer base, to be alert for changes, and proactive in identifying new customer opportunities.

Assessing the customers' perceptions

Once the manager knows who the customers are, he or she should establish and monitor their views about the quality of the organization's services and products. This will require marketing research and established systems to monitor the quality of service and, more importantly, the customer's perceptions of it on an on-going basis.

Measuring customers' perceptions
Spend 15 minutes identifying as many ways as possible ways to monitor customer views.

(**See** Debriefing at the end of this unit.)

What is quality and total quality?

The local doctor cannot evaluate quality simply by examining the service that patients receive during the consultation. Quality, to the patient, will include the time spent in the waiting room, as well as the service levels when making an appointment, the timekeeping of the doctor, the comfort of the waiting room, the accessibility of the surgery, and the general attitude of everybody who is a part of the doctor's support team. The decor, style, ambience and cleanliness all combine to form part of the total experience in which the patients make their judgement.

Consider the origins of the key terms 'patient' and 'practice'. A patient is so-called because of the need to be patient when waiting for the doctor. A doctor 'practises' on patients and therefore never admits to being a fully skilled person.

The very use of these terms shows how product centred the doctors' view of their service has been. Perhaps this is beginning to change in some countries where sick people are beginning to regard themselves as clients – and with the greater availability of private medicine there is some evidence that doctors are beginning to adopt a more client-centred approach.

Total quality involves all staff by encouraging them to see that it is the whole operation which determines the quality of the final output. All those employed have to be quality experts, monitoring the quality of their own contribution to the process.

Measuring quality

The first step is to identify what the customers perceive to be the key components of service. Research can be used to:

- Assess the importance of each component to the customer.
- Measure how the organization's performance measures up.
- Measure how competitor's performance compares.

The resulting profile may be assessed on the pro-forma shown in Figure 9.4. The objective of this is to ensure that the customer's stated importance is matched by the organization's performance strength. The relative strengths compared with competitors in these areas represent the basis of competitive advantage.

Organizations need to take care *not* to invest heavily in improving performance in areas *not* valued by the customer. Priority must be given to improvements in the areas which matter

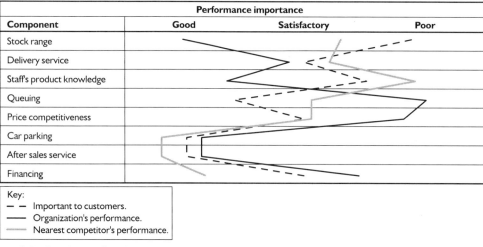

	Performance importance		
Component	**Good**	**Satisfactory**	**Poor**
Stock range			
Delivery service			
Staff's product knowledge			
Queuing			
Price competitiveness			
Car parking			
After sales service			
Financing			

Key:
- – Important to customers.
— Organization's performance.
···· Nearest competitor's performance.

Figure 9.4 Pro-forma for determining closeness of match of the customers stated importance and the organization's performance strength

most to the customer. The relative strengths and competitive advantages are likely to become the focus of positioning and of promotional activity. Areas of weakness vis-à-vis the competitors represent the areas of vulnerability. These are obviously aspects of customer service which can be targeted for improvement.

Self-check 9.1

Use the following questions to assess your understanding of the material in this unit so far:

1 What do you understand by the term 'relationship marketing'?
2 What is the difference between a market orientation and a relationship market orientation?
3 To which aspects of customer service should organizations give priority?
4 What is 'mystery shopping'?
5 What are the main responsibilities of the marketing manager working at the interface between the organization and the customers?

(**See** Debriefing at the end of this unit.)

The importance of quality and of customer care

Quality is the mechanism by which firms sustain their position as their customer's preferred supplier. It is critical to the organization's on-going success in the intensively competitive markets of the 1990s.

It is important for marketing managers to recognize quality across the breadth of their activities. Any variance between what customers need and the benefits they expect from your product offering represents a shortfall in the quality of your activity – which needs analysing and correcting if quality improvements are to be maintained, and competitive performance is to be enhanced.

The concepts of quality and of customer service are at the heart of the marketing concept and require managers to:

- Identify customer needs.
- Use their knowledge, experience and expertise to create systems and processes which will deliver benefits that the customer perceives will satisfy those needs.

Quality breakdowns

Spend a few minutes looking at the following scenarios. What do you feel may be the cause of the organization failing to deliver the quality required?

1 The Keepit Bank has invested heavily in researching the market to identify customer needs and has committed itself to improving customer service. Investment in new technology and refurbishing of the Bank's outlets has been extensive. Staff have new corporate uniforms and there has been intensive promotional activity highlighting the superior performance of the Bank in the area of customer care.

   Senior Management are very disappointed by the results of a recent mystery research project in which in eight out of ten customer service issues they scored below their nearest competitor. These results have been confirmed by research amongst customers who have indicated that they perceive little improvement and complain particularly about waiting time for service, difficulties in speaking to senior managers and unhelpful staff with inadequate product knowledge.

2 The Boxit packaging company has been a family-run business for three generations and little has really changed. Recently the company has lost a number of orders because they were unwilling to replace their old, but much more secure, closing systems with a new technique being asked for by their clients. The Managing Director had assured the buyers in these organizations it was simply a 'fad' and that she was confident they would return when they had experienced the inferior performance of the competitive offerings. Six months later there is no sign of this forecast proving correct.

3 The Budget Wear Company produce a wide range of women's clothing at very attractive prices. They use cheaper materials, purchase in bulk and distribute directly using a mail-order catalogue approach. They have been successful and grown steadily over the last 5 years. Recession made many of their customers more price sensitive and clearly helped to boost business. Research has indicated that their customers recognize the products as good value. Unsatisfactory goods can be returned within 14 days and about 5 per cent returns are normal – this is similar to other companies in the direct-sell sector. The Managing Director recently made a decision to improve the quality image and to change the positioning of the company.

   As a first step in this process the spring and summer catalogue for this year has been redesigned. Fashion-shot layouts were produced using clever presentation techniques which enhance the clothes and present the collection against a background of exotic locations. Orders increased by about 10 per cent but returns peaked at over 17 per cent in July.

Delivery of a quality offering can break-down in a number of places:

- Not knowing what the customer's needs are.
- Managers not making the changes or developing the systems to satisfy those needs.
- Raising the customer's expectations of benefits over that which is actually offered.
- The break-down of service and quality at any point in the process, but most particularly at the customer contact point.

The job of the manager in this context is the same as the basic task we identified at the beginning of this workbook – it is to use the available resources efficiently and effectively in order to win competitive advantage and achieve the organization's goals.

Any mismatch between customer need and the perceived benefits offered by the organization reduces either effectiveness or efficiency. In the instance shown in Figure 9.5(a), the company is wasting resources by providing benefits at a higher level than the customer needs.

The customer in case Figure 9.5(b) is disappointed with the offering as they perceive it to be below the level they need. This gap is the opportunity for competitive activity, and represents an ineffective use of resources – producing products which do not satisfy customer needs. Only when the needs and perceived benefits coincide (Figure 9.5(c)) has the manager achieved the objective of satisfying needs and expectations.

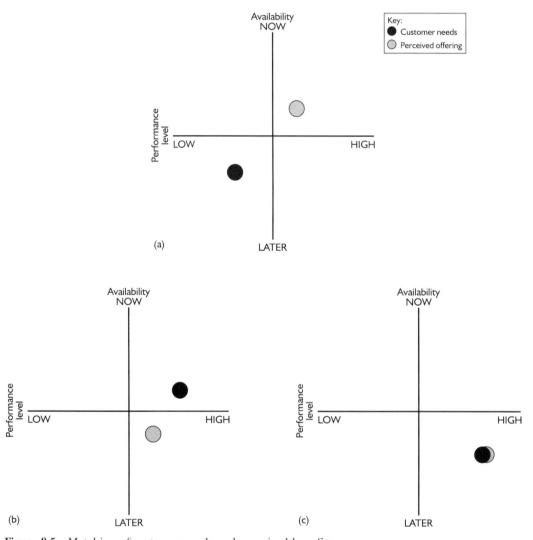

Figure 9.5 Matching of customer needs and perceived benefits

Even this is not the end of the story. As we know only too well the market is constantly changing, so customer needs will shift over time. The effective manager must be proactive in forecasting these changes and flexible in changing the organization to meet them.

The significance of the customer?
We use customer care to focus on the points of direct customer contact. The starting point is to identify which staff have direct contact with the customer. The list may surprise you.

Besides sales teams, receptionists and office staff, there will be security officers, car-park attendants, porters, delivery staff and, in the service sector, operational staff such as, cleaners, waiters and nurses. The team extends to a far wider extent than many imagine – as we saw in Unit 5.

QUESTION 9.1

Look at the following types of organization, and from your own experience produce a list of all the staff likely to have *direct* customer contact.

1 A college.
2 A local supermarket.
3 A major motor dealer.
4 A national charity.
5 A manufacturer of computer software systems.
6 Your own organization.

These are the individuals who make a lasting impression on customers and potential customers. Customer care is essentially in their hands. These staff are the front line of the organization's activities. The rest of the organization must be developed to provide them with every support and assistance if they are to provide the service needed to win and retain loyal customers.

ACTIVITY 9.5

How can management help?
Spend 10 minutes creating a mind map indicating ways in which management can help front-line staff in providing quality customer care.

(**See** Debriefing at the end of this unit.)

As you will have seen from your work on this last activity the operational staff are not isolated in their responsibility for customer care, but should be empowered and facilitated in their endeavours in this area.

Improving customer care

As we have found, often the process for improvement in the area of customer service is relatively straightforward. Implementation of effective plans is rather more demanding.

- Audit the current situation. Research to establish the current perceived care levels and identify the criteria by which the customer judges care levels in this market.
- Establish benchmarks to act as objectives and a basis for monitoring improvements.
- Target appropriate training and support on the relevant staff to enable them to perform satisfactorily.
- Devise mechanisms to empower and motivate these groups to act effectively.
- Monitor progress and modify systems as necessary to ensure that once embarked on the road to improving quality there is no temptation to stop. There is only progress on the quality path – no destination!

Developing plans for managing key accounts and customer segments

The marketing manager has limited resources and so has to make decisions to ensure that they are deployed effectively. Establishing objectives and plans for key segments or accounts is an important part of this process.

A life cycle of customers

The life cycle is a useful planning tool as it can be used in a number of ways. Below are plotted customers' positions on their life cycle with an organization.

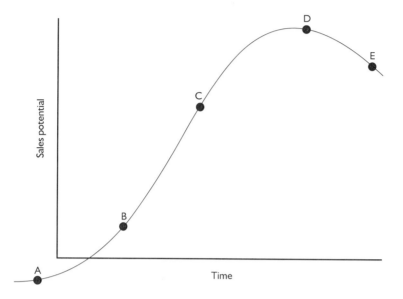

1 How would you describe each of the customer groups marked on the cycle as A–E? What would you expect to be the current status of their business relationship with the organization?
2 What sort of objectives might you set for customers B and D? Why?
3 Is customer E of no more value to the organization?
4 Why might the sales person who is effective with customer A be less successful with D?

Planning for a key-account meeting

Step 1   Know the customer

The first task involves audit and research. What do you know about this customer?

- How long have they done business with you?
- What products, in what volumes, at what intervals do they order?
- What contract terms have they negotiated?
- Who are the key people in their business and who are our main contacts there?
- Which of our staff have regular dealings with them and what are their experiences?
- What is the current business position:
    (a) Orders outstanding?
    (b) Invoices outstanding?
    (c) Invoices disputed?
- What is the nature of their business, who are their key customers and what are their future plans?
- Do we know how they rate our service? How we can improve? Which other suppliers do they use? Why?
- What proportion of our business does this client represent?
    (a) Percentage of turnover?
    (b) Percentage of profit?
    (c) Percentage of product sales?
    (d) Percentage of management time?
- What stage of the client life-cycle is the customer in?

- What are the advantages and risks of increasing business with this customer?
- Produce a SWOT analysis for the client identifying the strengths and weakness of the relationship and the opportunities and threats facing it.

Step 2 Set objectives

On the basis of a full analysis of the current position it is possible to set objectives for this account. The objectives must be quantified, realistic and expressed over time if they are to be of value.

Note: *The impact of profitability* Marketing managers must recognize that their objectives and actions directly influence the profitability of the business. The P of price is the only P which brings revenue into the business. The other Ps incur expenditure. Therefore, marketers have to achieve ratio of return to investment. Normally incremental profits should exceed incremental cost ... any planned actions which will not achieve this are probably contra-indicated.

Likely changes will be in the areas of:

- Promotional spend.
- Volume discounts.
- Mix of products sold.
- Mix of customers:
  - (a) More smaller value clients each costing less to service may, in total, be a viable option.
  - (b) Generating an equivalent sales volume from a few large customers may produce a lower level of profit because the large clients get a volume discount and may demand a higher level of service.

Special discounts should be negotiated only if they have specific, measurable benefit. (See Unit 10.)

Increasing business with one group of customers might influence the balance of products sold. A builders' merchant who actively promotes business with plumbers might expect to sell more copper pipe, whereas an increase in business from builders would raise the sale of cement. Copper pipe attracts a different profit margin than cement and is less bulky, but requires different storage and handling. Given this understanding a marketer must set objectives for different market segments with a careful eye on profitability, not volume.

Step 3 Strategy

A decision must be made on how you are going to achieve your objective. Whether you offer discounts or added value to attract the extra business, the basis of your negotiating position needs to be established.

- An fmcg manufacturer may offer to supply own-label products in exchange for greater shelf space for branded products.
- A conference centre may offer a special rate for the spring sales meeting if it is confirmed at the same time as the annual conference.

Step 4 Tactics

These have the details of your plan. Tactical planning identifies who is responsible for what and when it must be done. This can usefully be turned into a timetable of activity relating to that client, which is also useful as a basis for control (Figure 9.6).

Budgets

A budget of staff time and additional costs must be established for your plan. These costs must be justified in terms of your objectives.

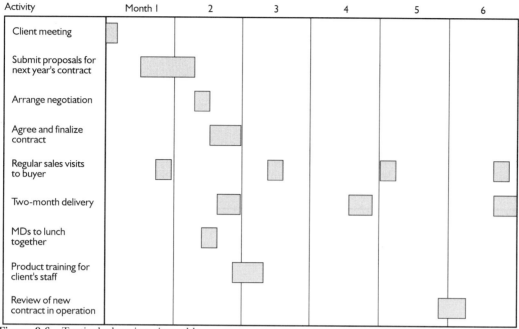

Figure 9.6 Tactical planning timetable

Control

Through an information system you would monitor the implementation of your plans against both the timetable and objectives to provide feedback on:

- Order numbers.
- Order values.
- Order quantities.
- Payment history.
- Complaints.
- Overall profitability.
- . . . and so on.

Only when you know where you are, and what your objectives are, can you identify the size of the opportunity or challenge.

(**See** Figure 9.7).

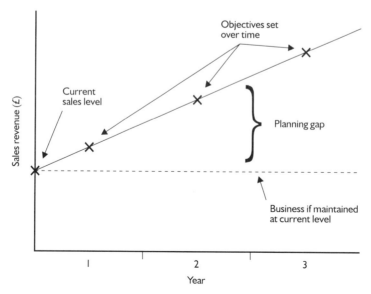

Figure 9.7 Sales revenue over time

The planning gap

You can plot your actual performance against that planned or budgeted. Feedback will help you to monitor progress and modify your approach to improve the likelihood of achieving your objectives (Figure 9.8).

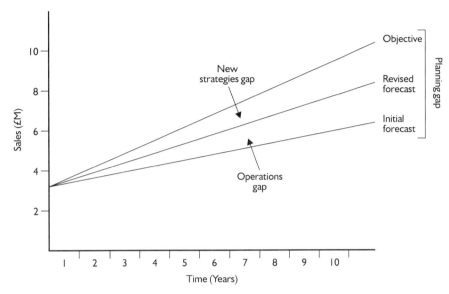

Figure 9.8 The planning gap

To identify a planning gap:

1 Determine where you are now.
2 Forecast where you will be in a given time if current situations remain unchanged.
3 Compare this to where your corporate objectives say that you should be.
4 If there is no variance, continue with present plans.
5 If there is a variance, consider what tactical changes can be made, and what the results will be. This reveals the operational gap.
6 If this is still insufficient you are forced into strategic change(s) in order to fill the strategic gap.

Select a market segment or key account for your business, or one with which you are familiar. Undertake a thorough audit of the current position and produce a complete plan for the next 12 months.

 Present this to your manager, if possible, and include a brief note on how the available client information could be improved.

The subject of quality and of relationship marketing is very much at the forefront of current management thinking and is a topic which you are likely to encounter both in this and other CIM papers. Much is written about the subject in the quality and marketing press. Make sure that you compile a cuttings file of *specific examples* to help you extend your knowledge of the subject area and to provide a useful source of current examples and illustrations for use in the exam.

A recent mystery shopper research survey has indicated that the quality of customer care in your hotel is significantly below that of two direct competitors in the town. Prepare a report to your managing director recommending a plan of action to improve the situation.

(**See** Debriefing at the end of this unit.)

Douglas McGregor: social psychologist

Douglas McGregor was professor of management at the Massachusetts Institute of Technology and is best known for formulating his theories X and Y. In his key book, *The Human Side of Enterprise*, he kept his argument commendably brief: 'Every management decision has behavioural consequences. Successful management depends – not alone, but significantly – upon the ability to predict and control human behaviour.'

McGregor's work has provided a focus, and a powerful springboard for later management gurus. His basic principles, that theory X managers believe that people resist work whilst theory Y managers believe that work is itself motivational have been described as simplistic. Peter Drucker wrote that 'Theory X assumes immaturity, theory Y assumes that people want to be adults.' Abraham Maslow (of hierarchy of needs fame) ardently supported the theory Y view. In his consultancy he endeavoured to put it into practice, but reported that theory Y makes inhuman demands on the weak members of the organization.

Drucker developed his critique by asserting that things are far less simple than McGregor says. Theory Y, says Drucker, is not of itself adequate because it places too high demands on both manager and worker. Other academics have commented that theory X and theory Y neatly encompass the key issues of business management – but they cannot so neatly and crisply be employed. They are, however, absolutely fundamental to modern-day management thinking and management practice, and have provided a solid foundation for the work of such as Peters and Waterman.

Key publication:
The Human Side of Enterprise, 1960

In this unit we have seen that:

- There is need to review your study notes as you come towards the end of the course.
- Satisfactions are delivered directly and indirectly. Even service providers rely on both tangible and intangible factors.
- Relationship marketing extends the marketing concept by showing the interactive and on-going nature of successful marketing relationships.
- It is very important to have detailed information about organizations, and individuals with whom relationships are possible, forming or formed.
- Quality is determined in the perception of the user.
- It is more cost-effective to retain existing customers than to seek new ones, although new customers are always needed.
- Identifying each customer's worth and importance is an important activity, but smaller customers should never be treated with disdain.
- Tracking research to monitor customer reactions is highly beneficial, providing that it is entered into with full commitment.
- Customer care must be understood, subscribed to and delivered by all members of staff.
- Feedback on results, with specific motivational plans built into the system, is an essential generator of long-term success.
- Strategic objectives may be achieved through tactical (operational) change – or there may be need for strategic change.

Debriefing

Activity 9.1

You may have other factors in your lists, depending on your experience, but the following indicates the broad areas of benefit and possible costs.

To the suppliers

Advantages:
- Long-term contracts reduce risks and enable long-term planning.
- Increases involvement in the 'whole process'. Generates more interest and facilitates the flow of market information. Suppliers, in effect, get closer to their end-users.
- Buyer becomes more sympathetic to supply problems and will tend to seek joint solutions.
- Relationship should be symbiotic – both parties growing as a result of it.

Disadvantages:
- May lead to overdependence on a small number of clients.
- Could become increasingly seen as a department of the organization, losing both the identity and the objectivity needed to make strategic decisions in their own right; i.e. investment targets on problem solving – not necessarily on the best opportunities.
- Relationship could become parasitic with the buyer pushing problems to the supplier.

To the buyer

Advantages:
- Less energy wasted in annual renegotiations of contracts and on the learning curve necessitated by a change in supplier.
- Closer knowledge of the supplier and their needs enables the buyer to have more confidence in their reliability and quality.
- Supplier works actively to help solve problems and to exploit new opportunities.
- New benefits such as targeted delivery can be offered – lowering operating costs and increasing flexibility.

Disadvantages:
- The supplier may become complacent. No annual negotiation could lead to higher prices and little incentive for proactive change.
- Long-term involvement will mean staff have on-going relationships with opposite numbers, possibly reducing their objectivity.

To the end-user

Advantages:
- Overall quality should improve.
- Increased flexibility in production might increase customer choice.
- Stock availability should improve.
- Range of choice should improve.

Disadvantages:
- Higher prices if higher costs of non-negotiated supplies are handed on.

Activity 9.2

1 No they are not. All are important and valued not only for current business, but also for their future potential. Given this, every effort should be made to satisfy the needs of all customers, but some – often referred to as key accounts – represent a significant proportion of business and so may be perceived to be more important to the stability and/or profitability of the business.
2 Not necessarily, the low value client of today may grow to be the big account of tomorrow. The large established client may itself be in decline – or because of a well-established relationship be more flexible or simply require less attention to maintain it.

Again, whilst attention to all clients is important, management's skills are often most valuable helping nurture the small accounts, developing the potential for tomorrow. A small account should never be snubbed or made to feel second class!

3 If the business is delivering quality, extra sales are often easier to win from established customers who are aware of and committed to the organization. Marketing costs of winning new customers from competitors or by converting unaware non-users are often very high.

4 There are advantages and disadvantages to each alternative. Costs of servicing a large customer base are higher, but small customers are more likely to pay premium prices as they are ineligible for bulk purchase discounts, etc. Profit margins are often lower with large accounts and there is greater risk if a large proportion of the business is tied up with a particular client. The large clients have more power and can dictate terms more effectively than can the small clients – a situation which can be observed in the on-going battle between branded fmcg manufacturers and the giant retailers.

5 The Pareto principle, or the 80:20 rule, indicates that 80 per cent of your business probably comes from 20 per cent of your customers. Identifying and targeting the top 10 per cent of the 80 per cent lower value customers are often very useful forms of segmentation.

Activity 9.3

There are a number of ways in which quality of service and customer perceptions can be assessed and monitored. Your list may include some of the following:

- Formal marketing research – qualitative techniques can be used to get customers to evaluate specific dimensions of service and to judge these either against their own expectations, or in comparison with competitors, to establish first a basis for bench marking and then on-going performance.
- Customer feedback – feedback at the point of service can be requested on an ad hoc or continuous basis. This must be carefully planned and only instituted if there is serious intent to take action, e.g. hoteliers can use in-room questionnaires to monitor guest satisfaction; telephone surveys can be commissioned; direct mail can be used; questionnaires can piggy-back along with invoices or statements.
- Sales force feedback – this can be routinely collected in sales reports or in specific debriefing sessions. Urgent information should come in through a special 'flash' priority route.
- Management information can be collected to provide feedback in relation to the relevant key indicators identified as important to the customers, e.g. waiting times, product failures, breakdowns, speed of service engineer response.
- Customer complaints are a key indicator which should be monitored and taken very seriously. Both the number and type of complaints should be monitored, and each complaint should be classified so that the 'genuine' are given urgency over the 'routine'.
- Informal customer contact is possibly one of the most underrated methods of collecting information about customer perceptions. Described by Tom Peters as 'management by walking about', getting back to basics and talking to both staff and customers at the sharp end of the business are very useful activities and can provide management with considerable insight.
- Mystery shopping is a research method widely used by retailers to assess service quality. Researchers appear as ordinary shoppers and are briefed to monitor specifics such as waiting time and product knowledge. This information can be focused specifically on the organization and/or used as a basis for comparison with competitors.

Self-check 9.1

1 'Relationship marketing' is the integration of quality, customer service and marketing focused on not only winning customers but also on retaining them.

2 Traditionally, marketing has focused on the winning of customers, not on their retention. Relationship marketing integrates the operational as well as marketing

dimensions to ensure that the organization is united in its objectives of delivering a quality service.

3 The aspects where customer priorities and their perceptions of the organization's performance are not in harmony. Also where the competitors have a relative competitive advantage.

4 A marketing research technique used to measure service levels and to compare service levels between competitors.

5 The marketing manager has a number of responsibilities:
- To monitor the existing customer base.
- To assess and measure the quality of service provided.
- To deal with customer problems.
- To ensure effective two-way communication between the organization and its customers.
- To identify new market opportunities and new potential customers.
- To identify the product offering(s) to meet customer need.
- To develop business from existing customers.

Activity 9.4

1 Keepit Bank has invested in identifying needs and in a range of systems to help deliver solutions, but they have failed to work at the critical customer contact point. Staff have to be trained and motivated to provide a quality service – they must be empowered to help customers solve their problems and involved in the processes of change they are expected to implement..

2 Boxit is a product oriented operation which has made the first mistake of quality – not knowing (or listening) to what the customer wants. Quality has to start from a solid understanding of customer need and then be backed up by a management team committed to making any changes necessary to delivering what the customer wants. Their system may technically be the best, but the rival is obviously at least adequate. Certainly, to the customers, it is the preferred choice. The need is to accept that, and change strategy.

3 External communication has to be developed in a way which does not raise customer expectations of the quality of product or service they can expect. Customer perceptions and expectations are the central measure on which quality will be assessed. The change in presentation set up a level of false expectation and the products which were perfectly acceptable within the previous perceptual framework are now being found wanting when judged against the new and higher expectation level.

Activity 9.5

See illustration on page 226

Activity 9.6

1 **A** Not current users – probably in the market, but possibly using a competitor's product. They are probably aware of us, and may have had contact with us, but have not yet placed an order. The sales person would describe this contact as a 'qualified lead'.

B A new user – trying out the organization's offering for the first or second time. Not brand loyal and no relationship established – very vulnerable to other suppliers at this time.

C Your growing customer has more potential business to offer. You have a well-established relationship and are likely to be working actively to help develop the potential.

D A key customer – a mature account. You have been working together for a long time and the relationship is well established. You have maximized sales from this account and business from them has settled into a level of repeat purchase.

E A previously mature client who has been with you a long time, but for some reason business is in decline.

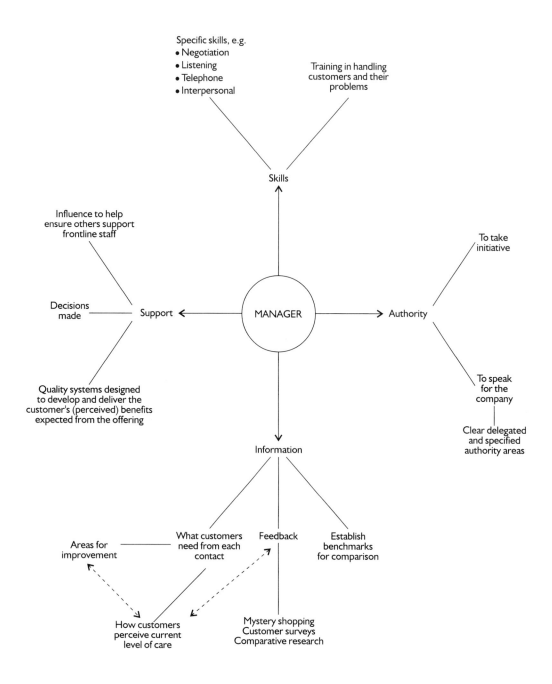

2 For customer B objectives are likely to be about the rate of growth in orders or order size. You would want to cement the relationship with them and work to ensure you remain their preferred supplier and retain the lion's share of their business.

For customer D, in the short term retaining the business, but working to maximize the length of the mature phase would also be an important goal. You would seek ways of extending business through the development of new markets or products with them.

3 Customer E is still generating a substantial amount of business and so is an important on-going source of income. The decline in business value may be temporary due to decline in their sales or them transferring business to a competitor. Investigate the cause of the decline.

4 Some sales people are very good at winning new business, but less effective at developing or maintaining it. The skills needed are very different. It is important to employ a sales person with appropriate skills and to make certain sales are not lost because the sales team do not have the empathy needed to build the business from existing customers.

Unit activity

Report to: Managing Director, Resort Hotel
From: Marketing Manager
Subject: Improving Customer Care   Date: XX.XX.199X

1 BACKGROUND

Following a recent research survey we have recognized that the quality of customer care offered by our front-line staff does not measure up to that of our key competitors in the town. The following report indicates my proposals for tackling this weakness.

2 PLAN OF ACTION

Any actions suggested will need to be implemented over a 12-month period to spread the cost and to reflect the real challenge of changing staff attitudes. Support from the project must come from the top, and the support, commitment and participation of all senior managers are critical.

2.1 Confirm Current Position

Further research with customers should be established to pinpoint specific areas of weakness.

We can monitor our customer care in four key categories:
- Staff:
  (a) Welcome.
  (b) Approachability.
  (c) Attentiveness.
- Atmosphere.

The research from our mystery shopper survey can be used to establish benchmarks to act as objectives for improvements.

2.2 Staff Input

A series of workshops to be implemented between now and the end of week 12 which all staff will attend. The objective being to:
- Discuss and identify the importance of customer care.
- Review the findings of the research.
- Gain staff commitment to improvements.
- Identify their ideas for improvement.
- Announce an 'employee of the month' and other motivational schemes.

2.3 Training

Specific skills training for customer care to be identified and implemented between weeks 13 and 24. Senior managers should be the first to attend and supervisors should be encouraged to take an active part in cascading skills through their teams.

2.4 Plugging the Gaps

Areas of weakness and pressure points to be reviewed thoroughly by management to identify systems and investments necessary to improve service levels. For example separating switchboard from reception or switching staffing levels to cope with peak times of demand.

2.5 Feedback

Regular feedback from customers to be obtained through:

2.5.1 Service level questionnaires in all rooms.

2.5.2 Research updates undertaken quarterly to monitor improvements.

2.5.3 Bookings and repeat booking levels to be monitored and results communicated to staff.

2.5.4 Suggestions for improvements to be sought.

2.5.5 Staff members recognized for their customer care performance to be rewarded.

3 BUDGET

If this outline proposal is approved I will submit a worked through plan, with full budget implications.

Tools for building better customer relations

In this unit you will:

- Examine the tools and techniques for improving customer relations.
- Identify the techniques for effective negotiation.
- Review the role of the manager as the coordinator and controller of the interface between the organization and the customer.
- Consider the challenges faced when trying to maintain customer relations through problems of change.

By the end of this unit you will:

- Be able to plan and participate in negotiations with a client.
- Understand the importance of maintaining effective communication and be aware of the options available.
- Recognize customers' worries and needs during times of change or difficulties.
- Understand the manager's role in supporting staff at the organization/client interface.
- Be able to propose plans to build on the existing customer base – winning more business and longer relationships from today's customers.

Managers throughout the organization need to recognize that the current customer base represents a considerable investment over the time taken to build goodwill and effective relations. It makes complete sense to focus strategies on maximizing the return from that investment by building and sustaining excellent customer relations.

Marketing managers, with their responsibility for the customer's interests, play a critical part in this activity. Responsible for both communication with external audiences and often for the negotiation of contracts, you can expect questions covering the building of customer relations to appear regularly in the Effective Management for Marketing paper.

You should allow 2 hours to complete this Unit and a further 3 hours to undertake the activities.

You will need a sample of the 'communications' which routinely take place between your organization and its customers. Collect an example of a letter, press release, instruction book, newsletter, statement, brochure, and advertisement which has been used recently. Alternatively, in your role as a customer, make the same collection, perhaps of communications from your bank to you personally as well as their public communications such as leaflets, media advertising, etc.

Effective managers need to demonstrate their empathy for customers, be they internal or external. Their needs should always be identified and considered. The most successful marketers and managers are those who take the trouble to put themselves into the other person's shoes. Taking time to see it from their view will help to smooth problems, anticipate worries and develop a style which ensures a quality relationship – establishing loyalty and support from both customers and team members.

The examiners will be looking for and rewarding evidence that you are able to put yourself in the other person's position within the context of the scenarios and questions set. Take time to think about the needs, and communicate these to the examiner.

- The member of staff participating in their first appraisal interview may feel threatened, nervous and lack the confidence to talk openly.
- The student audience at a presentation may feel bored or disillusioned by their course and cynical about the value of your contribution.
- The customer may be more concerned with ease of use than a 'sophisticated' range of options.

By recognizing these personal issues you can take them into account when developing your strategy, and so improve the effectiveness of your actions.

Explanations and definitions

1 *Negotiation*   Negotiation is a process by which parties to a conflict, or disagreement, attempt to resolve the matter by agreement. Disagreement can be over relatively straightforward matters such as price, or more complex issues such as the award of a detailed contract for a 'turnkey' MIS system.
2 *Turnkey*   In current usage – to set up a system from scratch to the point where it is running and fully tested. It is then handed over and will run with a simple 'turn of a key', i.e. switch it on and it works.

The current customer base

We have already considered the importance of the current customer base. It is an expensive activity to take a possible purchaser through the decision-making process from unawareness to action. It is therefore important that this investment is recognized and the maximum return extracted from it. As we saw in the Unit 9, provision of a quality service will help to establish long-term relationships. Success in this can be enhanced by the marketing manager taking care when negotiating and by proactively working to improve customer communications. Developing systems to support staff who have direct contact with clients is an activity which must be high on his or her agenda.

Throughout this unit you should bear in mind that investment in the customer base will be rewarded by:

- More repeat business.
- Closer working relationships with customers.
- Word-of-mouth recommendations.
- A steadier and more predictable flow of business.

We have established the critical importance of knowing who your customers are and of using the available technology to keep a well-designed and well-managed customer database readily available for managers to call upon.

How are customer records kept in your organization? Take time to find out who holds what information and how (or if) these data are shared?

- Does the sales team guard their information and records?
- In what format do finance keep records on order values and payments?
- Go on a fact-finding mission collecting information about a named client as a basis to determine:
    (a) What are the strengths and weaknesses of your information system?
    (b) What information is unavailable?
    (c) Whether the data could be integrated and be available more centrally?

Prepare a brief report recommending three improvements for your customer database.

Maintaining effective customer communication

Communication is the key to any relationship. Misunderstanding can be resolved and problems overcome as long as there is communication. Product and sales oriented companies have had the problem of being good talkers but poor listeners. As a result, communication has tended to be rather one sided. The firm that tells customers about product features and, in a sellers' market, dictates the terms of business, leaves little or nothing open to negotiation. As importantly, it never learns how its offerings may be improved and is often surprised to be superseded.

Increased competition has changed the nature of marketing because of the number of buyers' markets. Armed with greater bargaining power, and helped by improved knowledge of their rights, customers from all industries are increasingly vocal in their relations with suppliers.

- The supermarkets are demanding that manufacturers work with them to identify new sales promotion offers which target increasing average spend.
- British Rail and other public-sector operators have produced customer charters which empower their users.
- Environmentally conscious consumers are winning changes in both the product and packaging from companies across a wide range of sectors.

Identifying the communication options

Effective communication can take many forms and the manager needs to have the whole tool box of options from which to select.

Communicating . . . How?

Spend 10 minutes producing a mind map which identifies the methods by which the organization can:

- Send messages to the customers.
- Receive communication from them.

(**See** Debriefing at the end of this unit.)

Your mind map perhaps shows, like ours, the imbalance of the communication options. It is easy to visualize why the louder and/or stronger messages from the firm can drown out the response from the market.

Marketing research is the most obvious tool for the firm to use to find out about the customer, but the market can only be reactive to research. Individuals must wait to be asked and they may then be faced with questions which do not fully reflect the areas upon which they would wish to comment. The other options indicate the methods the customer can control and so can be proactive within. They are still dependent, however, on the manager to be listening actively!

Complaints (and compliments!)

Complaints and compliments are a valuable source of customer communication. However, managers need to take action if they are to even hear about them:

- They will often be addressed to operational staff with whom the customer deals and will be handled at that level.
- Few customers will actually complain (or compliment), they simply take their business elsewhere (or return for more).
- Managers may be biased in their perceptions of complainers and so the messages are 'decoded' in a way which marginalizes their value.

To overcome these barriers managers must do a number of things:

- Establish systems so that all complaints or comments are reported, especially those given orally.
- Positively seek feedback through questionnaires, suggestions and by actually meeting customers, talking with them, and listening to what they have to say.
- Treating all customer communication seriously and valuing it as direct response. Genuinely welcoming comments as opportunities for review – not being automatically defensive.
- Establishing customer panels and user groups, specially selected to provide objective responses.

QUESTION 10.2

Develop a short self-completion questionnaire which could be used at your distribution point to stimulate customer feedback. Suggest ways in which you could encourage customers to use it.

ACTIVITY 10.2

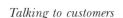

Talking to customers

Earlier in this workbook you reviewed a selection of communications to establish consistency of image and tone. In this exercise we would like you to consider the content of the documents you collected. Initially, put yourself in the customer's shoes. What will he or she feel and believe on receipt of each of them? To what degree do they make the customer feel valued and informed?

Next move on to a more detailed study by taking each example and producing a list of its strengths and weaknesses. Identify ways in which it could be improved in order to make communication with the client more effective.

(**See** Debriefing at the end of this unit and consider our checklist of questions, which should stimulate additional thoughts on the subject.)

The frequency and extent of communication between the organization and the customer will depend on a number of factors:

- Amount and importance of the business being transacted.
- Experience and length of the relationship. Repeat orders for regular clients may require less discussion and probably no negotiation.
- The potential value of future business.
- The complexity of the transaction.
- The degree or extent of change within the sector.

Effective communication does not imply daily contact. The key is to provide sufficient interaction to ensure the customer feels properly informed and valued. The extent of communication contact should be planned – perhaps focused around the sales-call pattern, supported by briefings, mail shots, promotional activities and social contact.

QUESTION 10.3

In Unit 4 you examined a range of communication alternatives. Use this exercise to complete your notes on this topic and to revise your understanding of that earlier work.

Take each of the following communication options and identify:

- Its strengths and weaknesses.
- An example of when each should be used:
  (a) Client/user newsletter.
  (b) Presentation.
  (c) Telesales.
  (d) Invitation to a sponsored event.
  (e) Give-aways, such as calendars and desk diaries.

Building good relations through effective communication

Communication is the cornerstone for building strong business relationships. It is not surprising, therefore, that it should be considered and planned with care. As with most relationships, trust is important. Communications which mislead or cover over a problem may reduce short-term pressures, but will be expensive in terms of the long-term relationship.

Hints and tips for maintaining effective communication

1 Establish from the outset the frequency and extent of contact and updating the client would like. Review this on a regular basis.
2 Ensure the client has a single named contact whom he or she knows and can call upon to deal with any aspect of the business.
3 Take care to avoid misunderstanding by specifying details. Avoid vague statements such as 'the product is not very heavy'. Be clear: 'the product weighs a little under 3 kilos'.
4 Do not try to ignore problems, they are unlikely to go away. Proactively dealing with the issue by activating a contingency plan and, if necessary, discussing the problem with the client will help you to retain his or her support.
5 Do not assume things have happened – check. For example, follow up the installation of new equipment with a phone call to make sure all is well and to actively seek feedback.
6 Always give customers every opportunity to communicate with you and *remember to listen to them.*
7 Reply promptly. Always acknowledge communication.

8 Meet to review past business and to discuss future possible activities in a general sense. Use your contact to build up a picture of their business to help identify emerging opportunities and potential threats to you. Also, of course, potential opportunities and threats to all parties.

. . . And the customer's role?

Communication is a two-way process and as a customer you have a responsibility to ensure it is effective.

1 Be clear about your objectives and requirements. Specifications and briefs need to be thorough – or the fact they are not should be clearly indicated.
2 Suppliers, agents and middlemen need to be trusted. They must be given all the background information which could be of value to them. Do not force, for example, your advertising agency to undertake secondary research which you already have available! Do provide them with the results of your latest relevant customer research, etc.
3 Give suppliers as much warning as possible about fluctuations in orders, the possibility of rush orders, cancellations, and so on. Help them to help you by keeping them informed.
4 Deal with any complaints and problems quickly and directly with your named contact. Give them a chance to put it right. Note: Ask for a named contact if one is not provided automatically.
5 Pay promptly. Do not lie that the cheque is in the post or has been lost by the Post Office. Saving a few days interest charges is unlikely to compensate for the loss of goodwill which you may want to call upon in the future.

Negotiations

One of the most direct examples of communications with customers and suppliers involves negotiation. This can be a relatively straightforward negotiation of the details of a purchase or work to be carried out, through to complex negotiations leading to the establishment of a contact spelling out the basis on which the relationship between the two parties will be conducted.

Negotiations lay the foundation of the relationship and so must be firm if they are to support a growing volume of transactions. Unfortunately, the negotiation process can easily break down because it involves the bringing together of two parties with their own needs and objectives. Negotiations should not be viewed as a battle or a competition from which will emerge a single 'winner'. Negotiation is undertaken to establish the basis of exchange – if that is not mutually profitable it will be a short lived commitment (see Figure 10.1).

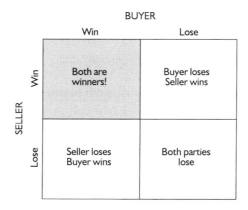

Figure 10.1 Buyer/seller negotiation

Only if both parties recognize the long-term benefits of win/win negotiations will they be focused on ensuring that negotiations lead to an optimum conclusion with the needs and objectives of both parties being satisfied. This is particularly important when there is an imbalance of power between the buyer and the seller.

Planning for negotiations

There are a number of stages or phases for the successful negotiation which should be followed through:

Setting the scene

The background against which negotiation takes place needs careful preparation. The participants should be relaxed and comfortable. It helps if they get the chance to meet before the negotiation starts. The ice-breaking stage is important because it can help to establish a cooperative approach to subsequent proceedings.

Opening negotiations

Getting down to business usually entails the parties agreeing the negotiation process, establishing the objectives and agreeing a timetable and approach. The ground rules of the negotiation are agreed, those involved introduced and their roles made clear.

Negotiation

Within the negotiation phase there are a number of stages.

- *Exploration* The research stage of the process. It ensures that everyone involved has the same basic understanding of the situation. Normally, each party will state their position, interests, priorities and attitudes. During this stage clarity and brevity are important. Whilst listening, do not argue or counter. Ask for clarification if you are not clear.
- *Creative solutions* The aim of both parties should now be to identify the creative options – generating a range of ideas which could show the way forward. Clearly, the personality of the managers involved in negotiation is important if a flexible approach and a broad view are to be achieved.
- *Framing the deal* This evolves from the broad solution identified – it clarifies the basis of the deal so that both parties can assess the relative costs and benefits to them. This is critical before bidding commences, as the parties need to know the 'value' of the contract on which they are bidding. Within the deal there may be details which themselves require negotiation. The parties need to keep a clear picture of the progress of the deal and the agreements as they are made.

- *Bidding* Traditionally, the opening bid or price is high and represents the ceiling for the negotiations. It is not possible to inflate this later. The bid may be high, that is expected, but it must be realistic or it can in itself offend the other party. The counter bid or offer is traditionally low – establishing the floor for negotiations. Between these two extremes the parties will now bargain to reach an agreement. Thorough preparation before the negotiation will now pay off because the manager will know the priorities and interests of his opposite number. These can be used in this part of the process. A new offer can be made, or the deal may be modified as part of a give-and-take round.

The golden rules
- Never agree a concession without securing a concession in return.
- Move into an agreement by summarizing the possibilities: 'If it were possible for me to . . . would you be able to offer . . . ?'
- Always give what is valuable to your customer, but cheap for you. For example, a lower price may be a costly move; offering shorter delivery times may be much more valuable to the customer and less expensive for you.

- *Bargaining* The negotiator must be well briefed and thoroughly prepared for this stage of the process. He or she needs to know the extent of their authority and the limits within which they are able to negotiate. Offering faster delivery may help to reach an agreement now, but will do little for long-term relationships if the company does not have the capacity to meet that commitment.
- *Closing* Once complete the negotiation should be summarized. Test both parties' understanding of what has been agreed. The agreement will simply be confirmed in writing or by formal legal contact, as appropriate.
- *Follow up* Both parties, singly and collectively, must monitor the agreement to ensure it is progressing as planned.

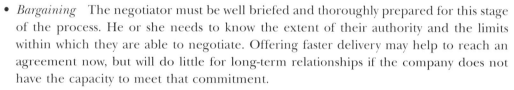

We are all actively involved in negotiations throughout our lives. Children learn the art of negotiation from the time they first question their bed time or the amount of pocket money they receive.

Identify an opportunity for negotiation at home or work and try out your skills. Perhaps you could negotiate with your children to tidy up their rooms, or with a manager to support your application for a training programme.

Do your preparation thoroughly and remember to think about the needs of the other party. What are you offering in exchange? The objective is a win/win situation. Do not abuse your power. (Both parents and children have power bases – the parent of control, the child of rebellion.)

Take time out to review your progress and to identify ways to improve your negotiating techniques.

Self-check 10.1

Review your understanding by tackling the following questions:

1 Why do organizations have to improve their listening skills?
2 How would you encourage and stimulate customer feedback?
3 What would be the value of introducing a newsletter for your customers?

4 What preparation would you do before attending a negotiation meeting with a new potential client?

5 Why should the target of negotiations be win/win outcomes?

(**See** Debriefing at the end of this unit.)

Managing through problems

One could argue that maintaining strong relationships is straightforward when everything is going smoothly. The challenges really arise when there are problems and managers have to cope with crisis or adversity. Relationship marketing implies that the two parties will work together to develop opportunities and to solve problems. This partnership approach requires considerable effort on the part of all those involved.

Spot problems early

Effective channels of communication will pay dividends in such circumstances because you will be aware of the pending problem at the earliest time – giving the maximum opportunity to find solutions and so retain the loyalty of the customers.

- Well developed information systems will also provide an early warning system which can help to alert managers to possible problems. An unexpected reduction in sales through a particular outlet or a lower volume of orders from a client should be identified and responded to by the management team.
- Managers should be alert to changes which may generate problems both in their environment and the environments of their customers. Recession, lowering demand, high interest rates, reducing disposable incomes affect all, but sometimes particular markets suffer whilst others proceed unaffected. Noticing and responding to these changed circumstances can be crucial to on-going relationships and to the profitability, both short and long term. Creative companies are those who help their customers that are in trouble by producing economy models, leasing options or offering credit schemes.
- Managers should appreciate how their actions may cause problems. A change of key account manager, an altered delivery or administration procedure, the discontinuation of a product or a change in specification might all create problems for the customer and should be anticipated and tackled proactively.

When supplies are short

A fire has caused extensive damage at your central manufacturing base. Stocks have been destroyed and it is expected to be 3 months before operations can recommence. Short-term leasing of factory capacity, along with double shifts at your second plant will enable you to supply 80 per cent of your order book. What action would you recommend be taken?

(**See** Debriefing at the end of this unit.)

Tactics for tackling problems

As we indicated earlier in this unit, honest and open communication is essential if trust is to be maintained.

Organizations can easily become very inward looking, failing to recognize that their actions have an impact on customers. The case of the fire described above seems obvious, but equally problematic and more frequent may be the change of key contact staff.

If the change is caused by promotion within the company the client may feel unsettled but pleased for the contact. A smooth transition to the new contact person should not be too difficult. If the contact is changing employer there may be a strong risk that the buyer might re-evaluate suppliers.

It is important to remember that for the customer the staff who are the key contacts don't just represent – they are the organization. The relationship with the organization is often personified in that individual. Organizations with a policy of frequent staff changes, such as the clearing banks, often fail to recognize the impact this has on their customers.

Handling staff changes

1 Managers should not try to pretend the change is not happening. They should brief the customer about the change and who their new contact will be.
2 Where possible, a hand-over period should be arranged so that the new contact person can be introduced to the client.
3 Sales managers can play an important role in smoothing the passage from one person to another. They should take particular care to review customer reactions to the new contact and to check out customers unhappy with the new arrangements.

With foresight, tact, creativity, information and good communication systems the manager should be able to retain effective relationships, even during difficult times.

The marketing manager – a coordinator of others

It is perhaps appropriate that we conclude the syllabus coverage for this course by coming nearly full circle. We began by investigating the role of the manager as a coordinator of resources. We conclude by reviewing the specific role of the marketing manager in building relationships and customers as a coordinator of the marketing activity and of customer contact staff. Marketing is at the sharp end of the operation, dealing extensively with customers and other external stakeholders. As we have seen, the expertise of marketers is being increasingly called upon to help market plans and to motivate staff within the organization.

Marketing's role is to match demand to supply – to ensure there are customers for the output of the organization. It does that by ensuring resources are used to provide goods that the customers need and will value. Marketing opens up the channels of communication between the customers and the company.

It may sound simple, but in a large organization there are many people involved in the complex process of delivering customer satisfaction. Marketing brings about a coordination of the efforts of these individuals through the planning process. A clear plan, communicated and disseminated throughout the operation means that everyone:

- Understands his or her contribution to customer satisfaction.
- Has quantified and relevant objective(s).
- Has benchmarks against which to monitor the performance and quality of their work.
- Is empowered with the authority necessary to be responsive to customer needs.
- Is motivated to care about customer satisfaction.
- Has the skills necessary to do their job.

The marketing plan will be central to ensuring the coordination of effort at the marketing and sales level.

Marketing's unique position, in close contact with the customer and able to influence the strategic decisions of the business, give it this particular responsibility for ensuring that the scarce resources of the business are allocated in a way which creates the perceived benefits needed by the customer.

Both the tools and skills of the manager, and the specialist knowledge of the marketer, are necessary to ensure that this is achieved efficiently and effectively.

Questions

Use these questions to review your understanding of the work in this unit.

Indicate True or False against each of the following statements:

1 When negotiating it does not matter how high the opening bid is.
2 The more communication you have with your customers the better.
3 Managers should be proactive in looking for possible problems and client difficulties.
4 Coordination of individual activities in an organization must be planned.
5 The plan is a focus for motivation of staff.
6 Investing in improved customer liaison and communication will increase customer loyalty.
7 The customer is always right.
8 Winning new customers uses more resources than retaining existing ones.

(**See** Debriefing at the end of this unit.)

Section A of the exam paper will be a mini-case scenario or an article extracted from a business publication. Managing and maintaining the customer base is so important that you will not be surprised to learn that this topic is likely to be highlighted in the case scenarios.

When tackling Section A take time to analyse the situation thoroughly. Assess the nature and extent of any problem(s) before making specific recommendations for its (their) resolution.

Work in report format unless otherwise specified. The following unit activity gives you an example to practise on.

Tackling problems

You have been recently appointed as the Marketing Manager for a company importing fabric and clothing from Asia. The recession has had a particularly dramatic impact on the large number of small clothing manufacturers supplied by the company. A significant number of them failed over the last 3 years, causing bad debt problems which greatly concerned your company. As a result ordering and payment systems were tightened, but unfortunately with little notice taken. Complaints from regular customers were not really resolved. Now business is picking up there is evidence that some of the regular clients are looking elsewhere for suppliers.

Your initial research indicates a number of problems, including lack of availability of certain fabrics and slow delivery times as well as difficulties in getting decisions or responses from the supplier.

1 What is your assessment of the situation and how might it have been prevented from developing?
2 What actions would you take in the first 3 months of your appointment and why?

(**See** Debriefing at the end of this unit.)

Tom Peters and Robert Waterman: Consultants

The management-book market was transformed in 1982 by Peters and Waterman's book *In Search of Excellence*. It has sold well over 5 million copies world-wide, and spawned money-spinning excellence movement. The book has been severely criticised for its extreme simplicity – the very factor which has made it such a runaway bestseller! The problem appears to be that, whilst it appears very simple to apply the principles of excellence, they are in reality extremely hard to bring to fruition. Just as one can read how to perfect a golf swing or a tennis service, so one can read how to be a good manager – but how many actually work hard enough to translate the simple theory into practical reality?

Peters and Waterman say that their approach broke the mould of 'line and staff' which was evident in previous material. Other models had been written about, they say, but with no evidence that they were working, nor associated with success. The book came about because European multi-national companies with US operations that were not doing too well wanted to know what to do about it. From their work with blue-chip consultants McKinsey, Peters and Waterman were able to draw on practical examples, and refer directly to the success achieved.

Peters and Waterman refined their research down to eight essential points which were identifiable characteristics of excellent companies:

1 A bias for action – for getting on with it.
2 Closeness to the customer – a genuine belief that the customer is king.
3 Autonomy and entrepreneurship – an environment that encourages innovation.
4 Productivity through people – treating the rank and file as the root source of quality and productivity gains.
5 Hands-on, value-driven management – leaders who make their presence known, who tell employees about the values they hold.
6 Stick to the knitting – staying close to the business they know.
7 Simple forms, lean staff – very simple structures and a minimum of headquarters bureaucrats.
8 Simultaneous loose–tight properties – they are both centralized (around their core values) and decentralized (with regard to other values).

The backbone of the original book was reduced by Peters over time until, with Nancy Austin, he produced *A Passion for Excellence*. In this the concept was encapsulated in a simple triangle. On the three sides are: care of customers, innovation, people. Central to these is leadership – what Peters calls 'management by walking about' (MBWA).

Waterman continued from *In Search of Excellence* with *The Renewal Factor*, which concentrates on the need to learn from the best. It took over seven person-years to write and over 20 drafts. Described as 'inspiring and elegant in its simplicity', it shows in eight points how to make a company 'renewable':

1 Informed opportunism – information is a strategic advantage.
2 Direction and empowerment – everyone is a source of creative input.
3 Friendly facts, congenial controls – facts are friendly and controls liberate.
4 A different mirror – step out of the business and put it into perspective.
5 Teamwork, trust, politics, power – the first two must be commonplace, the latter two taboo.
6 Causes and commitment – grand causes expressed as small actions secure commitment.
7 Attitudes and attention – visible management attention gets things done.
8 Stability in motion – constantly review, break habits.

Key publications:
In Search of Excellence, 1982
A Passion for Excellence, 1985
Thriving on Chaos, 1990
The Renewal Factor, 1987

In this unit you have seen that:

- The existing customer base represents an investment, but it must be nurtured and cared for if it is to produce greater returns.

- Many organizations keep customer information in a variety of systems and departments, making intelligence gathering difficult.

- Effective communications are central to developing relationships with clients.

- Organizations are naturally good senders of messages but must work at being good listeners.

- There are range of options for communications. They should be identified and selected with care.

- Negotiations are important. They must be planned and the research stages should be understood and carried through.

- Negotiations should lead to win/win situations.

- Managers should always bargain with variables which are valuable to the customer but relatively cheap to them.

- Managing relations through difficulties requires patience and planning – as well as creativity and a good communications system.

- Marketing managers play a critical role in helping to bring the organization and customer together in order to achieve mutually profitable exchange.

Debriefing

Activity 10.1

Evaluate our thoughts and use them to stimulate additions to your mind map.

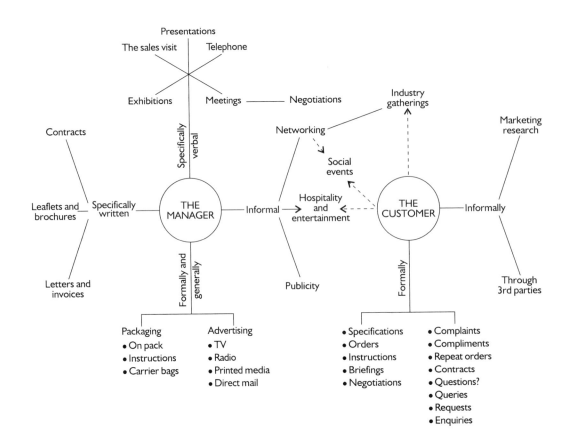

Activity 10.2

Checklist Use these questions to stimulate your review of the communication examples collected:

1 Is the purpose and the message of the communication clear?
2 Is the medium appropriate to the message?
3 Is the content, verbal and visual, appropriate to the message?
4 Does it encourage two-way communication?
5 Is the receiver named? Does the communication indicate an established/cordial relationship?
6 How would you feel if you received this document?
7 Does the communication include jargon or generalities which might be misunderstood or misinterpreted? For example 'delivery will be a.s.a.p.' could mean a few hours – a few days – even a few weeks!
8 Does the communication summarize key points and spell out the required response?
9 What improvements would you make to each of the examples?

Self-check 10.1

1 Organizations have built up their experience as 'talkers', but only since they have become more customer oriented have they needed to become 'expert listeners'. As a result the systems and procedures for 'listening' are less developed. Accurate listening is how companies can start the process of winning competitive advantage.
2 This has to be actively developed. Give customers every opportunity to provide feedback, through research, comment forms and user panels as well as taking customer complaints seriously and encouraging both managers, operational and sales staff to meet with and talk to customers.
3 It would provide a regular focus for news and information. It would provide a format for informing customers and users about new products, developments and services. It could carry customers' letters and enquiries and so, to some extent, offer two-way communication opportunities. To be of value to the customer it would have to be relevant and provide real value – not simply become a showcase for the company's products.
4 • Use secondary research to find out as much as possible about the firm, its business and strategies. Have knowledge about the industry and the likely problems and opportunities faced.
   • Identify the key staff and negotiators and research their backgrounds, authority and interests. If possible, identify past or current suppliers and any other contenders for the contract.
   • Establish the potential for negotiation, what the organization is able to and will offer.
   • Be clear about the value and potential value of this client to you.
5 Win/win negotiations are the only ones which offer a long-term framework for developing the relationship. A win/lose situation leaves either the buyer or seller unhappy and at least open to alternative partners. Lose/lose means the needs of neither party are satisfied. Mutually profitable exchange is a win/win scenario.

Activity 10.3

1 A decision must be made about how available stocks are to be allocated, e.g. rationing, first come first served, or key accounts given priority. The criteria for allocation should be clearly stated.
2 The priority is to communicate with all customers to tell them of your ability to maintain some service, the time span of the problems and your strategy for handling the crisis.
3 Discussions with key accounts should be undertaken to identify the minimum levels of delivery which they can accept over the next 3 months.
4 Sales teams should actively source, negotiate for and supply alternative products where possible. This reduces probable interaction between your clients and competitive sales teams.

5 Customers should be kept updated on progress following the fire.

6 Management might consider a loyalty bonus to reward and/or compensate clients who coped through the shortage.

Activity 10.4

1 *False* Too high a bid may simply be rejected with no further negotiation. It may be seen as offensive. Bids must be realistic and defensible.

2 *False* There could be too much communication, a weekly sales visit for example. There needs to be an agreement on the appropriate level of communication.

3 *True* Foresight gives forewarning, allowing time to evaluate and plan.

4 *True* It focuses on the effective and efficient use of resources and its objectives tells everyone what is the target and the strategies clarify how they are to be achieved – thus ensuring a synergy of effort.

5 *True* The plan can be used in internal marketing and the motivation of staff.

6 *True* Better communication leads to greater understanding, stronger relationships and enhanced chances of repeat business.

7 *False* Not always. Solid partnerships are founded on an equal balance of power. Some customers may be more trouble than they are worth, but they should never be marginalized without great care and only after many attempts to satisfy their needs.

8 *True* It takes time and costs considerably more marketing resources to win than to retain. Looking after the existing customers makes good financial sense.

Unit activity

1 *Background*

1.1 Management has responded reactively to difficult trading conditions. They have failed to communicate with their customer base and not negotiated with them over the changes imposed.

1.2 As a result the customers feel resentful and undervalued. They feel as though they have been placed in a win/lose position, with the supplier abusing its power.

1.3 It seems that all customers have been treated the same, with no attempt to identify the degree of risk associated with specific customers.

1.4 As a result, there is a motivation for these users to seek alternative sources of supply when the environment improves. Possibly made more critical by their experience, they are also identifying a number of weaknesses they perceive with this company – associated with both stock availability and the length of delivery times.

1.5 The company could have taken a number of actions to have avoided this current problem. They could have:

(a) Forecast the impact of the recession on their small traders and taken action to identify high risk companies earlier.

(b) Discussed their worries and problems with the customers and sought to find a possible solution.

(c) Been more aware of other weaknesses through customer research, and taken steps to rectify them.

(d) Been more discriminating rather than treating all clients the same and imposing a blanket policy change.

(e) Forecast the problems and feelings such an action would generate and taken steps to forestall the changes, or prepared customers for them.

(f) Informed customers of the changes and the necessity for them. Offered to discuss any possible problems caused.

2 *Course of action*

2.1 Complete audit – analyse the current position. Identify the key accounts, collect relevant records and correspondence and prioritize those most in danger of going elsewhere.

2.2 Set objectives – set a series of objectives

(a) To retain 95 per cent of current customer base over next 12 months.

(b) To retain at least 75 per cent of all their orders.

2.3 Establish strategy – how this should be achieved will require a considerable change in the approach of this importer to the customers. We recommend winning support for developing a relationship marketing partnership with a number of key accounts, offering:

(a) Priority selection and ordering.
(b) Speedier delivery.
(c) Less bureaucratic systems with an identified key account contact.
(d) Simplified payment terms.

In exchange for:

(a) A contractual agreement for an agreed volume of orders.
(b) No further 'shopping around' for 3 years.

To set up a series of presentations and negotiations for month 3 to discuss this proposal with the clients.

2.4 Other actions – improved systems for information and communication should be identified and, where possible, implemented. Undertake a review of logistics to identify means for speeding up delivery.

2.5 Timetable

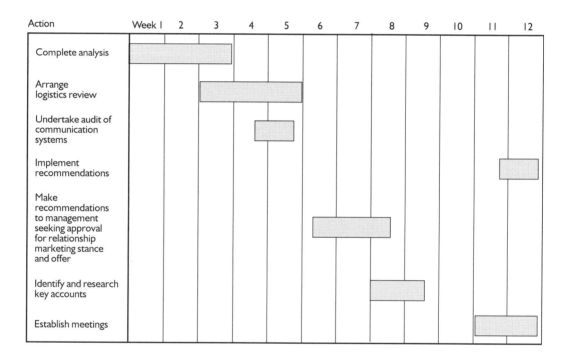

Focus on the examination

In this unit you will:

- Examine the tools and techniques for improving your learning and thinking skills.
- Identify the examiner's requirements.
- Discover the techniques needed to ensure a pass in your examination.

By the end of this unit you will be able to

- Produce effective revision notes.
- Understand the importance of meeting the examiner's requirements.
- Manage your time before and during the examination.
- Select questions and plan your answers.
- Present your answers effectively.

Students have to make a major behavioural change when approaching an examination. It is necessary to metamorphose into a *candidate*.

As a student you have been used to absorbing information, to following the lead given you by your workbooks and your tutors. You have been writing notes that only you have to understand. As a candidate you have to convince an examiner that you have credibility in a given subject. In the case of Effective Management for Marketing you must show that you are a credible manager who can be trusted to respond positively to the challenges, opportunities and threats that face a marketer in the course of his or her daily routine. This means that you have to take charge of your response. You have to make decisions regarding the examiner's requirements, be able to select the appropriate response in terms both of content and style of presentation and manage your time so that you fully answer all the questions asked.

Examiners' Reports are published after each examination and these regularly comment on two key candidate failures:

- To present their material appropriately, i.e. to write reports, memos, notes, or whatever the examiner calls for – *not* to write essays unless specifically called for.
- To answer the questions asked.

From the examining and tutorial side of the examination process it is easy to see why so many candidates make these two cardinal errors. The difficulty is in getting students to:

- Acknowledge the importance of good presentation (in all its aspects).
- Practise answering so that they are experienced in the process.
- Take the time to read and thoroughly understand the questions.
- Plan their answers before starting to write them.

It is not difficult to pass any examination, providing you have a minimum of basic knowledge and are well versed in exam technique. This unit is devoted to helping you build the needed competence to handle yourself well in the examination itself.

You should allow 2 hours to complete this unit and a further 4 hours to undertake the activities which include a full mock examination as the Unit Activity.

Explanations and definitions

Examiners are precise in their use of the English language. They say what they mean, and you must take it that they mean *exactly* what they say, e.g. market and marketing research are often interchanged in everyday speech. To a marketer, however, they have special and precise meanings. The one is, as we know, contained within the other. Take the examiner's wording literally – be extra careful to read and fully understand each question.

Be quite clear about the exact meaning of the following terms:

1 *Briefly* Short, concise.
2 *Compare* Look for similarities and differences – perhaps reach a conclusion about which is preferable.
3 *Contrast* Set in opposition in order to bring out differences.
4 *Compare and contrast* Do both of the above.
5 *Criticise* Give your judgement about the merits of the subject. Back your views with evidence and/or reasoning.
6 *Define* Write the precise meaning of a word or phrase. Quote a source if possible. Show that the distinctions contained or implied in the definition are necessary or desirable.
7 *Discuss* Investigate or examine by argument, sift and debate, give reasons for and against. Examine implications.

8 *Describe* Give a detailed or graphic account of.

9 *Evaluate* Make an appraisal of the worth of something, in the light of its truth or usefulness.

10 *Explain* Make plain, interpret (see below), and account for. Give reasons for.

11 *Identify* Recognize, establish; select the key issues.

12 *Interpret* Expound the meaning (or possible meaning) of; make clear and explicit.

13 *Illustrate* Give examples to make clear and explicit. Demonstrate understanding.

14 *List* Number of names, items, things set out clearly in order.

15 *Outline* Give main features, or general principles. Omit minor detail. Emphasize structure and arrangement.

16 *Relate* Show how things are connected to each other, and to what extent they are alike, or affect each other.

17 *Specify* Name expressly, mention definitely.

18 *State* Present in clear, brief form. (**Note:** brief!)

19 *Summarize* Give a concise account of the chief points; omit details and examples.

20 *Trace* Describe development or history of a topic from some point of origin.

You must also be able to write in *report* and *memo* styles, and to produce *notes* for your manager and *presentation notes* for yourself.

During the examination you are likely to be faced with setting budgets for your proposals, and so you need to be up to date with basic prices charged in your market. You do not need to be precise, but it is important that you feel comfortable with market prices.

Take the time to research your marketplace and fill out the grid below.

Service	Period/ Quantity	Price charged
Consultancy (marketing, management, PR)	Day	
Training course (in-house)	Day	
Training for an individual on an external course	Week (5 days)	
Individual's attendance at a workshop or course	Day	
Advertisement in your local paper	Half-page	
Advertisement in a quality national paper	Half-page	
Advertisement in a trade magazine	Whole page	
Printing – eight-page A5 leaflets in four colours	2000	
Production of two-page A4 questionnaires in black and white	500	
Marketing research interviewer	Hour	

Lateral thinking

Edward de Bono is the creator of the concept of lateral thinking. Lateral thinking is most easily understood by contrasting it with the linear thinking which occupies us for most of our lives. Linear thinking works in straight lines, it is logical, and it assumes a logical and unchanging world. Linear thinkers are slow to react to change, they are self-programmed to a predicted course of action. For much of our lives we depend on linear thinking to reduce the workload on our mental faculties. If every perception had to be tested we would never have time to do anything. In crossing the road we assume that an approaching car is travelling at a certain speed and decide to cross or to wait. If the driver is behaving differently than our experience leads us to believe, we make a misjudgement – but we cannot possibly measure the speed of every car on every road crossing.

de Bono asks 'What is the purpose of thinking?' and answers 'To stop thinking'. This is not as crazy as it sounds at first. We are constantly faced with new experiences, and for each novel situation, however trivial, we have to make one or more judgements. We have to think our way through to a solution. Once we have solved the problem we adopt our solution and add it as a routine response that requires little or no fresh thinking. Thus the purpose of thinking is to clear the way for us to move more effectively through our lives.

Managers have a particular need for advanced thinking skills since a major part of their role is thinking through problems and making decisions. A manager without lateral thinking abilities is less effective than he or she could be. Mind mapping and lateral thinking are powerful tools that link strongly to help the manager – especially the creative marketer. The mind map stimulates a multidimensional view of a situation; lateral thinking encourages an unconventional approach.

You are encouraged to explore this fascinating and worthwhile area as part of your own self-development – two examples must suffice in this Unit to whet your appetite:

1 *Look back to the problem.*
   When you can't see your way through a problem it helps to imagine that you have solved it and arrived at the destination. Then look back. Often you will see at least part of the route. You will have narrowed the gap, isolated the area that contains the problem, reduced the magnitude of the difficulty, put things into perspective. It is unlikely that your first route will be the best. It will be refined in the light of experience . . . but someone has to go first. Often this is the manager – the leader. (See Figure 11.1)

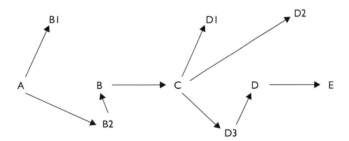

Figure 11.1   The linear route A–B–C–D–E may well have resulted from lateral thinking. Teaching will be along the route A–B–C–D–E but, whilst effective in giving a basic understanding, this route does not impart the ability to see what might be.

2 *What if?*
   Asking 'What if?' about even the most mundane items can lead to exciting results. de Bono gives the example of himself wandering into Woolworth's one day on a 'What if?' expedition. He picked up a penny whistle and asked 'What if it had no holes?' A silly question! But it stimulated a line of thought that resulted in the invention of a device that measures the lung strength of asthmatics. They blow down a tube and a restrictive device indicates the strength of their efforts. The invention is in widespread use because it met an unfulfilled need which had not been met by linear thinking.

Lateral thinking

It is often best to write the answer to an examination question before writing the question itself. Take 15 minutes and test the validity of this statement. Consider its importance to you as a student about to become a candidate.

(**See** Debriefing at the end of this unit.)

Learning

Much work has been done on learning theory, but you don't need to delve deeply unless you get hooked on the subject. What you need to understand fully is that what most people call 'learning' is actually only memory. Revision, for example, is of little use to many people because they treat it as a passive activity and read and re-read their notes. Learning is actually understanding and use:

The double U principle:

- To truly learn anything you have to *understand* it.
- To remember you have to *use* it.

There should never be any shame in not understanding something. Everybody has a different make up and all find some topics easier than others. Share your particular skills of understanding with others, and benefit from their abilities in return. You will find that this mutually supportive activity greatly enhances your own understanding because you will be using your knowledge. So it is worth helping others, even if they can't help you back.

If you are in a job where you can use your learning then you have the ideal situation. If you are not, then you have to create opportunities so that you can put your learning to use. **Note:** If you don't use learning you are extremely unlikely to remember what you have 'learnt'. How many times have you gone back to your notes at revision time, and found that material covered in the first part of a course is coming at you almost as new? What a waste!

Exercise is important

It is necessary to schedule both physical and mental activity into your learning. The mind needs time to assimilate and process new data and the body needs to rid itself of the physical and mental tension that builds up during concentrated periods of study.

Research indicates quite clearly that more learning takes place if the periods of study are brief and interspersed with physical activity. An effective break can be as little as 5 minutes, but it must be taken outside the study area, preferably in the fresh air. It must certainly involve physical stretching – perhaps a short walk.

Does this situation ring true to you? One of the Computer Technicians in a large College wanted to improve her memory, so she got a book on how to do it from the library. She discovered that her memory could be improved, but that it would take effort. Her comment was 'It'll take so much time to learn the system that it's better not to bother'. Recognize the situation?

It is the same when a boss does the work himself because 'it takes too much time to show anyone else'. The argument is not sound for the boss (he cannot do everything) and it is not sound for the technician – just think how much time she would save over the next 40 years if she invested 3 months work now.

Be very clear about your needs both short- and long-term.

Review

Tony Buzan's research shows that if you don't review your work regularly you will forget most of it very quickly. You have to impress your subconscious mind with the importance of the material and of keeping it both stored and accessible.

It may seem like hard work, but you really only have to glance over your notes. If they are set up with good triggers and you understand the material you will get to know the notes very quickly. You will also be able to recall them in the exam room.

Studies show that properly spaced review, as part of planned learning, can keep recall constantly high.

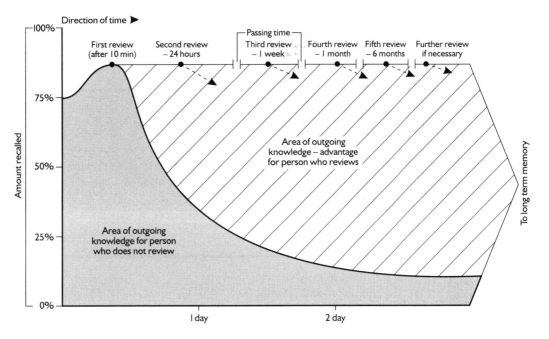

Figure 11.2 How properly spaced review can keep recall constantly high (from *Use Your Head* by Tony Buzan, reproduced by permission)

Revision notes

Notes made whilst learning form the basis of your revision notes. They should be full of triggers – key points that stand out and stimulate a mental response. Triggers should be memorable, unique, and link into your preferred learning style. They can be humorous, dramatic, stylish – anything that makes them stand out to stimulate a recollection when you come across them in review.

You should actively seek to build triggers into your notes so that they are there as associative links which your subconscious mind can identify and index. Your aim should be to establish key issues as triggers and links so that a flow of association is stimulated whenever any one of the triggers in an associative chain is activated. Mind maps, of course, work on exactly this principle.

Trust your memory

Your learning notes are too long for effective revision. They must be reduced to the key points – the triggers and associative links. But you cannot really go in one bound from lengthy notes to abbreviated Flash Cards. Reduce your notes in stages over time. As you pass through each stage you will be moving from passive student to active candidate. The aim is to have a set of postcard-size notes, each with a key area of learning on the front as a trigger, with the key points briefly extended on the back.

Revise actively

Whatever you do, *avoid* the standard form of 'Revision' used by almost all candidates. Do not sit for hours on end with textbooks trying to cram knowledge into your head. It is not subject knowledge that is most important. You need skill in pulling out and presenting the right knowledge at the right time.

Pat Cash, the Australian tennis star, was being interviewed about his ability to win. 'You can't win', he said, 'until you have time to read the game and get to where the ball is going to be before it gets there. Then, if your shots are in the groove, you can pass the other player.'

Having time is what distinguishes the professional from the amateur. You have to become professional at passing examinations. That can only mean practice, rehearsal, to get your skills 'in the groove'.

Skill comes only from practice. So revision has got to be active – you trying, failing; trying again, getting better; trying again, getting confident; trying again, getting it right; trying again, getting it perfected; trying again, getting it to a routine.

Take a little time to learn how to learn. Learn how to make notes so that they will help your revision. The work of both Tony Buzan and Edward de Bono is very helpful (and fun).

Preparing to pass

Preparing to pass begins at the second you decide 'I'm going to pass', not before. Not at the moment you sign on for a course, not when you enter for the exam, not when you hope to pass, not if you expect to pass, not if you think it would be a good idea to pass. Only when you decide to pass. When you set passing as a specific objective.

Why do you want to pass?
Take 15 minutes and clarify why you want (need?) to pass this examination.

(**See** Debriefing at the end of this unit.)

Physical presentation

The examiner must be impressed by your paper. The first response is critical. It is likely to be 'This is good, how good ?' or 'This is bad, how bad ?' The successful candidate gives the examiner every opportunity to award marks. The actual layout, crispness and overall impression are powerful influencers for good, or ill. The basic rules are:

1 Write your personal details clearly and neatly on the front of the answer book. Enter the numbers of the questions you have answered in the order you have answered them.
2 Do all your rough work in the *back* or *centre* of the answer book. (No matter how professional the examiner, it is better to keep the rough work out of the way.)
3 Start your first answer on the right-hand page. Use white space, do not crowd your work!
4 Never use red or green ink! (These are the examiner's colours.)
5 Do not use liquid paper – neatly cross through any work that has been replaced.
6 Always underline, draw diagrams, cross through with a ruler. Never freehand!
7 Label the axes of graphs and matrices.

What does the examiner require?
Take 10 minutes and jot down the things that the examiner requires of you. What should you do to make a good impression?

(**See** Debriefing at the end of this unit.)

First impressions count

The whole aim and purpose of your overall presentation must be to communicate marketing credibility to the examiner. The reaction you are seeking is – 'This is a good paper – I wonder how good?' From that beginning it is very difficult for an examiner to give a fail grade. On the other hand, a start of 'Oh dear, wonder how bad this will be?' is very difficult to turn into a pass!

Therefore, the cover should be pristine – you have ample time to get that right. And your first three pages should be written with special care. It is probably best to write your second best answer first. This allows you to relax into the paper, yet presents a good first impression to the examiner.

The best answers are planned answers. The best planned answers are those where a candidate's knowledge is displayed so that it will gain most marks. It is too easy to throw all one's best material into the first two questions, and then be short when it comes to the third answer. Play the percentages – it is much harder to increase a 14-mark answer to Question 2 than to secure 6 or 8 marks from Question 3.

Use the Checklists at the end of this unit to self-evaluate your work between now and the examination.

Eight months ahead of the examination

When it is 8 months ahead, the exam is a very long way off. It will either seem very frightening, or so unreal as to be of little concern. Either way you will be tempted to blot it out of your conscious mind. Unfortunately, your subconscious isn't going to forget. It'll worry away, nag at the problem, and throw up all kinds of mental blockages at the most unexpected times.

You have to be clear in your thinking, and be sure your subconscious is clear too. Then, if you set your objectives and make an action plan, your whole mind will be working in the same way, on the same things, at the same time. Your action plan must provide for these issues:

1 *Get the routine out of the way*:
   - Check you are a registered student.
   - Note the date for exam entry – and make a note in your diary of the need to enter three weeks before.
   - Obtain past exam papers, Examiners' Reports, Guidance Notes, etc.
2 *Learn to learn* Plan time into your studies so that you are able to learn easier, and to retain what you have learned. Try to learn something just before you have a real-life need for it. Or organize a real-life usage immediately after a topic has been covered on your course.
3 *Learn the subject* Your study of learning will show you how to set out your notes so they are memorable. It will also show you ways to keep your learning fresh.

There is no question that review plus use ensures little forgetting. One effective way to review is:

   - Whilst learning make notes (linear or mind map), work on the activities, note the explanations, relate to your practical experience. Let the material flow into and around you. *Ensure that you understand.* If necessary, ask questions of anyone who can help. Most people are flattered to be asked for their assistance.
   - The next day rewrite your notes into an organized format. One that works for you. It is now that you are setting up your revision for months ahead. You do not want page after page of notes that all look alike, there have to be associative hooks and triggers, and you must build them in – now.
   - The next week flip through your notes before you start to study; and again before you write up that week's work.
   - Always do the activities. Do more as voluntary work; and get a second opinion on it from somebody that you trust.*

* If you are learning alone, with no tutor, you will still find that there are people near to you who will help. (Sometimes they may not know your subject, but if they are intelligent and look at the Examiners' Reports and Guidance Notes they will be able to comment on your style; and on whether they have learned something from your work.)

- Always put your learning into the context of your main motivation – work, or whatever it is for you.
- Don't worry about exam question technique too soon. If you know your subject, and you know how to learn, you will pick up exam technique quickly.
- Once a month quickly review all your notes on each subject. Take time to rework examples, and/or to check understanding.

It is good to have someone with whom you can share part of your learning. So make it your business to find one or more.

One month ahead of the examination

Assuming you are working, and that your exam is in four subjects, taken in the same week, here is what you do:

1 Clear your social calendar, except for Saturday and Sunday evenings.
2 Secure a quiet area in which to work undisturbed. If necessary, get down to the local College library (you don't have to be registered as a student).
3 Programme 2 hours and 10 minutes into each weekday evening, and the same into either Saturday or Sunday morning.
   - In each session work 35 minutes on one subject. Then take 10 minutes out of your study area. In the open air if possible. (You need to blend academic and physical activity.)
   - Then 35 minutes on subject two, 15 minutes for coffee. (No television!)
   - Back for one more 35-minute session, and stop. Roll the subjects around day-by-day. (This gives 13 hours work, per week, for four subjects.)
4 Ensure that your support team are on your side – your spouse, parents, and close friends, must know that it is only temporary, but that it is definite. No exceptions. You only have just over 2 hours blocked out each evening for only a month – there is still time available for priority things (you can get out socially). And there are video recorders so you don't miss important television programmes.
5 Plan answers to all the past questions you can get hold of. Refer back to this workbook after your first plan – then improve the plan. Refer back to your first plan as an aid to your second attempt to plan the question – then use the workbook to improve your plan. Always work from your mind and your notes first, and from the workbook only if needed.
6 Reduce your learning notes to key points. Put these onto A4 sheets first. Then reduce to A5, and finally to postcards. It is a good idea to have a question on the front, and an outline of the answer on the back. Carry these cards everywhere – and use them as flash cards, as self-testers, when on the bus, the underground, waiting to see a client.
7 Do not *read* a textbook – refer to texts by all means; extract what you need; but don't read chunks of text. To pass you have to understand. To understand you have to use.
8 You are practising when you work on exam questions, but you also need to practise under exam conditions. Plan, in your third week, to spend two full, 3-hour evenings, in a library. Set yourself up exactly as for an exam. With a paper you haven't worked on before (one is provided at the end of this unit). Self-evaluate, as described later.
9 Check your exam answer plans against your flash cards. Go back to the book(s) at this stage only if absolutely necessary.
10 Keep your flash cards going up until the evening of two days before the exam.
11 Do no exam work at all on the day before the exam. Your mind needs the time to absorb and categorize the material, and to begin to unconsciously prepare for the exam itself. It has things to do which are beneficial, and you can use a break! So remind yourself that the world is still there. Relax in your favourite way (don't overdo it). Get a good night's sleep.

The day of the exam

The most important thing to develop is self-control. Do not get flustered! This is, of course, very easy to say, but very hard to do. Yet it is vital. The best way to control your nerves is to understand what is happening to you:

- You are putting yourself into risk, into danger.
- You are going into the unknown.
- You are going into an atmosphere of stress and tension.
- You badly want to do well – whatever you might say to friends to keep up appearances.

It will be the same for everyone else, one cannot avoid it – but *you* can control it if you understand what is happening, and why.

Why does it happen?

We possess very old-fashioned bodies, and very old-fashioned mental systems. They were not designed for this century, nor have they adapted to it. So far as our autonomic (subconscious) systems are concerned, nerves are just a form of physical fear. There are only two responses to fear. One is to run away; the other is to stand and fight.

Both responses call for the same protective measures – which are completely automatic. The blood supply is taken back into the main body cavity, leaving just sufficient for function in the parts most at physical danger. The blood-carrying vessels tighten down, to make them both smaller and tougher. A surge of adrenaline is automatically released. This substance (a hormone) is a very powerful stimulant. The whole body goes into a state of alert. Secondary systems such as digestion are shut down – the body is ready to run, or to fight. Unfortunately, the exam candidate can do neither. There is need for calm; for confident relaxation.

It is very important to recognize this, and to take action to control the nervous energy that the body will provide for you.

The advantages of nervousness
Take 15 minutes to work through the advantages that controlled 'nerves' offer. What are the implications to you – personally?

(**See** Debriefing at the end of this unit.)

ACTIVITY 11.5

Preparing for the exam

The basic rules are:

1 Find out the location of the exam centre a week ahead. Check travel details (bus and train timetables, parking, etc.). If possible, visit the centre; use the route you intend to use on the day. Buy the ticket the day before if you can, and ensure that you have enough small change on the day to cope with tickets you have to buy, and any emergencies. If the exam is in your College be sure to visit the exam room days ahead. Walk around it, get the feel for it. Be sure *not* to decide where you want to sit ! (This can be a great let down if you are told that you have to sit in another place on the day.) In everything you must have one aim – to know what is about to happen, and to be prepared for as many eventualities as possible.

2 You may have to sit near a radiator, or in a cold room, so you will need to be able to vary your clothing. A shirt or blouse, with sweater and jacket gives you a range of options on the day. You have to be comfortable in yourself.

3 You know what equipment you will need, but make a list well ahead of time, and prepare two easy to carry bags at least 24 hours before. (One can fit inside the other.) You will need to pack under two headings:

(a) What you need on the day – basic day-to-day materials, packed lunch (can only go in on the morning), revision notes for the exam, and perhaps for a second exam after lunch. This bag will have to be placed at the front of the exam room, out of your reach throughout the exam.

(b) What you need in the exam – special materials, e.g. pens, pencils, rulers, and calculator; study notes and/or reference book(s), (if allowed). This bag you can keep with you on your desk or table, so you should also include some sweets, a small and carefully sealed drink – whatever is going to help you through the length of the exam. The guideline here is *not* to include anything that may upset other candidates (apples are noisy, oranges are messy and smelly).

If you need to add anything on the morning of the day – make a note of it the night before when you make your final check. In the morning you do not want to be harassed with detail – so get as much behind you as possible.

4 Good-luck mascots – be very careful about mascots. The good candidate makes sure of doing well with careful planning. Candidates' confidence can be shattered by simply forgetting a mascot!

5 The day starts early for most candidates; their nerves see to that! Fine – expect it. Be sure to have something to eat and to drink, whatever your normal breakfast habit. An exam day is a different day – give your system something light to work on.

Avoid any tranquillizers, anti-sickness tablets, and so on. They may quell your tummy, but they slow down your mental processes. Is it better to be sick? Probably – but if you have planned carefully you should be in charge of the situation and should not be so nervous as to need medical aid. (Don't say, 'But it always happens to me, I can't help it'. You can help yourself to overcome the problem, if you think and plan ahead.)

Often parents are the worst problem. They are so anxious that they can infect you with their nervousness. You should have dealt with this problem much earlier – by getting your support team on your side. If not, you must be prepared to cope with it now. (Probably by forcing yourself not to argue, it will do no good – it will only set your adrenaline flowing in a negative, tightening, frustrating way.)

6 Leave home in good time, you will know how long each part of the journey takes, so you should be able to be reasonably relaxed about the travel.

7 On the journey you will probably feel better if you go through your flash cards one last time. Or glance through your notes. But by now it is too late to affect your true knowledge. You are filling in your time, and reinforcing the knowledge you already have.

8 At journey's end you should have some time in hand, so plan to use it well. Don't go into the Centre and stand around with the other candidates. Don't stand around outside. Go to a coffee shop, or for a walk in the park. You must *not* become infected with the nerves of the other candidates. You cannot expect them to be as well prepared as you. There will be nervous ones, troubled ones, upset ones. The organized ones will be off, like you, securing their own peace of mind.

9 Take possession – this is important. The space around you, your desk and chair should become yours, psychologically. Your seat may have been allocated – but you can still take charge. All you have to do is move the desk very slightly, to a different position. A position you have chosen. Move the chair too. Again, a very slight movement is all you need. By taking charge and creating your own space you will exert a very strong psychological boost to your ego. It is a small technique, but a most valuable one – remember you are playing a psychological game, and you have to play to win.

10 Fill your time by carefully entering your name/number on every piece of exam stationery that is waiting for you.

Your examination paper

You are sitting in the exam room. All is quiet now that the candidates are settled. Any time now and the invigilators will bring round the exam paper. It can get very tense. Fine. No problem. Why shouldn't you get tense? It is natural and you are prepared for it.

Then they make it worse, they give out the paper, face down, and you can't touch it. Then they look at the clock and wait for the second hand to sweep around. It's agony, can time ever move so slowly ?

Be prepared for this anguish. Wait it out. It will all go in a rush when you can get to the paper, you just have to sweat through.

At last – 'Turn the paper over, begin'. This is when many candidates lose control. They rush – all their good intentions are forgotten in the excitement of the moment. It is a very powerful psychological release! This will not happen to you, because you will have thought ahead and planned exactly what you are going to do.

The Effective Management for Marketing paper is in two parts. A mini-case worth 40 marks, and a requirement to answer three 20-mark questions from a choice of eight. It is necessary to know in advance exactly how you are going to tackle the paper. That is the only way to move smoothly and effectively when under exam pressure. Go into the exam knowing exactly what you are going to do.

Two exams

Effectively you have two exams to sit. For each you have 50 per cent of the time, i.e. 50 per cent of 180 minutes = 90 minutes. When you allow a time for preliminary reading through we can say that you have 85 minutes for the mini-case and 40 minutes each for the two questions.

There are effectively two exams in one paper because the technique for answering the mini-case is different from the technique needed for the two questions. Thus you need to put your mind into gear for the first half of the paper, take a short break midway, and then gear up slightly differently for the second half. You may therefore plan your time like this:

Minutes

0–2	Quick read through.
3–88	Mini-case.
89–94	Break.
95–175	Two questions.
176–180	Final read through and correct.

Alternatively, you may prefer to take the questions first – the choice is yours. Do not, however, mix questions and the mini-case. Keep the two parts of the paper separate.

A second, and compelling reason to separate the two parts is the benefit to be gained from a single planning session within each half of the exam.

Planning your answer to the mini-case requires a lengthy period of analysis and synthesis as you determine the interrelationships within the case and structure a planned answer that will meet the examiner's requirements. It makes complete sense to then write your answer, whilst the plan is fresh in your mind. You may well feel you need to divide your mini-case time:

Minutes

0–2	Quick read through.
3–10	Detailed penetration.
11–30	Answer planning.
31–79	Answer writing.
80–85	Checking through.

After the midpoint break, where you stretch the cramped shoulder muscles, relax the fingers, take a drink and clear the mind, you can get straight in to the second part of the exam.

Choosing two from five questions to answer can cause anguish as you find that there are questions that you prefer to avoid. (There always are questions you'd prefer to avoid!) The tick, cross and question-mark technique prevents the anguish and gets you into answer planning very quickly and confidently.

Tick, cross or question-mark

The technique relies upon your intuitive sense of knowing which questions are OK, which are possibles and which are best avoided. It works like this:

1 With a pencil in hand read down the questions very quickly. Don't try to analyse them, don't ponder over them.
2 Against each put either a tick, a cross, or a question-mark. (A tick means you can do the question; a cross 'no way'; a question-mark, 'possibly'.)
3 Count the ticks. If you have two or more you are on your way to a good pass.
4 Count the question-marks, if you have a further two you have a paper with which you can do well.
5 Ignore *totally* the crosses. For you they *don't exist*. They are no problem, they do not get in your way.

So you are, within 45 seconds, in a position to know how good a pass you can get. And you have eliminated the difficult questions and don't need to worry over them. There is no agonizing over an early question that you hate when an easier one is waiting further down the page!

The maths works out like this:

Each question = 25 marks   Pass = 50 per cent

	Marks achieved			
Ticked questions	18	2 × 18 = 36 marks	1 × 18	= 18 marks
Question-mark questions	10		1 × 10	= 10 marks
		Total = 36 marks		= 28 marks
		Safety margin = 6 marks		= 3 marks

But you should do better on question-mark questions than 10 out of 25!

You should be able to guarantee a minimum of 25 from the mini-case because of the time you have to devote to it, and the fact that it asks for your recommendations. *Your* personal recommendations that come from your understanding, background and experience. Providing that you have practised and write a report you shouldn't have any trouble.

Plan your answers

Plan all your answers in each section before starting to write. Ignore the many other candidates who will start straight in to answer without planning first. In the mini-case, if there is a sectioned question, plan the answers to each section first. In the questions part, plan your answers to both questions at one time. Why?

Because you must have your mind doing one thing at a time. When it is switched into planning mode it is actively searching for pertinent information. Mind maps provide an excellent stimulus to this process. When in active search mode you will find that thinking about one question will trigger ideas for another. Getting these ideas out before you switch to writing mode enables you to make better plans, quicker, and you will not find excellent ideas for the first question popping up whilst you are writing the second or third answer.

So plan your answers on a double-page spread of your answer book, and remember to neatly cross through the rough work before you hand the answer book in at the end of the exam.

It is worth repeating that first impressions are vital. An examiner is likely to have a strong first impression – 'This is a pass paper, how good?' *or* 'This is a fail paper, how bad?'

How, then, to discover what the examiner requires?

There are *key words* that you must first look for in a question. (These were listed earlier in this unit.) Key words are about *style* – they tell you what type of answer is needed. They are also about *content* – they tell you on what subject knowledge to focus the answer.

Always look for style words first because they tell you what has to be done. They indicate much of the context of your answer. Turn back and check on 'Discuss', 'Outline', and 'Evaluate'. Do you agree that each requires a different approach?

An examiner will give you a variety of questions to choose from. You can see that some will be easier in style for you; they will require less work. Always choose the ones with the minimum of work (provided you know the subject, of course). Let us take three similar questions, using the key words you have checked.

1 It has been said that general management is a skill that must be learned by any Manager who intends to attain and secure a position on the Board of Directors. Discuss.
2 Outline the skills of general management that are necessary for a Director of a Company to possess.
3 Evaluate the general management skills that are needed if a Company Director is to be successful in his post.

Many candidates would target on 'general management' only. Some would write all they knew on the topic. Some would present an essay, very few would give a report. Some would write about 'general management skills' – again in a standard essay. Yet the examiner is asking the candidate to put his or her knowledge of general management into a context. To show three things:

1 Knowledge of management and of the skills a general manager needs.
2 Skill in using the correct style so that the set task is carried out – a discussion is very different from an evaluation; an outline is again a different requirement. An essay would be correct for the discussion answer, an essay or report for the evaluation, a report better for the outline.
3 Presentation of the knowledge, skilfully used, so that it is comprehensible. The candidate's command of language both in comprehension, and use, is being tested. This is a necessary skill for anyone who wishes to become a manager.

Note: The examples show how the same knowledge could be tested in different ways. Obviously the same topic will not appear three times on a paper. (If you think it has, then you are misunderstanding the examiner.) These questions are not typical of the Effective Management for Marketing paper. They have been used as examples because they are simply presented and easy to understand.

Presenting your answer

It is crucially important to present your answer in the form that the examiner requires. To do this requires careful analysis of the question, followed by careful planning of the answer. There is also a need for good physical presentation of your answer. A shorter answer that directly responds to the examiner's need, and which is presented in a clear style will impress – and attract high marks.

As we explained earlier in this unit, there is need to look for key words for style and for content. Look at these three typical questions and decide two things:

1 What presentation style is called for?
2 What subject knowledge is required?

A There is a very high turnover of sales representatives in your sales region. This is beginning to adversely affect customer relations.
In a report to the National Sales Manager, set out the remedial actions that you propose to take.
B 'The manager of the future will need to be a very different person than the manager of the past.'
You have been asked to support this statement at a discussion held by the local Chamber of Commerce. Provide the outline of your contribution. You may include the draft of up to three visual aids.

C A member of your team has recently been promoted to Marketing Research Supervisor with a team of four office and ten field staff. You have noticed she has been working very late to get the project completed to deadline, but the grapevine tells you her team is underutilized.

Briefly identify what the problem might be. What actions would you take?

Presentation-style	*Subject-knowledge (content)*
Key Words:	*Key Words:*
A Report.	A High turnover; sales reps.
B Outline; draft of visual aids.	B Manager; past; future.
C Briefly; identify.	C MR supervisor. Team of four office and ten field. Working very late, team underutilized.

Once the key words have been identified it is possible to plan an answer that meets the requirements of the examiner. The key words help you firstly to identify style, secondly to target relevant theory and practical examples. Remember it is *never* acceptable to write all you know about a subject! It is *essential* that you give just enough knowledge, demonstrate the required skills and use the correct style. A short answer that does this will always beat a rambling unstructured response.

In these questions you would need to bring in specific content – which the key words would trigger. To illustrate:

A Need to show understanding of a geographically remote team, of motivation and incentive coupled to morale and, probably, to clear objectives and good leadership.

B Manager versus leader. Requirement for flatter structures and knowledge-based workers who are better educated and have very different motivations and expectations than those of even 20 years ago.

C Delegation and control. Self-confidence. Need for development plan, possibly some coaching and mentoring.

Edward de Bono: thinker

Defined as 'seeking to solve problems by unorthodox or apparently illogical methods', lateral thinking was devised by Edward de Bono and has formed the basis for his 28 books which have been translated into 21 languages as diverse as Russian and Korean, Hebrew and Japanese.

Describing himself as 'what philosophy stopped being some 600 years ago', de Bono is a thinker about thinking. This may appear an esoteric occupation but, to use one of his own examples, how many hours in one's entire academic career are devoted to learning how to learn? The usual answer is – none. Even the frantic activity before traditional examinations has a focus of short-term retention of crammed material – not learning.

'Thinking', says de Bono, 'is a skill and like any skill it can be developed and improved if one knows how'. He has conclusively shown how to think creatively and constructively – how to maximize learning. His work has been invaluable – and yet it has not been picked up by the main body of educationalists who prefer to stay with the traditional methods of imparting knowledge.

Much of de Bono's efforts have been devoted to encouraging the adoption of his exciting and dynamic concepts within the world of education. In management he has been extremely successful in fields where innovation and creativity are valued and his work, coupled with that of Tony Buzan (see Unit 4) is invaluable to a marketing manager.

The summary from his introduction to his seminal book *Lateral Thinking* encapsulates the concepts that underpin his work:

The purpose of thinking is to collect information and to make the best possible use of it. Because of the way that the mind works to create fixed concept patterns we cannot make the best use of our new information unless we have some means for restructuring the old patterns and bringing them up to date. Our traditional methods of thinking teach us to refine such patterns and establish their validity. But we shall always make less than the best use of available information unless we know how to create new patterns and escape from the dominance of the old ones. Vertical thinking is concerned with proving or developing concept patterns. Lateral thinking is concerned with restructuring such patters (insight) and providing new ones (creativity). Lateral and vertical thinking are complementary. Skill in both is necessary. Yet the emphasis in education has always been exclusively on vertical thinking.

The need for lateral thinking arises from the limitations of the behaviour of mind as a self-maximising memory system

Key publications:
Lateral Thinking, 1970
Lateral Thinking for Management, 1971

- Learn about learning.
- Set up your learning notes so they have triggers and associative links.
- Review regularly.
- Understand and use.
- You have to decide to pass – nothing less will do.
- A plan is essential, a plan in writing which you will follow.
- Clear your diary for the run up to the exam, schedule practice sessions, work up to exam speed.
- Get your support team on your side. Don't try to do it alone.
- Work from your notes, not from text or workbooks.
- Reduce your notes, gradually, to Flash Cards. Trust your mind.
- Work on the skills of communicating what you know, impressively.
- Examine your own work. Would it impress? Would you pass it?
- No exam work on the day before – if you don't know it by then an extra day won't help; and your brain needs a break.
- Use 'nerves' to your advantage. Channel them into heightened perception, and an ability to concentrate and work for a longer stretch than is usual.
- Rehearse the day. Plan it ahead.
- Don't mix with ill-prepared candidates before the exam.
- Take possession of your exam-room space and equipment.
- Take charge of the question paper. Use ticks, crosses and question-marks to quickly select the questions you are going to answer.
- Do not worry about crossed questions, they do not apply to you, they are not your problem.
- Plan your time. Maximize your marks by planning all answers at the beginning, despite what the other candidates do.
- Key words clearly identify the examiner's requirements.
- Length is *not* needed, nor is volume.
- Share your knowledge around the questions.
- The best answers are well planned and well presented.
- Make certain that the first three pages are impressive. You must catch the examiner's attention, early and positively.
- Plan a 5-minute break at about half way.
- Be sure to read through and catch as many errors as you can.
- Make certain you have named everything you are handing in, and that all loose papers are tied into the main answer book.
- If in doubt, always write in report style. In a marketing exam this is never wrong.

Debriefing

Activity 11.2

Writing the answer outline first enables an examiner precisely to target the area(s) of the syllabus that are to be tested. With this objective established it is possible to draft a question that guides candidates to the anticipated answer.

If the question is written first it will almost inevitably be open to several interpretations and have to go through many more redrafts than a targeted question will need. Even a question written to elicit an answer can be ambiguous in the perception of some candidates, in which case the examiner will take the answers that are genuinely based on a logical interpretation of the question.

The implications for students and candidates are that the questions contain clear and specific clues to the expected answer and that a logical interpretation will be accepted even if it is unexpected. The need is to read, understand and interpret each question carefully.

Activity 11.3

Only you will ever know the full reasoning behind your need to pass this examination. As this is the case you can be completely honest with yourself. If status and/or pride are the motivators well and good. If you are only entered because of somebody else's expectations (perhaps your boss has insisted) you need to consider that if it is inevitable perhaps you ought to gain from it and not resist? Only when you know your motivations can you locate and tie in incentives that will work for you. Given clear objectives your task becomes so very much easier.

Activity 11.4

A survey of Examiner's Reports from a whole range of examinations shows a consistency in requirement. The key factors an examiner requires are:

- Prepare before the examination – subject and exam skills.
- Read and understand the questions.
- Do as instructed in the questions.
- Answer the questions set.
- Do not force your knowledge into your answers, despite the questions set.
- Attempt an answer to the full number of questions.
- Allocate time and effort to the available marks.
- Write answers that are long enough to cover the question.
- Show command of subject through practical examples.
- Read through and eliminate careless mistakes.

We are constantly told that many candidates are ignoring the Examiners' advice. It must therefore follow that an Examiner is going to be so pleased to receive a well presented script that answers the questions asked, that the natural inclination is to pass it! The only question is 'How good a pass to award'.

Activity 11.5

The advantages are likely to be:

- You will be alert, perceptive, full of energy, ready to accept the challenge of the examination.
- Your alertness will sharpen your mental skills and strengthen the associative links.
- Your subconscious will know that it needs to become fully active.
- Your whole system will be poised to 'fight', not run away from the exam paper.
- Above all you will be in control of your destiny.

You, if you think about it, will form your own best solution to the problem of control over your own destiny. But you have to learn to harness this major strength – learn to use it to your advantage.

Assignment checklists

Use these two checklists to help you self-assess your own work. Apply the questions (and the answers) to future assignments and work hard to improve your presentation so that the key points are routine when you reach the examination room.

Checklist one – overall impression

Turn the pages on your work:

1	Is it well laid out?	Yes	No
2	Have you used report format?	Yes	No
3	Have you used a ruler to underline headings, key points, etc?	Yes	No
4	Is there plenty of white space on the page – making it easy to identify sections of your arguments?	Yes	No
5	Does it look professionally credible?	Yes	No
6	Can someone else read it easily?	Yes	No
7	Would you accept this piece of work from one of your staff?	Yes	No
8	How many person hours went into the assignment, both of analysis and decision?	_____ hours	
9	Would you be prepared to show your work to your manager as the output of that amount of work and effort?	Yes	No
10	Would you pay a consultant £60 times the hours in (8) if this was submitted as the end result of a project?	Yes	No
11	Overall – is it a creditable piece of work?	Yes	No

Any 'no' and you are throwing marks away. Commercial credibility is the acid test of a management report and that means professional standards. Make sure the same mistakes don't happen again!

Now examine the content . . .

Checklist two – content

1	Does your answer *directly* respond to the actual question: as asked?	Yes	No
2	Does your answer contain:		
	a Clarification of assumptions?	Yes	No
	b Clear decisions and recommendations for action?	Yes	No
	c Quantified objectives?	Yes	No
	d Time scales?	Yes	No
3	Are your decisions practical and realistic?	Yes	No

4 If you were an examiner or a line manager how would you evaluate the competence demonstrated in this answer?
And say why?
Excellent _____
Good _____
Fair _____
Poor _____
Awful _____

5 Make lists of:

   a Three things which you can improve in your style and/or exam technique.

   b Three things you are pleased with about your style and/or exam technique.

6 Reserve a time in your diary to produce a personal action plan which will build on your strengths and eradicate your weaknesses.

REMEMBER:

Examiners have needs too . . .

. . . are you satisfying them?

Practice examination

This examination paper is produced by the Senior Examiner as a guide to what may be expected to be set in the examination room.

You should not attempt to answer any questions until you have set up as close an approximation to exam conditions as you are able. You need:

- 3 hours uninterrupted time.
- A clear workspace.
- A supply of A4 paper – wide lined if possible.
- A clock.
- Other materials you would normally take with you into an examination.

When you are ready, note the time of start, and the time that you must finish. Then take the paper and work it as in a real examination.

Note: You should answer the case in Section 1 and two questions from Section 2. Later, as part of your revision, you should attempt answers to the other questions in Section 2.

When your 3 hours are up note the fact in your paper – but continue to finish the question on which you are working.

Review

Immediate:

Review in writing how you believe you have done in answering each question. Do you feel that you would have passed in each? If not, where are your shortcomings?

Next day:

- Read through your paper as if an examiner. Grade it using the materials in this unit.
- Check through the suggested answers, and then re-grade your paper.
- Compare your initial feelings with the two gradings. What have you learnt? What changes will you make before the real examination?

Action plan

Produce a detailed action plan to consolidate your strengths and repair your weaknesses.

THE QUESTION PAPER
CANDIDATE'S INSTRUCTIONS

Section 1 is compulsory and carries 50 per cent of the available marks.
Section 2 requires you to tackle two from a choice of five questions, each worth 25 marks.

Credit will be given not only for your ability to demonstrate the relevant knowledge and understanding of the subject area, but also for the level of skill you demonstrate in tackling this paper; time management, presentation and effective communication of your arguments and ideas will be rewarded, as will the approach you recommend in tackling the various issues and scenarios described.

SECTION 1
This is a compulsory section

The Garden Design and Landscape Company – Getting More Out Of Less
The early 1990s have been tough for businesses of all sizes. Markets have been increasingly competitive and demand sluggish. Survival has been the goal of many and the need to get the best out of all available resources paramount to that goal being successfully achieved.

The Garden Design and Landscape company is one such organization – it has survived for over 18 years and has a turnover of some £2.5 million – about £1 million from household contracts, new drives, patios and garden layouts. The balance from a mixture of public sector and corporate work – mainly maintenance contracts but some new project work. Sales revenue has fallen slightly over the last few years, but has declined in real terms by over 15 per cent since 1989. Average order values have fallen and so has the operating profit.

Based in the South East of England the company has three centres, each with a small sales office and showroom. There are currently some 120 full-time staff, but a number of casual workers are employed as necessary to meet the seasonal shifts in workload. Staff numbers have fallen from 160 in 1988.

Having attended a recent seminar which examined the value of a strategic marketing approach to planning, the Managing Director approached you to act as a consultant and undertake an objective review of the current position of the business and to make recommendations for the changes which might be necessary if they are to be ready to meet the challenges of the rest of the 1990s and improve the overall financial performance of the business.

You have completed your initial audits and the following summarizes some of your key findings:

- The business is operationally/product oriented.
- There is little use of available information and no real information system.
- Planning is ad hoc and its value not really understood.
- The organization is hierarchical in structure with no real incentives for the individual work teams.
- Absenteeism is high, averaging over 1.5 days per month per manual worker.
- There is a small field sales team of a sales manager and four sales staff and six full-time administrative support staff. There is also a marketing manager who is mainly responsible for sales literature and advertising and reports directly to the Managing Director.
- There is increased competition and the market is increasingly price competitive.
- There are no clear links between sales and marketing and little coordination of effort between the sales teams in the three centres.
- Enquiries generated are high, but the conversion from sales visits to orders are low at only 1 in 7. In the past they have been as high as 1 in 3.
- Only the most basic customer records are maintained.

Questions:

1 Bearing in mind that any available budget for change will be limited, what proposals would you make to help the firm change to a more market-oriented culture? Provide an indication of the time-scale, and likely costs for your recommendations. (*25 marks*)

2 What actions would you recommend to improve the effectiveness of the marketing and sales team? (*25 marks*)

SECTION 2
Answer two questions

3 You have noticed that a recently promoted member of your marketing team seems to have been finding the new responsibilities and workload difficult. Although a reliable and thorough worker over the past 3 years, in the last months several deadlines have been missed, and a few silly errors have been made. You know he has been working late in order to try and keep up, and that he was planning to start his studies for a CIM qualification next month.
   (a) Explain briefly how you would handle the situation and give your justification for adopting this approach. (*7 marks*)
   (b) What advice would you give this staff member to help reduce the pressures and improve his time management? (*18 marks*)

4 As assistant to the Marketing Director in a large manufacturing company you have been asked to help with the plans for recruitment, selection and induction of three graduate trainees.
   (a) Produce a profile of the characteristics and competencies you would recommend be included as a basis for the job specification and explain briefly your justification for their inclusion. (*10 marks*)
   (b) Prepare a detailed plan, indicating the actions which should be undertaken to successfully recruit these three trainees. Include a timetable and budget expressed in terms of the management time required. (*15 marks*)

5 You have recently been appointed manager of a sales and marketing team of 25 people, having won the job over two internal candidates. Your initial review indicates that the department's performance has been deteriorating for some time, and there is a lack of motivation and enthusiasm evident across all areas and grades within the team.
   (a) What options are available to you in tackling this problem? (*17 marks*)
   (b) What steps would you take to help decide the best approach to adopt? (*8 marks*)

6 As part of a company-wide quality initiative a programme of staff appraisal is to be introduced. The Directors have asked for your suggestions as to how best to present this development to the staff.
   Prepare your proposals, and a plan for their implementation, for presentation at the next Board meeting. (*25 marks*)

7 Relationship marketing is becoming a very important dimension in cementing client, supplier and customer relations. Explain briefly what is meant by relationship marketing and outline both its advantages and possible disadvantages to a firm operating in a rapidly changing marketplace. (*25 marks*)
   (a) How would you persuade a firm about the value of investing in improved information? (*5 marks*)
   (b) Describe how a firm should go about evaluating and improving the information available to their managers. (*15 marks*)

The Examiner's answer plans follow.

Turn to them only when you have completed your self-review.

SUGGESTED ANSWERS

These are not included as complete answers but are intended to signpost the sort of things which the examiners would be looking for in each question area. There are no uniquely correct answers, but a number of alternative ways of tackling many of these questions which if supported and justified would be accepted.

General

You should have:

- Worked in report format.
- Paid particular attention to the specific audiences indicated in each question.
- Emphasized the action-plan dimension of your answers and provided an indication of timetables and budgets, where appropriate.
- Used the guidelines provided to assist you to indicate budgets. Fully quantified budgets are not required, but an awareness that costs will be incurred in, for example, the selection process is important. Budgets expressed in terms of staff time or simply indications of tender requirements for major projects are acceptable.

Section I

General

Good candidates will be those who use the case study information in answering the question and take these factors into account when making their recommendations.

Question I

1 *Background*
- Garden Design and Landscape Company is well established operating in both consumer and business-to-business markets.
- Their marketplace is becoming increasingly competitive and the company is not doing as well, with sales conversions having fallen from 1:3 to 1:7.
- Faced with an increasingly competitive environment, management need to change the focus of their business – becoming more customer oriented to ensure resources are not wasted.
- The company is currently product oriented so this will require a significant culture change.

2 *Changing to a marketing-oriented culture*
- Reorienting the culture of the company takes time, costs money and can be a painful process.
- It will only be possible if the change has the support of senior managers.

3 *Proposals*
- To review the current organizational structure – to consider a structure:
  (a) Based around customer groups.
  (b) Flatter structure with delegated responsibility and targets for work teams.
- To establish a system of improved management and marketing information, including marketing research to provide the basis for improved decision making, and to ensure future decisions are made based on customer's needs. To keep costs to a minimum the first priority would be to review the current internal data and to identify ways this can be managed more effectively. The company has the advantage of knowing its customers – by location, type of work required, order value, etc. – and so is well placed to undertake fairly simple research in-house.
- To introduce a customer-care programme for all staff. This should be undertaken gradually, using cascade training within the organization to keep costs down.

- Management to be encouraged to consider going for a quality standard certificate such as BS 5750 although this will entail a substantial cost and so may be deferred for a year or so.
- Over the longer term, to review the scale and organization of the sales and marketing department and consider appointing a marketing director.

4 *Time scale and budget*

Activity	Time	Budget
Review current organization structure	2 months	
Proposed and agreed changes with all staff	4 months	
Implementation of changes	3 months	
Consultancy time	10 days	
Management time	30 days	£8000 (assuming no redundancies)

Customer care training starting immediately with managers, 1-day course for each work team of 10

	Time	Budget
Spread over	12 months	£7200 (trainer costs)
Review of internal data	3 months	
	20 staff days	
	5 consultancy days	£4000
Development of improved database and MIS	24 months	To be tendered
BS 5750	18 months from year 2	To be tendered
Appointment of a marketing director (year 2) estimated salary £40 000	8 staff days	£6400
		£5000 (selection costs)

Question 2

- Revise organization away from area sales offices towards customer segments.

- Evaluate current customers to identify target segments.
- Use ratio analysis to identify strengths and weakness of current sales and marketing effort.
- Establish clear, realistic sales targets for each sector.
- Provide support to ensure maximum benefit of sales effort – telesales, direct mail to generate qualified customer leads and follow up on enquiries.
- Establish a basis for monitoring performance of sales and marketing effort.

Section 2

General

This section requires you to tackle two from a choice of five questions. Examination technique and answering the question in context are very important to achieving good marks in this section.

The comments given below are not full answers, but indicate the kind of issues and views the examiners might expect to be covered.

Question 3a

- This is a potentially sensitive situation – this team member could be feeling vulnerable and lacking in confidence about his abilities to cope with his new responsibilities.
- He is likely to be feeling stressed and is probably well aware of the missed deadlines, etc.
- An informal friendly and supportive approach should be adopted, to avoid any possible implication that this is a disciplinary or grievance interview.

Question 3b

- Encourage the completion of a time diary to identify the critical and routine tasks and current use of time.
- Encourage him to produce a plan of activities for each day.
- Offer to help identify areas of particular difficulty and provide support or training to bridge any skill gaps.
- Encourage delegation to the other members of the team – to reduce the work pressures.
- Discuss arranging a training course in time management for this member of staff.
- Arrange regular meetings to provide support and monitor progress.

Question 4a

The graduate selected will need to have the characteristics and aptitudes which:

- Suit the company culture.
- You would expect in a marketing manager.

Characteristic justification:

- Creative – adding broader dimensions to problem solving.
- Analytical – able to evaluate situations and information.
- Good communicator – able to get ideas across and enjoy communicating in all situations.
- A strong team player – appreciative of the contribution of others; able to work effectively together.
- Interested in satisfying customers – a belief in the fundamental concept of marketing.

Question 4b

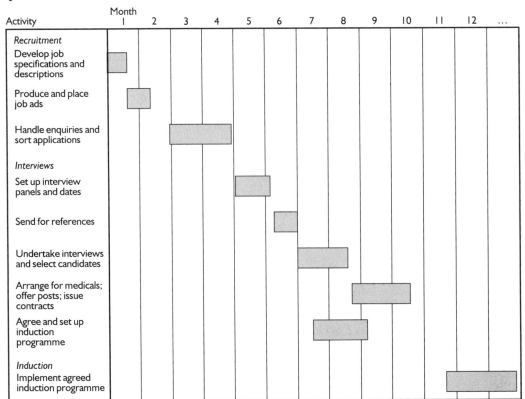

Question 5a

There are two main issues, which could be cause and effect – poor motivation leading to lower performance. But this needs clarifying. There may be other factors leading to poor performance, e.g. the economic climate or inadequate resources, and this could, in turn, be leading to low levels of motivation.

There are a number of approaches open to you as the new team manager:

- Review the organization of the team, establish working groups with identifiable areas of authority and responsibility.
- Involve the team in planning for the group – establishing realistic targets and specific goals. Short-term objectives will generate more immediate results and so be more useful in these circumstances.
- Establish team-building activities – perhaps some training or even a common interest such as generating funds for charity or organizing a departmental social event.
- Informal interviews with all team members to identify their views, worries, expectations, etc. Particular sensitivity will be needed with the two failed internal candidates. Winning their support could be critical.
- Consider the alternatives for motivational schemes – these need not be major financial incentives to be effective.
- Establish regular team meetings to encourage communication and involvement.

Any combination of the above would lead towards an open and consensual approach to management based on a McGregor's theory Y organization. The alternative approach – adopting a theory X style of team management – would mean hierarchical systems, tight targets and controls, with management disciplining those who fail to achieve.

Question 5b

A thorough audit and analysis of the situation to clearly identify cause and effect:

- Detailed appraisals with team members – possibly incorporating techniques to assess management styles and assess the current and preferred culture of the team.
- Discussion with team members to identify both their needs and their views.
- Establishment of controls and feedback mechanisms to monitor the effectiveness of any changes implemented.

Question 6

Internal marketing of company appraisals.

Background – the appraisal scheme:
- Board has agreed to implement a company wide programme of appraisals as part of our ongoing drive for quality.
- We need to recognize that this is a change and is likely to be resisted by some or all staff unless the benefits to them are clearly presented. Appraisals can appear to be a threat.

Objectives
- To have successfully introduced the appraisal scheme within 18 months.

Strategy
- We need to take care how we present and position this scheme to the staff.
  It is important that it is not seen as confrontational/disciplinary or 'one way'.
- We need to identify the various segments within our workforce who may have similar worries or interests regarding the scheme:

  (a) Managers.
  (b) Production staff.
  (c) Customer contact staff.

  It is possible that different age groups of staff will respond differently and should be targeted.

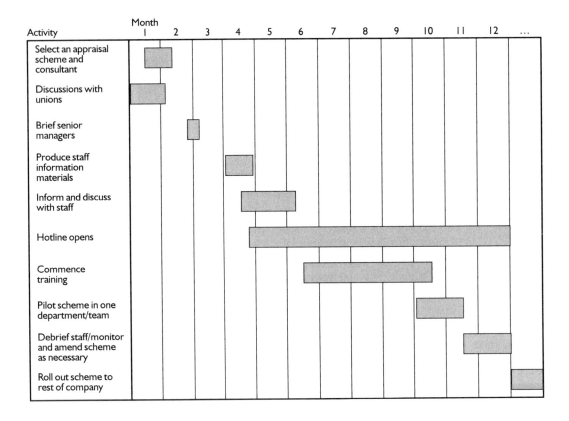

- Those involved in influencing or advising the staff need to be identified and targeted (trade union representatives, staff committee members, and so on). Identifying and using informal as well as formal communication networks will be important.

The plan

- The product is our appraisal scheme. The features and benefits it offers must be clearly identified for the staff. Benefits to them:

    (a) Personal development.
    (b) Two way communication.
    (c) Opportunity to influence corporate/departmental policy.
    (d) Provide quantified objective feedback on performance in a structured way – controlled by an agreed set of procedures.

- Promotion – successful implementation depends on communication being coordinated and effective:

    (a) Staff briefings – co-ordinated so the scheme is launched simultaneously.
    (b) Advance information and discussions with the unions to ensure their endorsement and support.
    (c) Written details circulated to all staff enclosed in their pay advice notification.
    (d) Notice boards for posters selling scheme benefits.
    (e) Member of the personnel team to operate an enquiries hotline handling personal enquiries for the first weeks following announcement, and when first appraisals are conducted.

- Price – there is a price staff are being asked to pay and we need to recognize they are giving their time, support and trust if they 'buy' this scheme.
- Value for money has to be evident. We should ensure that adequate resources for staff development exist to support development in areas of agreed need.
- Training, to ensure all participants get maximum out of the process, must be in place before the start of the scheme.
- Place – when and where information about and training for the scheme will be available. This must be coordinated across the company to avoid rumour and misinformation.

Control
- Research, either informal or formal can be undertaken to assess and monitor staff attitudes before and after appraisals have been conducted.
- Monitoring of some key indicators over time would also be helpful:

  (a) Changes in the number of training days.
  (b) Proportion of internal promotions.
  (c) Improved measures of efficiency.

- A budget of training and staff time to prepare for and undertake appraisals will be needed. Quantification of this would depend on staff numbers. Allowance of about £4 per head to provide for internal promotion of the scheme.

Timetable: year 1/year 2

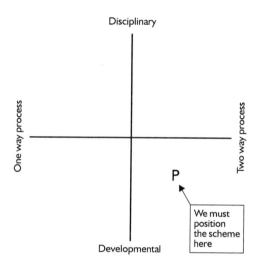

Question 7

- Relationship marketing is being widely adopted by many organizations as part of a quality initiative – where the emphasis is on building strong links with suppliers as a strategy for improving and ensuring quality. It has been particularly important for companies wishing to establish just-in-time deliveries etc.
- It is an equally valid and important approach when trying to build repeat business with clients. Building a long-term relationship reduces the threat of external competition and provides the firm and its customers with the opportunity to build a longer term partnership, with both parties seeking to resolve any problems.

Advantages
- Reduces the need and cost of constantly seeking new suppliers.
- Allows problems to be tackled in partnership – often sharing the costs of implementing solutions.
- Enables the supplier to be treated more like an internal function of the business – trusted and involved in developments.
- Quality targets can be assured and costs lowered through, for example, just-in-time delivery.

Disadvantages
- Possibility of complacency from the supplier. The lack of competition may mean that over a period of time prices will rise above the market rate.
- In a rapidly changing environment the supplier may, over time, no longer be the best suited to the needs of the business.
- Long-term relationships may mean personal loyalties influence managers' commercial decisions.

Index

your chance to bite back
Effective Management for Marketing

Dear student

Both Butterworth-Heinemann and the CIM would like to hear your comments on this workbook. All respondents will receive a FREE copy of a CIM marketing book.

If you have some suggestions, please fill out the form below and send it to us at:

Business Books Division
Butterworth-Heinemann
FREEPOST OF/1639
Oxford OX2 8BR

Name and address: _____

_____

College/course attended:

_____

If you are not attending a college, please state how you are undertaking your study:

_____

_____

_____

How did you hear about the CIM/Butterworth-Heinemann workbook series?

Word of mouth   ❏
Through my tutor   ❏
CIM mailshot   ❏

Advert in _____

Other _____

What do you like about this workbook (e.g. layout, subjects covered, depth of analysis):

What do you dislike about this workbook (e.g. layout, subjects covered, depth of analysis):

Are there any errors that we have missed (please state page number):